Deep Splendor

Deep Splendor

A Study of Spirituality in Modern Literature

ROBERT P. VANDE KAPPELLE

WIPF & STOCK · Eugene, Oregon

DEEP SPLENDOR
A Study of Spirituality in Modern Literature

Wipf & Stock
An Imprint of Wipf and Stock Publishers
199 W. 8th Ave., Suite 3
Eugene, OR 97401

www.wipfandstock.com

PAPERBACK ISBN: 978–1–6667–3631–1
HARDCOVER ISBN: 978–1–6667–9443–4
EBOOK ISBN: 978–1–6667–9444–1

NOVEMBER 22, 2021 4:48 PM

To Orlando
most courteous of gentlemen,
"a poet, I dare say."

Beauty and terror are very real things,

[but they are also] related to a real spiritual world;

and to touch them at all, even in doubt and fancy,

is to stir the deep things of the soul.

—G. K. CHESTERTON

Contents

Preface

HUMANS ARE SPIRITUAL BEINGS inhabiting physical bodies for a time. For this reason, our lives are caught in a tidal pull between vast forces, one physical, secular, and temporal, the other spiritual, sacred, and eternal. While I cannot speak for your experience, this tug of war has produced in me a curious restlessness. During my youth and early adulthood, I loved adventure, engaging in activities that pushed me to my physical limits. Hikes in the woods, climbing mountains, long bike rides, participating in sports, playing with friends, these are the activities I cherished. However, I also loved reading, playing the piano, and studying theology, for these activities fueled my insatiable curiosity. Not yet appreciative of poetry, I yearned for a story with an adventurous plot, inspiring characters, and a happy ending, including elements of mystery and surprise. Many of these qualities were present in short stories, novels, historical fiction, science fiction, fantasy literature, and biographical writing, and I gravitated to this literature. As son of missionary parents, I also read the Bible, biblical commentaries, missionary stories, devotional material, Christian classics such as John Bunyan's *The Pilgrim's Progress*, and other inspirational literature.

As a thirteen-year-old, my life was turned upside down when I learned that my parents were asked to relocate to a new country, exchanging idyllic Costa Rica for war-torn Colombia. Their relocation changed my life, for it meant I would be separated from my parents prematurely. Staying in the United States, I enrolled in The Stony Brook School, a select Christian preparatory school in Long Island, not far from New York City, and that school became my home for the next three and a half years. My transition from dependence to independence happened rather quickly, aided by an active sports life and a demanding academic program. At Stony Brook, I developed an appreciation of literature, and by the time of my graduation from high school, I had acquired a sizeable personal library, consisting largely of inexpensive paperback copies of classic novels purchased through yard-work and other remunerative activities available to high-school seniors.

In college, love of literature led me to major in modern foreign languages, and my personal library expanded to include volumes in Spanish, French, and German, in addition to a growing collection of English-language literature. Prior to my PhD work in biblical studies at Princeton Theological Seminary, I completed a master's degree in Latin American Studies, during which time I added dozens of Spanish classics to my expanding library. At Princeton Seminary, in addition to courses in speech, homiletics, ethics, practical and historical theology, biblical studies, and Hebrew and Greek, I enrolled in an elective on Religion and Literature, further expanding my appreciation for literature while exploring the questions that framed my spirituality, namely, what it means to be Christian and what it means to be human.

In retrospect, love of great literature made me a better husband and parent, a healthier cleric, and a more effective teacher, for it kept me open to lifelong learning, an advantage I imparted to many students along the way. Literature also contributed significantly to my wellbeing, for it helped me outgrow fundamentalist and dualist perspectives and kept me open to spiritual growth and ongoing transformation.

QUALITIES THAT MAKE LITERATURE GREAT

What is it about literature that make it great, qualifying some books as classics and excluding others? When I first thought about this project, I wanted to include representative literature throughout history and across cultures, including the Homeric literature, the writings of ancient Greek and Roman authors such as Aeschylus and Virgil, and later literary masters such as Augustine, Dante, Shakespeare, and Milton. In addition to being impractical for a one-volume work, I felt such a project would eliminate from consideration much of modern literature. For that reason, I limited my selection to nineteenth- and twentieth-century authors, avoiding those with obvious political or religious axes to grind, while recognizing that avoiding bias was not altogether possible, since every writer of necessity has personal, social, and cultural preferences and points of view. While political, religious, and theological bias is evident in some of my choices, my rule of thumb is to bypass or dismiss such distractions where possible to get to the greater spiritual core. Since all humans are flawed, I decided to adopt a forbearing stance, addressing lifestyle issues where possible while focusing on positive rather than negative elements, responding with inspirational and informative rather than critical commentary.

In this regard, the winnowing process led me to the following genres and authors:

1. literary fiction: James Joyce, T. S. Eliot, Joseph Conrad, Nathaniel Hawthorne, Herman Melville, Fyodor Dostoyevsky, D. H. Lawrence, Herman Hesse, and Miguel de Unamuno

2. literary fantasy: J. R. R. Tolkien and J. K. Rowling

3. historical fantasy: Marion Zimmer Bradley, Evangeline Walton

4. theological fantasy: C. S. Lewis.

Most are novelists, but at times it is to their essays, novellas, short stories, or poetry to which we must go in order to find their most promising contribution to the topic of spirituality.

Classical literature is often considered the literature of ancient Greece and Rome. However, the term "classical" has a broader meaning, for it includes literature of any language notable for its excellence and enduring quality. A classic novel, for example, introduces a memorable protagonist. Such characters have distinct personalities but often strong points of view about the world, serving as the reader's eyes and ears.

Books also become classics because they say something profound and lasting about the human condition. Whether it is the coming-of-age story of Stephen Dedalus in James Joyce's *A Portrait of the Artist as a Young Man*, or the themes of social and class struggles in the novels of Charles Dickens or Alexandre Dumas, classic novels and short stories tend to express universal truth about human life.

Classical literature endures because these are the books we reread. The classics are great because they beg to be read multiple times, revealing new depth and meaning upon each subsequent reading. Reading *To Kill a Mockingbird* as a young person for the first time might cause us to identify with Scout, a curious kid trying to make sense of the complex world around her. However, as we transition to adulthood, a further reading might cause us to relate to Atticus, a man trying to protect his children while grappling with the moral ambiguity of society. Either way, a true classic of literary fiction can be read and reread, demonstrating new layers each time.

A true classic stands the test of time, regardless of when it was written. Shakespeare's writings find modern audiences despite having been written in the sixteenth and seventeenth centuries, largely because his themes, characters, and storytelling are timeless. While read and reread, his works have inspired countless retellings and adaptations in the world of theatre, opera, radio, television, and film.

For the most part, the books I select are stylistically unique, contextually vivid, and thematically timeless, with universal themes. Whether it is about coming of age, self-integration, human relationships, the eternal struggle of good versus evil, the nature of change, or the corruptive aspects of power, a classic novel examines enduring, immutable truths about how humans behave, what they believe, how they respond, and how they are unique, all components of spirituality.

When we think about great literature, it is easy to focus objectively on the literature itself, on what makes literature "bad" or "good." However, another essential distinction involves the reader, replacing the category "good" or "great" book with that of "good reader." In that respect, I rely on the advise given by the popular author, critic, and master teacher C. S. Lewis, who, in one of his last books, *An Experiment in Criticism*, judged books in terms of readers rather than the other way around. Thus, he begins by proposing that "we try to discover how far it might be plausible to define a good book as a book which is read in one way, and a bad book as a book which is read in another."[1]

To accomplish his intent, Lewis identified four main features of a good reader: (1) frequent rereading of favorites; (2) giving priority to reading as an essential activity; (3) fundamental change of consciousness as a reaction to some books; and (4) permeation of the mind by the vivid recollection of reading.[2] Applying these criteria, Lewis noted that "bad" readers—those who do not give priority or full attention to reading—typically find good writing either too spare or too full. Furthermore, their innate responses to literature might be obstructed or overly influenced by critics, scholars, and other "experts," and not guided primarily by their own judgments. As a master teacher, Lewis regularly encouraged students to make their own judgments, which would in turn be open to challenge. Unlike those who read Lewis in search of answers or certainty, I am attracted to Lewis the teacher, who guided readers without claiming to know all the answers. To

1. Lewis, *Experiment in Criticism*, 1.

2. Lewis, *Experiment in Criticism*, 2–3.

seekers after truth, he recommended risk rather than security. Lewis's *Experiment in Criticism* is an attempt to define "good" literature in a new way. In the final chapter, while not claiming to have discovered a rule by which "good" literature can be measured, he rather affirms, "the nearest I have yet got to an answer is that we seek an enlargement of our being."[3] Though we cannot see light, it is by light we are able to see. In this regard, if you find anything in this book or in its recommended reading useful, use it; if not, set it aside until a better time.

Despite favoring a theistic and medieval model of reality, Lewis notes in his last book, *The Discarded Image*, that his fundamental intention in reconstructing this model is to induce readers "to regard all Models in the right way, respecting each and idolizing none. . . . No Model is a catalogue of ultimate realities, and none is a mere fantasy."[4] Herein we find the core of Lewis's teaching. Though we may have "discarded" models of the past as no longer valid, we need not give them up. We can still respect and enjoy past models, recognizing that our own models, in turn, will be superseded. Lewis's idea of replacing models generally implied adding rather than discarding; since "none is a mere fantasy," all may have value. In relying on "myth" (a story out of which various meaning emerge over time) over "allegory" (a story into which one meaning is placed), Lewis was admitting how much human beings do not yet know.

Shortly before coming to America in 1940, The Russian author Vladimir Nabokov wrote a novel entitled *The Real Life of Sebastian Knight*, in which he noted that there are three sides to every book: "shaped by the teller, reshaped by the listener, concealed from both by the dead man of the tale." In his lectures, Nabokov famously noted a variant of his three perspectives: your side, my side, and the truth, thereby making clear that there are many lenses through which we view reality. As we read great literature and ponder themes regarding spirituality, I encourage you to question the lenses through which you view truth: the bias shaped by family, reshaped by culture, and concealed from both by your religious indoctrination. As you read, your own heart will identify the lenses that distort your truth and prevent you from seeing the universal truth hidden deep within these texts. If possible, remove these lenses, one at a time. It will be a difficult process, perhaps even impossible, but if you persist, the results can be transformative.

3. Lewis, *Experiment in Criticism*, 137.

4. Lewis, *Discarded Image*, 222.

ALL LITERATURE IS FICTION

When my friend Georgia—who recruits, convenes, and facilitates study groups on my writings—read my segment on racism in the second chapter of *Walking on Water*, she felt triggered and to some extent betrayed, because in that chapter she sensed that I had crossed a boundary that jeopardized my "brand." As an entrepreneur who runs her own business, she believes it is important for people in business to offer a consistent product, and she felt that by siding with those who condemned white supremacy, I had been naïve, for my discussion only represented one side of the debate and ignored alternative perspectives. She was right; I had deviated from the path of biblical studies and traditional spirituality into the arena of current events and partisan politics, divisive topics she wished to avoid. In my mind, I was being faithful to my spiritual journey, but from her perspective, I had opened a Pandora's box that might jeopardize the unity of our study group and threaten recruitment and retention.

In my way of thinking, faith never stands alone. Rather, it leads to action, and authentic spirituality inevitably calls us to take sides and make stands, to follow our conscience into risky territory. As an author of spirituality, I feel called to a journey of risk-taking, following a path into the unknown, with no clear goals, guarantees, or results. In *Walking on Water*, I understand spirituality to be counter-cultural and hence indifferent to ideology, theology, and dogma. As I wrestle with the topic of spirituality, I realize that spirituality is not concerned with facts, with being right, or even with producing a product, a perspective, or point of view.

My books, I told Georgia, are designed to get people on a spiritual path and keep them on the path. That path is not charted or controlled by any individual or religious point of view, but is designed to produce wholeness, healing, unity, and peace. It is the path of love and grace, a spiritual path designed and maintained by no human hand, certainly not by me or by members of my race, religion, creed, nation, or clique.

All literature is fiction; even nonfiction is fiction to some degree. Every literary endeavor, ranging from poetry and novels to newspaper reporting to books on spirituality, is filtered through the lens of human subjectivity, ingenuity, and creativity. The same can be said of courtroom testimony. To some degree, all human activity is biased. Every author has a point of view. Some authors have a clear sense of perspective, and some maintain that point of view more consistently than others do.

When I began writing, I had a story to tell; one story led to another, and soon I was on my way to a literary career. To some extent, my intent changed with *Beyond Belief*, my fifth book. At that point the focus of my story changed, from external to internal, from stories with endings to a journey with no discernable goal or ending. Occasionally, of course, I was more in charge, such as in my biblical commentaries, but otherwise, one book led to the next, and now, nearing thirty volumes, there seems no end to the journey.

Desiring to promote my books through social media, I am told that I need to identify my "brand," my point of entry, my product. For that reason, I call myself a "progressive conservative," a label I can live with, partly because of its paradoxical nature. However, don't ask me what it means, for today's answer may not be tomorrow's; what is true in the morning may be a lie by afternoon. For that reason, I am content with metaphorical labels, logos, and usernames such as "Into Thin Places," "Iron Sharpens Iron," "Dark Splendor," and "Adventures in Spirituality," all titles of my books. Authentic spirituality, however, is not Timothy Leary self-transcendence. If I seek a spiritual motto, it is "Love and Service," associated with Matthew 25 spirituality, which encourages me to enjoy God's gifts and share them (see Matt 25:34–40).

People concerned with spirituality are seekers. They do not possess truth; rather, truth possesses them. Our task is to let our heart speak its truth. As my friend, Jess reminds me, "the minute we stop learning, we rent our house to an old person." Truth is never ours, for we have not arrived, nor will we ever, at least not until we see, to use the apostle Paul's metaphor, "face to face." For the time being, we are an unfinished painting, though the painting we are becoming is indeed wonderful. If, in the interim, we need an answer, it is "42." However, if "42" is the answer, what it the question?

When we live in our heads only, we are isolated from the God who resides within, closer than our next breath. To subject truth and love to rational analysis eliminates awe, surprise, and mystery. The restoration of wonder is the beginning of the inward journey toward the awaiting God. Literature, as all art, is a gift of divine grace, a pathway to mystery. Each literary experience is slightly beyond our horizon of understanding. What a gift literature is! When it enhances spirituality, each literary moment confounds in order to keep us going and growing, forever enthralled, forever longing.

In the past, when people asked me what I do in my retirement years, I responded, "I write about theology and spirituality." Now, when asked, I respond, "I write spiritual fiction." *Deep Splendor* is another volume in this series.

NOTE FOR LEADERS AND PARTICIPANTS

Deep Splendor is useful for individual or group study. As you read this book, consider journaling as a way to grow spiritually. A good place to start is with your hopes and dreams. As you reflect and write, be honest with your thoughts and feelings, without ignoring your fears. Transparency facilitates the process of becoming healthy and whole.

As you read this book, it will be helpful for you to become acquainted with the extraordinary literature examined in each chapter. While I have included summary, overview, or synopsis of the literature for each chapter, you are encouraged to read the original material when possible. Because some of this literature is difficult, dense, or lengthy, I encourage you to select one or two authors or works you initially find most interesting, intriguing, or compelling, and obtain copies from an available library or through purchase. Later, you may wish to add to that list. In this regard, be aware that reading and analyzing great literature can be daunting, but if you stay with it, your ability to read, analyze, understand, and benefit from this experience will expand your horizons and enrich your life.

Upon completing each chapter, readers will find the following questions helpful for review and reflection. If you are reading this book in a group setting, be prepared to share your answers with others in the group. If your study is private, I encourage you to write answers to each question in your journal for review and further reflection.

1. After reading this chapter, what did you learn about spirituality?

2. In your estimation, what is the primary insight gained from this chapter?

3. *For personal reflection*: Does this chapter raise any issues you need to handle or come to terms with successfully? If so, how will you deal with them?

DEDICATION

I dedicate this book to Jess Dale Costa, upon whom I relied throughout this project. As in *Wading in Water*, my volume on spirituality and the arts, I am indebted to this former student and longtime friend, a lawyer and independent writer. It is he who suggested the inclusion of Bradley and Walton's books as chapters 2 and 3, and for which he provided insightful comment. As iron sharpens iron, so agreement and disagreement—together—define true friendship.

CHAPTER 1

James Joyce's
A Portrait of the Artist as a Young Man

I BEGAN TEACHING RELIGIOUS studies fulltime in the Religion Department at Grove City College, a Presbyterian-related liberal arts college of some 2,300 students on a beautiful 170-acre campus in western Pennsylvania. There I joined a team of six faculty members who taught a required class for all freshmen, in addition to offering all-college electives and courses for students majoring in religion.

The religion faculty was an eclectic group, with PhDs in fields such as theology, philosophy, English literature, biblical studies, and sociology. One evening, department members were convened by the Rev. Bruce Thielemann, a world-renowned cleric who served as Dean of the Chapel. Before us were some fifteen members of the pre-ministerial club, and our individual assignment was to compile a list of five non-theological books we considered essential reading for students preparing for ministry. Following a brief presentation by the instructors, outlining their list and providing a rationale for the items selected, students were encouraged to engage in a question-and-answer conversation. I don't remember the items on my list, but I do recall that two of the faculty had on their list James Joyce's *A Portrait of the Artist as a Young Man*. I was familiar with the book, but had not yet read it. Despite the difficulties posed by Joyce's innovative stream-of-consciousness style, aspects I still find daunting, I can see why theologians, philosophers, and scholars from many fields consider this book essential reading, not only for pre-ministerial students, but also for people interested in their own spiritual growth, as I hope to make clear in the pages that follow.

A century after its publication in 1916, Joyce's *Portrait of the Artist* endures as a modern classic. The first novel by the author who wrote two of the first truly experimental novels of the twentieth century—*Ulysses* and *Finnegans Wake*—*Portrait* explores the psychological, spiritual, and artistic development of its young protagonist, Stephen Dedalus, Joyce's fictional alter ego, whose surname alludes to Daedalus, Greek mythology's consummate craftsman, and whose first name derives from the first Christian martyr. Like Joyce, our protagonist bears the conflict between religion and hedonism, the sacred and secular, the modern and the mythological, Christianity and paganism. Like Joyce, Stephen questions and rebels against the Catholic and Irish conventions under which he has grown, culminating in his self-exile from Ireland to Europe.

Setting the novel against the background of Irish culture and the drive for Irish independence, Joyce (1882–1941) used the evolving consciousness of Stephen to examine such issues as the patriarchy of Irish culture, the relationship between traditional and symbolist art, and the role of the artist in the modern world. On the face of it, *Portrait* is a coming-of-age story, a tale of a boy growing up in an Irish-Catholic family during the last part of the nineteenth century. He does what a typical boy might do: he goes to school, initially to a boarding school because of his family's social position (chapter 1); he experiences an initiation into sexuality (chapter 2), he experiences guilt and returns to the church in his teens, becoming fanatically pious (chapter 3). Ultimately losing his faith, he gains a new sense of artistic direction (chapter 4), which requires him to discover his life's purpose (chapter 5). While the details of the experience are unique, the story is universal, for each generation faces the same patterns of growth and development.

While the story is somewhat conventional, what is startling about Joyce's novel is its technique. Using the stream-of-consciousness style to describe the development of individual consciousness as a way to overcome, thwart, or dismiss the overwhelming power of external authorities—family, church, school, social class, political orientation—to shape our lives, beliefs, and values, this novel stands out as a new beginning, a new way of writing novels. The experiments initiated by Joyce in *Portrait* reflect the map of twentieth-century novels; Joyce, like others of that century, enacted a spiritual and philosophical "discovery," that truth resides only within the individual and within the perceptions humans choose to call shared. Joyce's insistence that nothing is "real" outside the human imagination became an existentialist manifesto of his time. The novel insists upon this view and is one of the early dramatic statements of that reality. Through Stephen's character, Joyce explores the ways we shape and help create our own realities.

Readers may find the publishing history and initial reception of *Portrait* bizarre. On January 7, 1904, Joyce submitted a work of philosophical fiction entitled *A Portrait of the Artist* to the Irish literary magazine *Dana*. Its editor rejected the work outright, telling Joyce "I can't print what I can't understand." Later that year, Joyce began a realist autobiographical novel, *Stephen Hero*, which incorporated aspects of the philosophical aesthetic he had expounded in *A Portrait*. He worked on the book until mid-1905, taking the manuscript with him when he moved to Trieste (then part of Austria-Hungary) to escape the influences of his religious, cultural, and political upbringing. At 914 manuscript pages, Joyce considered the book half-finished, having completed 25 of its 63 intended chapters. In 1907, however, he abandoned this work, and began a complete revision of the text, producing by 1909 a complete draft of what became *A Portrait of the Artist as a Young Man*, abbreviated to five carefully chosen chapters. In 1911, angered over refusals by publishers to print the stories that made up his *Dubliners*, Joyce flew into a fit of rage and threw the manuscript of *Portrait* into the fire, whence it was rescued with only minor damage by a family member.

Whereas *Stephen Hero* had been written from a realist third-person narrative, in *Portrait* Joyce adopted the free indirect style, a change that subjectivized and interiorized the narrative. Thus, characters, events, and salient details were no longer mentioned according to their external, linear value, but only as perceived from Stephen's point of view.

In 1913, the Irish poet W. B. Yeats recommended Joyce's work to the avant-garde American poet Ezra Pound, who was assembling an anthology of verse. Pound wrote to Joyce, and in 1914 Joyce submitted the first chapter of *Portrait* to Pound, who was so impressed that he managed to have the work published serially in the London literary magazine the *Egoist*, where it appeared in twenty-five installments in 1914 through 1915. In 1916, Harriet Weaver (editor of the *Egoist*) agreed to publish the novel in book form, but printers refused to set the type, frightened by the recent censorship of D. H. Lawrence's *The Rainbow*.[1] The novel was eventually published in November, 1916 by an American publisher in New York, where British libel laws did not apply. Earlier that year, a small band of Irish republicans, standing on the balcony of the General Post Office, prematurely declared Ireland a republic. The British put down the revolt and executed the leaders, and the cause for Irish independence continued.

At the same time, a debate continued between two competing views of art—nationalist and symbolist. One task of any twentieth-century writer was to choose from among these notions about art. Joyce clearly opted out of that decision, trying to fuse the two. The author explores this fusion by examining Stephen's struggle between the influence of his environment and his yearning for the transformative effects of art. Stephen claims in the last chapter that the Irish soul is imprisoned by nationality, language, and religion, what he calls "nets" that hold the soul from flight (5.1049). These are cultural modes of life, nets perpetuated by environment, while Stephen's escape, in his view, will occur through art, a timeless, placeless, magical gift. His choice to be "a priest of eternal imagination, transmuting the daily bread of experience into the radiant body of everliving life" (5.1677–79) clearly aligns him with the symbolists. Stephen believes that he can escape environment, yet Joyce's depiction of his character demonstrates that environment does determine character, and that even Stephen's decisions to transcend Dublin and to turn to symbolist art are environmentally conditioned. Ultimately, Joyce surmounted obstacles in his life through his own realistic and symbolic art.

For many first-time readers of *Portrait*, their age affects the story they read. To read this novel as an adolescent or young adult is to find one's own frustrations with the world. Authorities threaten to destroy our youth and freedom as they attempt to mold us into properly socialized adults whose thought and spirits contribute unthinkingly to the status quo. In Stephen's case, as with most of us, the authorities are biological, literary, spiritual, even ancestral. Finding a young rebel who opposes those codes that threaten his freedom, or one whose experience with religion mirrors the experiences of many adolescents, or one who is intelligent and misunderstood, appeals to anyone who has experienced rebellion at a similar age. Young males in particular identify with Stephen. No matter how jaded, sophisticated, mature, or cynical readers become, this first response to the trials and growth

---

1. Joyce's *Portrait* contained some obscenity, and one of the peculiarities of English libel and obscenity laws was that typesetters were personally libel.

of Stephen Dedalus remains, namely, the feeling that they too have found a way—however unpleasant it might have been for their churchgoing parents—of escaping that world, at least for a time. Escape remains not only for those who heard sermons on hell that Stephen hears, or who have found home life overbearing or depressing, but for all who have heard since childhood various voices telling them what to do with their lives.

Reading the novel later in life has different rewards. Some may identify their younger selves with Stephen while they detach their mature selves from the callowness of their youth. They may even despise Stephen, possibly due to some tendency they fear in themselves, tendencies toward solipsism, arrogance, or indifference to the emotions of others. We tend to despise what threatens us, and this hatred may depend on our degree of identification with this Joycean alter ego. Others read this novel because it allows them to enter a world different from their own. To get a sense of the political intrigues of Dublin, of the nationalist views of the English-Irish conflict, or of the enormous power of the Roman Catholic church in the lives of devout people as Joyce constructs them in this novel intrigues and rewards those of us who are curious about others and their lives.

Some read this novel because they are attracted to Joyce's topics or obsessions: the family, adolescent yearning for escape, the sexuality of men and women. All of these responses are valid and are perhaps the reason the novel lives in our literature. At the same time, the position assigned to this novel by literary history is owed to its experimental nature, its newness and modernity.

A PORTRAIT OF THE ARTIST AS A YOUNG MAN: PLOT AND RESPONSE

Joyce recounts the childhood of Stephen Dedalus using vocabulary that changes as he grows, in a voice not his own but sensitive to his feelings, from the childish language of the beginning to the rumination of a sophisticated university student. The reader experiences Stephen's fears and bewilderment as he comes to terms with the world through a series of disjointed episodes.

The story begins with peculiarly odd and yet familiar language, "Once upon a time and a very good time it was there was a moocow coming down along the road and this moocow that was coming down along the road met a nicens little boy named baby tuckoo." *Portrait* is not, as we know, a fairy tale, and yet it begins that way. The novel starts with an unidentified voice telling a kind of story whose formulaic beginning promises a formulaic ending. Perhaps, like fairy tales, this story will have a way of making the impossible possible or the intolerable tolerable. In fairy tales, the hero is rewarded only if he or she dares do the impossible. If heroes dare to engage in a fearsome task, benevolent powers will come to their aid, and they will succeed. Finally, the formulaic beginning promises a formulaic ending of survival and happiness, where "all lived happily ever after."

The opening of Joyce's story lets us hope that the impossible is possible, that the small, the marginal, and the private voice and its desires can triumph over the older and more powerful voices of authority, voices that contain threats. Yet, before we have finished the second page, we find Stephen hiding under a table. Apparently, he has proposed marriage to another toddler, and seeks refuge under a table. After that action, Stephen is told that he will apologize; "if not, the eagles will come and pull out his eyes" (1.33). Not only does this bizarre threat match the equally bizarre dangers of fairy tales, but also the lack of clear motive for the threat matches fairy-tale plots that similarly ignore linear, causal plot sequences. Like children who listen to a story and choose to identify with its hero, readers may feel threatened by the voices of authority that seem to limit their freedom and creativity. They can shape or change this story to suit their inner story, but in any sense, readers will add their voice to "make sense" of Joyce's tale.

At this point, the scene abruptly switches from the potentially blinding eagle to the playground of Clongowes Wood School, a Jesuit-run boarding school where the apprehensive, intellectually gifted Stephen suffers the ridicule of his classmates while he learns the schoolboy codes of behavior. Ever the underdog, Stephen identifies with the Protestant political leader Charles Stewart Parnell, the recognized leader of the Irish nationalist movement. Stephen's fantasy suggests that Parnell, too, is a figure in a fairy tale, a small and marginal being attacked and threatened by the powerful, malevolent voices of England and the Roman Catholic Church.

At this point the narrative shifts abruptly to Stephen's return home for Christmas. Stephen looks grown-up and is allowed to join the adults for Christmas dinner while the children remain upstairs in the nursery. The setting seems idyllic, but the conversation turns to Parnell and politics. Parnell has died, and church opposition to Parnell over an infidelity reduces Stephen's family to a shouting match in which two voices—one speaking the language of political need and the other of religious orthodoxy—tear at each other, reducing Stephen's father to tears. The terror of Stephen's Christmas break ends in silence, with no voice of reconciliation. Readers are left to fill in the space, to conclude from so little what Stephen or they are to make of the scene.

The scene ends abruptly, and once again Stephen is back at Clongowes, in the midst of yet another confusion, for word is spreading that a number of older boys have been caught "smuggling" (the term, while undefined, refers to secret homosexual horseplay in which five students are caught). Discipline is tightened, and the Jesuits resort to corporal punishment. Stephen is flogged when one of his instructors believes he has broken his glasses to avoid studying, but prodded by his classmates, Stephen works up the courage to complain to the rector, Father Conmee, who assures him there will be no such recurrence, leaving Stephen with a sense of triumph as chapter 1 ends.

What we make of the story thus far depends on how we focus and what we bring to our reading. The novel can be read in many ways, including as fairy tale, as a political and social analysis of Ireland in the late nineteenth century, as a psychological study of young children or of artistic children, even as an analysis of the effects of an Irish Catholic upbringing.[2] Nevertheless, the inferences we draw are at least as much our own as they are what Joyce implies; for we cannot be certain what he, or any other author, implies.

In chapter 2, Stephen's personal and familial world abruptly changes; his family fortunes dwindle, and he moves from childhood into adolescence. Here we learn that Stephen's father gets into debt and the family is forced to leave its pleasant suburban home to live in Dublin. Stephen now realizes he cannot return to Clongowes. However, thanks to a scholarship obtained for him by Father Conmee, Stephen is able to attend Belvedere, a secondary school where he excels academically and becomes a class leader. As Stephen enters adolescence, things seem to fall apart. Despite acquiring a large cash prize from school, Stephen squanders it on a lavish dinner for his family. As distance grows between him and his drunken father, he begins to visit prostitutes.

In this thoroughly patriarchal novel, Stephen's quest for identity focuses almost exclusively on the males he seeks either to identify with or to reject. Women stand in the shadows, important no doubt, but separate

---

2. In 1916, H. G. Wells proclaimed Joyce's novel "by far the most living and convincing picture that exists of an Irish Catholic upbringing." Cited in Harkness, *Portrait*, 21.

from the work of the world, or from the world of the fiction itself. Women exist in the novel as fantasies of men. They come and go, but none of them offers, as do Stephen's patriarchal figures, materials from which he draws to construct his world. And none of them is a storyteller, the guardian of words and hence of reality.

In the first chapter, Stephen perceives his world as simple. Obedience to the clerical fathers at Clongowes and to his biological father at home guarantee success. But fathers turn out not to be so simple a matter. The inadequacy of his biological father leads Stephen into literature and ultimately to the choice of literary authorities. Having read Alexandre Dumas's *The Count of Monte Cristo*, Stephen acts out the part and imagines that, like the fortunes of Dumas's hero, Edmond Dantes, his fortunes may change. Reading about Mercedes, Dante's fiancée, he fantasizes a secret tryst with a female, anticipating that through this encounter his adolescent "weakness and timidity and inexperience would fall from him in that magic moment" (2.185). His "strange unrest," "restless heart," dreams of Mercedes, and his longed-for transfiguration all promise an escape from home and from an increasingly inadequate father.

In *Monte Cristo*, Stephen discovers another proud, single, and maligned hero battling against odds to establish himself as wronged. In this identification, Stephen finds both hope in his social position and sexual fantasy. His normal adolescent uncertainty seems exacerbated by the family social situation, as the first section of chapter 2 ends with Stephen awaiting transfiguration through an encounter with "the unsubstantiated image which his soul so constantly beheld," and the second section begins with the family sliding further down the socioeconomic scale. His father dreams of fighting his enemies with Stephen at his side, but Stephen does not understand his role, or how he is to fulfill the demands of his family. Rather than enlist in that nebulous fight, he increasingly moves away from the disappointing material world of his father and into the world of his imagination.

The fourth section of chapter 2 ends with a Shelley quotation that soothes his despair: "Art thou pale for weariness / Of climbing heaven and gazing on the earth, / Wandering companionless . . ." The moon, in Shelley's verse, is a "chosen sister of the Spirit," an element of hope and companionship.

In chapter 3, Stephen finds another father in the church and God, who both threaten and forgive. As Stephen abandons himself to sensual pleasures, his class is taken on a religious retreat, where the boys sit through sermons by Father Arnall. Stephen pays special attention to sermons on pride, guilt, punishment, and the "Four Last Things" (death, judgment, hell, and heaven). He feels that the words of the sermons describing horrific eternal punishment in hell are directed at himself, and, overwhelmed, comes to desire forgiveness. Overjoyed at his return to the church, he devotes himself to acts of ascetic repentance, though they soon devolve to mere acts of routine, as his thoughts turn elsewhere. His devotion comes to the attention of the Jesuits, and they encourage him to consider entering the priesthood. Stephen takes time to consider, but has a crisis of faith because of the conflict between his spiritual beliefs and his aesthetic ambitions. At a beachside resort, he spots a girl wading, and has an epiphany in which he is overcome with the desire to find a way to express her beauty in his writing.

Initially, Stephen accepts the spiritual authority of the priests of the church without question. But even in chapter 1, their stature is diminished, particularly when Stephen overhears a conversation between his father and Mr. Casey, who speak of the failures of the priesthood that hounded Parnell to his grave. Later, Stephen wonders about their adequacy when he wonders what priests do when they sin (that is, when they are not—as they are supposed to be—perfect). In chapter 3 Stephen choses the authority of the church, not solely because of the power of Arnall's sermons, but also because of disappointment with his own sensual life. At the end of chapter 2, Stephen felt his initial transfiguration achieved in sexual contact as a freeing of the self, but almost instantly sexuality becomes lust, imprisoning Stephen in self-made labyrinths. In chapter 3, he feels he prefers the imprisoning maze of dogma, finding "an arid pleasure in following up to the end the rigid lines of the doctrines of the church and penetrating into obscure silences only to hear and feel the more deeply his own condemnation" (3.138–41).

In their labyrinth of language, his spiritual fathers become—as Shelley and Dumas in the second chapter—the progenitors of the newborn Stephen, who enters "another life," reborn into his faith. But that faith is only nominally the faith of Simon Dedalus, who, at this point, has been utterly usurped by more "appropriate" fathers. As we listen to the sermons of Father Arnall, we find him denying the maturity of his audience's potential artistry, repeatedly referring to the gathered students as "my dear boys" or "my dear little brothers in Christ." Such fatherhood proposes perpetual childhood for Stephen, perpetual submission to the views of others. It is no wonder that he finds these fathers inadequate in chapter 4, for they would enforce sexual regression, limit his verbal, physical, and spiritual freedom, and keep him in a world of "chill and order." To choose an authority who advocates regression or stifles growth halts maturation. In choosing the church and its reversion to a prepubescent, asexual purity, Stephen makes of the church's dogma and ritual another labyrinth, one designed to imprison his body and with it, mind and soul.

Like all human beings, Stephen is a hybrid, a combination of body and soul. However, in chapter 3 he is asked to set aside his physical body and restrict his life to the spiritual realm. Thus, in chapter 4, he devises a prison for his body, controlling his sexuality through faith and piety. This prison, this authority, too, must be escaped, for it offers no liberation; Stephen feels himself unable to love, unable "to merge his life in the common tide of other lives" (4.166). However much he strives to imprison his sexual being, his purity and piety provide no freedom, no release. The final spiritual father with any power over Stephen offers him a priestly vocation, but this vocation, and these fathers, now possess the language of discredited authority. The language of the church, with its voices and systems, now threaten to end his freedom, and he discovers that this father won't do either. Authorial language no longer inspires him.

In chapter 5, as a student at University College, Dublin, Stephen grows increasingly wary of the institutions around him: church, school, politics, and family. In the midst of the disintegration of his family's fortunes, his father berates him and his mother urges him to return to the church. An increasingly dry, humorless Stephen explains his alienation from the church and the aesthetic theory he has developed to his friends, who find that they cannot accept either of them. Stephen concludes that Ireland is too restricted to allow him to express himself fully as an artist, so he decides that he will have to leave. He sets his mind on self-imposed exile, but not without declaring in his diary his ties to his homeland: "Welcome, O life! I go to encounter for the millionth time the reality of experience and to forge in the smithy of my soul the uncreated conscience of my race" (5.2788–90).

When, at the end, Stephen announces to himself and to his readers his departure from Ireland, he proclaims a new authority in his diary, one rooted in his ancestry: "27 April; Old father, old artificer, stand me now and ever in good stead" (5.2791–92). The novel begins with a biological father and ends with an appeal to an imaginative father, Daedalus.

Stephen sees in his name a sign of his destiny. As Daedalus, the ancient master artisan who constructed a labyrinth in Crete to contain the Minotaur—a hybrid both human and bovine—and who became imprisoned within his own maze to protect its secrets, so Stephen Dedalus sees in his name his destiny as artist, used and mistreated by culture but ultimately triumphant. Stephen responds to his telos, his imagine call to what he hopes might be his destiny: "Yes! Yes! Yes! He would create proudly out of the freedom and power of his soul, as the great artificer whose name he bore, a living thing, new and soaring and beautiful, impalpable, imperishable" (4.810–13). Now, at the point in his life when he chooses, he apprehends in his name the sign of his vocation to create, to be an artist. At this point he chooses—or is chosen—by a father who replaces his original father.

One father opens this account with a story; another father closes it. The biological father is displaced by the chosen father, the latter invoked almost as a patron saint at the end, as Stephen Dedalus seeks to fly to the voices that call, "we are your kinsmen" (5.2782). Between these two poles, however, other authorities populate Stephen's world: his religious fathers, and more literary fathers (including Aristotle and Thomas Aquinas).

How should we interpret Stephen's choice of an ancestor? While most versions of the Daedalus myth paint Icarus, the son, as doomed to fall into the sea, the myth does not always speak with one voice. Can we view the Icarian fall as a fortunate fall, the fall crucial to genuine art, just as Christian theologians have constructed the human fall at Eden as a step up, not only because it makes possible the redemption of Christ, but because the expulsion from the Garden makes possible human creativity and growth? In chapter 5, Stephen refers again to the Daedalian myth: "When the soul of man is born in this country [Ireland] there are nets flung at it to hold it back from flight. You talk to me of nationality, language, religion. I shall try to fly by these nets" (5.1047–50). Trapped in the labyrinth, Stephen uses his only hope as flight, departure, transcendence.

As an artist, Stephen gravitates not only to his ancestry, but to a kinship with various authors of his culture, foremost among them his compatriot W. B. Yeats. When Stephen designates the artist "a priest of eternal imagination" (5.1677), we recall how Yeats claimed in "The Theatre" that artists would become a "priesthood," spreading "their religion everywhere." Yeats, who is alluded to in chapter 5, is perhaps the single most influential writer for Stephen Dedalus. In "Ireland and the Arts," Yeats told himself and other artists what they had to do as Irish artists: "We who care deeply about the arts find ourselves as the priesthood of an almost forgotten faith, and we must, I think, if we would win the people again, take upon ourselves the method and the fervour of a priesthood. We must be half humble and half proud."[3]

Stephen's journey can be seen as a quest for the father of his choice, an odd and paradoxical phrase in itself, for in one sense, we cannot choose our fathers. They preexist us. We certainly cannot choose our biological fathers. Stephen's sense, by the second chapter, that he is a "foster child" to his parents, stands as but one indication of his desire to do so. Just as crucially, we cannot choose the "pool" of metaphorical fathers. They are the given of our culture and of our circumstance, though with today's Internet, our choice is expanding. Perhaps we cannot choose what progenitors precede us, but we can and must choose from that pool, selecting "elders" and companions who best respond to our own needs and inclinations. When we choose mentors, influences, and spiritual guides, such choices involve rejecting other mentors, influences, and guides. Taking our cue from the opening and closing fathers of Joyce's *Portrait*, we can make one kind of sense of this novel by focusing on the authorities (the patriarchs and matriarchs) Stephen chooses and rejects.

The fifth chapter of *Portrait* proposes that artists must in some way destroy their patriarchy in order to create, agreeing with Friedrich Nietzsche, who once noted, "When one hasn't had a good father, it is necessary to invent one." Stephen's adoption of various literary and spiritual fathers stems from the inadequacy of his biological father. Ultimately, it is to Daedalus, the "old artificer," that he turns. As Joyce seems to indicate, artists must not only invent their lineage, they must also select their modes of life. Like Stephen, each of us must choose our aesthetics, our poetry, and our dance against the absurdity and despair in our world. Stephen's university companions seek universal peace and social betterment (MacCann), Irish nationalism (Davin), and the conventions of filial piety (Cranly). Stephen chooses art. Joyce's novel—with its gaps, breaks, sudden shifts, and indeterminacies—demands that we, the readers, become artists, accomplices in the act of creation, for "in the virgin womb of the imagination the world was made flesh" (5.1543–44).

---

3. Yeats, *Essays and Introductions*, 203.

CHAPTER 2

Marion Zimmer Bradley's
The Mists of Avalon

LONG AGO AND FAR away—late fifth- and early sixth-century Britain if you require specificity, but beyond the realms of time and space if you value fact and fiction equally—there lived a king named Arthur, a figure of such power and originality that his story became one of the most popular literary subjects of all time.

The Arthurian legends have always had a firm hold on British and Continental literature, due to the heroic and evocative picture of the past that they present. There is, however, little historical evidence about the real King Arthur. He seems to have been a minor king or warlord of the Celtic Britons who, in the confused and violent period following the withdrawal of the Roman legions from Britain around 410 CE, led his people in temporary resistance against the Anglo-Saxon invasion. Despite Arthur's legendary twelve battles, the Anglo-Saxons were ultimately triumphant and drove the defeated Britons into the remote regions of Scotland and Wales. It was in these areas that the Arthurian legends first arose.

A great number of these derive from the Welsh tradition. The most considerable collection of these Welsh legendary tales is known as the Mabinogion. The oldest poems in this collection have been dated to the sixth century CE. Whoever Arthur was, and whatever his real achievement, there is no question that he rapidly became the most important hero and the central figure of British legendary history. Over time, many Celtic myths and traditions became attached to his name, including such legend-ary figures as Gawain, Lancelot, and Tristram (Tristan), all originally inde-pendent characters. By the end of the Middle Ages, Arthur was the hero of romances composed in France, Germany, Italy, and Spain.

From the Arthurian tales there developed further tales about the Knights of the Round Table and their quest for the Holy Grail. Few leg-ends of the Middle Ages have had so strong an evocative power as those that developed about the Grail. Thanks to Tennyson and Wagner,[1] Galahad and Perceval have become knights of virtue, and the quest of the Grail has come to mean either a vain following after "wandering fires" or the arduous search for supreme mystical experience.

The stories of the Grail—and there are many—have fascinated leading literary figures of our time, with varying results. They inspired T. S. Eliot's poem *The Waste Land*, Charles Williams's fantasy novels on the struggle between the forces of evil and good, and films such as *The Da Vinci Code, Indiana Jones and the Last Crusade, Excalibur*, and the irreverent *Monty Python and the Holy Grail*.

Whence came this Christianized development of the Arthurian leg-end—a development of which the first record is found in a French poem dated about 1180, and which in the next fifty years produced so many varying forms—and how did it come to be linked with relics of Christ's Passion? When we ponder the Grail quest, many dualities come to mind, including social, psychological, cosmological, philosophical, and religious. Those acquainted with the history of Christianity are aware that during its first five centuries, there were many Christianities, many ways of being Christian. Eventually, in the late fourth century, the only religion allowed in the Roman empire was one version of the Christian religion—the orthodox form—wedded to the remnants of Roman imperialism in what became known as Christendom. The West's conversion to Christianity required the demise of paganism, and with it, the loss of nonduality as a way of thinking and living.

One of the interesting aspects of the Grail legends as we remember them is that they developed about five centuries after Christianity was

---

1. Alfred Lord Tennyson was the most important poet of the Victorian period, and his works include some of the finest poetry in the English language. The *Idylls of the King*, one of his best-known compositions, deals with an exciting age in English history, and with such fascinating characters as King Arthur, Guinevere, Sir Lancelot, and the other Knights of the Round Table. Perceval, another Grail hero, was the main inspiration of Wagner's *Parsifal*.

imposed upon Europe. Properly understood, these legends represent a coming together of two traditions, Celtic pagan and non-Celtic Christian traditions, an amalgam not unlike the earlier Canaanite pagan and Israelite traditions, or the later Judeo-Christian and Greco-Roman synthesis.

The details of Arthur's story, mainly composed of Welsh and English folklore, are unhistorical. The legendary Arthur developed as a literary figure largely through the popularity of Geoffrey of Monmouth's imaginative twelfth-century *Historia Regnum Britanniae* (History of the Kings of Britain). While some of Geoffrey's *Historia* (completed in 1138) seem to have been invented by Geoffrey, other material was adapted from earlier sources. According to Geoffrey's account, Arthur led the defense of Britain against Savon invaders and established a vast empire, but in earlier tales and poems, Arthur appears as a figure of folklore, defending Britain from human and supernatural enemies.

In the late twelfth century, the French writer Chétien de Troyes added Lancelot and the Holy Grail to the story, beginning the genre of Arthurian romance that became a significant strand of medieval literature. In these accounts, the narrative often shifted from King Arthur to other characters, such as the Knights of the Round Table and their quest of the Grail, associated with the death of Christ and the Eucharistic cup. Arthurian literature thrived during the Middle Ages but waned in the centuries that followed until it experienced a major resurgence in the nineteenth century. The legend continued to have prominence into the twenty-first century, not only in literature but also in adaptations for theatre, film, television, comics, and other media.

The Arthurian legend holds a unique place in the literature of the English language and seems to be capable of infinite interpretations. Perhaps the most imaginative—and insightful—of the recent versions of the account is *The Mists of Avalon*, a 1983 historical fantasy novel by American writer Marion Zimmer Bradley (1930–1999), which offers a feminist perspective of the Arthurian legends. Focusing on the life of Morgaine (Morgan le Fay), a priestess of the Goddess fighting to save her Celtic religion at a time when Christianity threatened to destroy the pagan way of life, the epic relates the Arthurian legends from the perspectives of Morgaine, Gwenhwyfar (Guinevere), Viviane, Morgause, Igraine, and other women of the Arthurian legend.

The lengthy novel, written in four parts, was a best-seller upon its publication and remains popular. The book was later expanded into the Avalon series. Bradley received significant praise for her convincing portrayal of the Arthurian legend and for her respectful handling of Celtic paganism, casting her story in a nondualist frame in which there is neither black and white nor good and evil, but various truths. Isaac Asimov, the American writer of science fiction and popular science, called Bradley's book "the best retelling of the Arthurian Saga I have ever read." The book also won the 1984 Locus Award for Best Fantasy Novel and spent four months on the New York Times best-seller list in hardcover. The paperback edition also ranked among the top five trade paperbacks for four years. In 2001, the book was adapted for television into a TNT miniseries. In 2010, J. S. Morgane examined religious aspects of the Avalon series in *The Spirituality of Avalon*, a study of the religion of the Mother Goddess portrayed by Bradley in her Avalon cycle.

THE MISTS OF AVALON: PLOT AND RESPONSE

Bradley's storyline comprises a multi-generational retelling of the Arthurian legend from its Brythonic Celtic perspective. The plot tells the story of the women who influence King Arthur, high king of Britain, and those around him.

The book's protagonist is Morgaine, priestess of Avalon, who is King Arthur's half-sister. Their mother Igraine married Uther Pendragon after Morgaine's biological father, Gorlois, is killed in battle. Uther becomes her stepfather and he and Igraine have a son, Arthur. When Morgaine is eleven years old and Arthur six, an attempt is made on Arthur's life. Their maternal aunt, Viviane, arrives at Uther's court in Caerleon and advises him to have Arthur fostered far away from the court for his own safety. Uther agrees, also allowing Viviane to take Morgaine to Avalon, where she is trained as a priestess of the Mother Goddess. During this period, Morgaine becomes aware of the rising tension between the old pagan and the new Christian religions. After seven years of training, Morgaine is initiated as a priestess of the Mother, and Viviane begins grooming her as the next Lady of Avalon.

Shortly after her initiation, Morgaine is given in a fertility rite to the future high king of Britain. Their union is not personal, but rather a symbolic wedding between the future high king and the land he will defend. The following morning, Morgaine and Arthur recognize each other and are horrified to realize what they have done. Two months later, Morgaine finds she is pregnant.

After Uther dies in battle against the Saxon invaders, Arthur claims the throne of Britain despite questions about his legitimacy. Since Arthur must now defend Britain against the Saxons, Viviane has Morgaine make him an enchanted scabbard that will prevent him from losing blood, and gives him the sacred sword Excalibur. With the combined force of Avalon and Caerleon, Arthur repels the invaders, his kingdom jointly representing and defending the old pagan values and the new Christian ones.

As Morgaine's unborn child grows within her, so do her feelings of anger and betrayal toward Viviane, whom she believes tricked her into bearing a child to her half-brother. Unable to remain in Avalon, Morgaine leaves for the court of her aunt Morgause, queen of Lothian, where she bears her son, naming him Gwydion. Spurred by her husband Lot's ambition and her own, Morgause tricks Morgaine into allowing her to rear her son. To escape Lot's unwanted advances, Morgaine leaves Lothian and returns to Arthur's court as a lady-in-waiting to the high queen Gwenhwyfar. She does not see her son again until he is grown and a Druid priest.

When Gwenhwyfar fails to produce an heir, she is convinced God is punishing her for her sins. Chief among them, she believes, are her inability to persuade Arthur to outlaw pagan religious practice in Britain and her forbidden love for Galahad, Arthur's cousin and finest knight, who is known as Lancelet. Although Lancelet reciprocates Gwenhwyfar's love, he is also Arthur's friend and an honorable man. The situation causes intense suffering and guilt to both Lancelet and Gwenhwyfar. On the eve of a decisive battle against the Saxons, Gwenhwyfar prevails upon Arthur to put aside his father's Pendragon banner and replace it with her own Christian banner. As her religious fanaticism grows, relations between Avalon and Arthur's court grow strained. Out of desperation over her inability to carry a child to term, Gwenhwyfar seeks Morgaine's help, threatening to have an extramarital affair so she can become pregnant. To keep her from doing so, Morgaine reveals that Arthur already has a son, though he does not know it.

After the battle, Arthur moves his court to Camelot, which is more easily defended than Caerleon had been. Seeking to free Lancelet and Gwenhwyfar from the forbidden love that traps them, Morgaine tricks Lancelet into marrying Gwenhwyfar's cousin, Elaine. Some time later, Gwenhwyfar unwittingly breaks Morgaine's confidence and tells Arthur he has a son. Horrified, Arthur summons Morgaine and orders her to tell him the truth. Gwenhwyfar and Arthur then arrange for Morgaine to marry into Wales, far from Camelot. However, through a misunderstanding, Morgaine, who thought she would be marrying the king's younger son Accolon, a Druid priest and warrior, finds herself betrothed to King Uriens of Wales, who is old enough to be her grandfather. Arthur yearns to meet his son Gwydion and possibly foster him at Camelot, but Gwenhwyfar refuses to discuss it.

Morgaine marries Uriens and moves to Wales, but in time begins an affair with Accolon. The "old people" of the hills, who keep pagan ways, regard Accolon and Morgaine as their king and queen, while King Uriens suspects nothing. When Avalloch, Accolon's older brother, confronts Morgaine about her relation with Accolon and tries to blackmail her, Morgaine arranges for Avalloch to die in a hunting accident. When Morgaine tells Accolon, who is now Uriens's heir, of the sacred marriage she made with Arthur years before, she persuades him to attempt to wrest the kingdom from Arthur and the Christians and bring it back under the sway of Avalon. The attempted coup fails and Arthur kills Accolon in single combat. As Uriens recovers from the shock of losing a second son, Morgain leaves Wales forever.

Gwydion, now grown, goes to the Saxon courts to learn warfare far from Arthur's eye. Impressed by his cleverness, the Saxons name him Mordred ("Evil Counsel"). Years later, at a Pentecost feast at Camelot, Gwydion introduces himself as Queen Morgaine's son. Because of his close resemblance to Lancelet, he must tell people that Lancelet is not his father. To earn his knighthood, Gwydion challenges Lancelet to single combat during a tourney. As they start to fight in earnest, Gwenhwyfar, who has warmed to Gwydion, protests, and Arthur interrupts the match. Lancelet makes Gwydion a knight of the Round Table, naming him Mordred.

During another Pentecost festival, Morgaine returns to Camelot under guise, with another sister of Avalon. Wielding great magic, Morgaine and her companion make manifest the Holy Grail—one of the sacred regalia of Avalon. The assembled court view the Grail as a Christian object, seeing the manifestation of the Holy Grail as a holy revelation. When the Grail disappears, the Knights of the Round Table leave to search for its location. Mordred, like Arthur, remains at Camelot, where he attempts to usurp the throne. In a climactic battle, the armies of Arthur and Mordred fight and Arthur is mortally wounded. Morgaine takes the dying Arthur through the mists to Avalon, reassuring him that he did not fail in his attempt to save Britain from the approaching dark times. Arthur dies in her arms as the shoreline of Avalon comes into view. Morgaine buries him in Avalon and remains there to tell the tale of Camelot.

Usually, when we look at the past, we only see a small part of it, and most often from a patriarchal perspective that excludes women or portrays them as villains, responsible for the failures of men. *The Mists of Avalon* paints a very different picture, providing a glimpse of the spiritual possibilities beyond male-dominated, male-defined religion. While this book inspires feminist views, it also enhances interest in folklore and primal spirituality.

While the story focuses on female characters, Bradley brings irony and nuance to her characters. Hers is not a fairy tale, or a story about beauty and the beast. Rather, it is the story of a smart girl who becomes a powerful woman. Yet Bradley shows Morgaine doing foolish, selfish things, and she makes clear that Gwenhwyfar's position is an impossible one. Doom hangs over Arthur's reign, just as fate rules legend. There is no happy ending for anyone at Camelot. Bradley depicts real people struggling against their destiny, and she demonstrates that it is not simply impersonal fate behind her characters' inevitable downfall, but rather, a system of oppression.

While one might label the system "patriarchy," the cause is never one-dimensional. In 2014, Moira Greyland, Bradley's daughter, told the world that her mother had sexually abused her and many other children for over a decade. Rumors about Bradley and her husband Walter Breen (Greyland's father) had circulated in the science fiction and fantasy communities for years, and Breen had died in prison after being convicted of molesting a child, but it wasn't until Moira's disclosure that the truth became clear. She had waited so long to tell her story out of respect for her mother's work and reputation.

As we know, all humans are flawed; men are not equally bad, and women are not equally good. Knowing what we now know about Bradley's life, we can detect elements of pedophilia in her writings. In *Mists*, one can easily dismiss episodes of pedophilia as simply elements of abnormal behavior linked to ancient fertility rituals. Should we discourage or prohibit reading *Mists* for those episodes that contravene modern standards of behavior or sexuality? The answer varies from person to person, and community to community. There will always be episodes in great literature, including the Bible, that we find questionable, deplorable, unwholesome, and profane. Should we ban reading such literature because of controversial episodes, or can we allow their reading for the sake of discussion and debate, to help individuals clarify or establish their own standards, values, and beliefs?

This is, of course, a version of the question we all need to ask at this moment. How do we separated the artist from the art, and how do we distinguish good or acceptable art from bad or unacceptable art? Who draws boundaries and establishes standards? At what age and in what context can youth be exposed to contrary opinions, standards, and perspectives? Can (or should) we watch movies directed by Woody Allen, or produced by Harvey Weinstein, separating good art from defective artists? Can we admire films portrayed by flawed actors, worship in churches and denominations led by flawed clergy, purchase items from corporations run by flawed directors, or maintain allegiance to governments run by flawed politicians? To some extent, we must, or else we would simply return to the cave, or better yet, remain unborn.

The question of separating abusers, perverts, and deviants from their work is not simple, and there are no easy answers. There is, however, one necessary response. When individuals declare they have been assaulted, abused, harassed, or mistreated, we must believe them and come to their aid, particularly if this mistreatment occurred in their youth or through violence. We can value *The Mists of Avalon*, its characters and story and what they add to our personal mythology, while rejecting Bradley's pedophilia, for however we might admire books such as Bradley's, life matters more than fiction.

POINTS TO PONDER IN *THE MISTS OF AVALON*

Bradley's central theme, found in the book's prologue and repeated throughout, is deeply spiritual and intrinsic to all wholesome spirituality, namely, that "all the Gods are one God, and all the Goddesses are one Goddess, and there is only one Initiator." To this principle of the interrelatedness, unity, and ultimate oneness of all reality, Bradley adds a corollary, "And to every man his own truth, and the God within."[2] By adding this corollary, Bradley is affirming not only the interconnectedness of all living things, but also their uniqueness. Interestingly, Bradley's thesis, unlike her corollary, correlates with primal spirituality.

The first humans were animists; they were conscious that nature was spirit-infused. Their life was holistic; individuals and groups alike viewed

2. Bradley, *Mists of Avalon*, x–xi.

the natural, social, and spiritual dimensions as profoundly integrated. Primal cultures—that is, tribes or communities having no scriptures, literate sources of guidance, or linear sense of history—represent primitive attempts to establish harmony with the powers such groups sensed directing human life. Spirituality, for primal peoples, meant direct relationship between human beings and the deeper realm around and within them, which they viewed as more powerful and real than the realm they experience through the senses.

As Bradley indicates in her title, Avalon is a liminality, a place of deep splendor, a "thin place" on earth diaphanous and permeable to the divine but inaccessible to the uninitiated behind a veil of mist. Like C. S. Lewis's Narnia and J. K. Rowling's wizarding world of Hogwarts and Diagon Alley, Bradley acknowledges that our world is alive with liminalities (threshold spaces between the sacred and the mundane). Adjacent to Avalon are two other worlds, the Christian Glastonbury and the realm of the fairies.[3]

To enter Avalon requires training in spiritual telepathy, whereby a select few are able to enter by summoning the barge needed to transport Avalonians to their ethereal island home. As the earthly abode of the Goddess and her priestesses, Avalon is led by a series of high priestesses, selected primarily because they possess the gift of "the Sight," an ability to foresee the future or to display deep awareness of the present. Like seers in the world's religions or recipients of the gifts of "prophecy" and "discernment" in the Bible (see 1 Cor 12:10), some people called or chosen to serve the Goddess are spiritually prescient.

On one occasion, Bradley acknowledges the limits of human discernment when she has Morgaine say, "I think the Sight is given to mock us— we see what the Gods give us to see, but we know never what it means."[4] On the other hand, Morgause, a spiritual skeptic, concludes that the Sight is not something connected exclusively with the Gods (religion), but is simply "a

---

3. According to ancient wisdom, to believe in fairies is to acknowledge that there is much human beings don't know or understand. Affirming the limits of reason and the senses as sole connectors or interpreters of reality, belief in fairies represents remaining open to the possibility that anything is possible, including the realm of spirits. For the Irish author W. B. Yeats, to believe in fairies is to take folk stories seriously and to acknowledge the role spirits play in human life. Morally ambivalent, the spirits are said to be invoked by music, poetry, and love.

4. Bradley, *Mists of Avalon*, 814.

part of life, there and accessible, nothing to do with good or evil, but available to anyone who had the will and the ruthlessness to use it."[5]

Most commonly, when we study religious history, the perspective given is that of Christianity missionizing, conquering, and converting the heathen. In Bradley's book, the perspective is switched, for here the perspective is that of the underdog, the marginalized, or the inferior. The world we encounter in *Mists* is an evolved form of primal spirituality, in which the world is under allegiance to a female power known as the Great Goddess. It retains the essence of paganism (called "the Old Mysteries"), but it includes vestiges of modern feminist matriarchy, evident when Morgaine declares, near the end of the book, "I have called on the Goddess and found her within myself," or when she reflects on previous priestly mentors such as Viviane and Raven and says, "They are the Goddess. And I am the Goddess. And there is no other." In such passages we discern Bradley's own religious perspective, particularly when she writes, "And Morgaine knew that never again would she have the ability to seek beyond herself for comfort or counsel; she could look only within."[6]

In passages such as these, Bradley is adapting neo-pagan ideals to criticize traditional gender roles and the misogyny of institutionalized Christianity. In her religion, sex is not a necessary evil, women are not seducers, nor should they be blamed as the means by which sin came first into the world, views she associates with Christianity. Contrary to Christianity, she dismisses belief in hell, affirming a process of reincarnation that culminates in union with the Gods. In her view, the essence of paganism is the struggle for enlightenment, attained over many lifetimes.

Writing historical fiction, Bradley portrays a time when Christianity entered Britain and had begun claiming undivided cultural allegiance, including the abolition of all pagan beliefs and rituals, which Christians attributed to demonic influence. Bradley portrays much that is true, Christian missionizing by force and through threat of damnation, but her perspective is one-sided, for rarely does one hear of the Christian God as the God of love, mercy, and grace. For Bradley, truth has many faces, and is related to an individual's character. There is no concept of original sin in paganism, and Bradley advocates an instinctual understanding of sin as "the wish to do harm." At a critical point in the narrative, when Gwenhwyfar, portrayed as a zealot Christian, forces King Arthur to confess of his incestuous sin,

5. Bradley, *Mists of Avalon*, 816.
6. Bradley, *Mists of Avalon*, 803.

Morgaine tells her, "Gwenhwyfar, you think too much of sin. We did not sin, Arthur and I. . . . The Goddess—for that matter, your God—is not a vindictive demon, looking about to punish somebody for some imagined sin."[7]

In her account, Bradley advocates coexistence rather than conquest, religious cooperation and pluralism instead of particularism and supremacy, nondualism in place of dualism. This, of course, is a modern emphasis, but one rooted in antiquity. As Taliesin, the harpist of Avalon and Merlin of Britain[8] tells Gwenhwyfar early in the story, "Dear child, you must remember—this country is for all men, whatever their Gods, and we fight against the Saxons not because they will not worship our Gods but because they wish to burn and ravage our lands and take all that we have for themselves. We fight to defend the peace of these lands, lady, Christian and pagan alike, and this is why so many have flocked to Arthur's side. Would you have him a tyrant who puts the souls of men in slavery to his own God, as not even the Caesars dared to do?"[9]

Bradley is correct in demonstrating that Western culture, society, and religion have leaned too far toward patriarchal domination, but the solution is not to lean excessively toward matriarchy. As she states clearly and persuasively, all the Gods are one, and all the Goddesses one, and the truth is within. The solution is balance, moderation, and the equality of all in a world ruled by love. The principle here is this, "go deep in any one perspective and you will find universal truth." As Bradley states, using the Merlin as mouthpiece, "I think you mistake the nature of Heaven . . . Do you really think mankind's quarrels and imperfections will be carried on in Heaven? . . . I have one thing in common with (Christian) priests. I have spent much time trying to separate the things of man from those that belong to the Divine, and when I have done separating them, I find there is not so great a difference. Here on Earth, we cannot see that, but when we have put off this body we will know more, and know that our differences make no difference at all to God."[10]

---

7. Bradley, *Mists of Avalon*, 551.

8. In Bradley's retelling, Merlin is a title and not a name. This legendary wizard, featured in Arthurian legend and medieval Welsh poetry, is said to have been the king's advisor until his untimely demise.

9. Bradley, *Mists of Avalon*, 386.

10. Bradley, *Mists of Avalon*, 37–38.

TWO WOMEN, TWO PURITANS, BOTH MISGUIDED[11]

The prologue to *The Mists of Avalon* offers a retrospective statement of Morgaine's viewpoint. She writes it after the events she describes in her story have taken place and been journaled. It offers us a view of a spiritually mature Morgaine, one who has endured great hardship in order to reach her level of understanding. The story itself begins with a far less wise storyteller, one who has many miles to travel to reach the wholeness she either must reach or be destroyed in the process of seeking.

The young Morgaine is a zealot, a puritan like Gwenhwyfar, consumed by fundamentalist zeal and evangelical fervor. Mindless of her own intuition and judgment, unable to differentiate the voice of her Goddess in her heart from her own voice in her own mind, Morgaine proceeds on the assumption that she is on a divine mission, and that her Goddess requires her assistance to accomplish her ends. It is always dangerous to assume that our God requires assistance, or that we can even know what ends our God is working towards. Gwenhwyfar is an extreme example of this. Morgaine, however, is far more guilty, because she knows the importance of intuition and wisdom but discards them in her fervor to advance her own perceived agenda; Gwenhwyfar is merely ignorant, simple and naïve. But Gwenhwyfar is as resilient to change—transformation, rather—as Morgaine. In the end, Morgaine is transformed, Gwenhwyfar is not.

The radical mistake both of these two make, the commonality that makes these two different people from two different worlds so similar, is their shared notion that somehow they can know the divine will, and the somewhat egotistical notion that the divine will requires their active participation in order to take place. The idea of an all powerful God or Goddess creates an oxymoron when expressed in the same breath as the idea that that God or Goddess requires our assistance to operate and achieve the divine will. In fact, it is even more striking that we think we can even know for sure what the divine will is. To act on our own will is to believe we are at the same level of omniscience and power as the inexpressible absolute we call God.

The mind is a death trap. In the most spiritual of matters, only the heart (only the intuitive senses) can see clearly, and only through these facilities

---

11. This segment is adapted (with minor edits) from unpublished journal material written by my friend Jess Dale Costa, a lawyer, independent writer, and a discussion leader of my books. Proficient in topics related to literature, the arts, and spirituality, it was he who suggested I include *The Mists of Avalon* in this study.

can we presume to understand the divine will. Even then, we remain human, and the self-willed mind has an annoying habit of intruding on everything. Acting on perceived understandings of the will of God is a dangerous undertaking. Both Morgaine and Gwenhwyfar assume they know the best path for others as well as for themselves, spreading the tragic effects of their puritanical zeal everywhere, and only impeding, never changing, the steady progress towards the divine purpose. Impeding the divine purpose never changes it; it simply causes unnecessary additional pain for individuals and everyone around them.

In the end, Morgaine achieves a vital transformation. It is eloquently expressed in the prologue. All of the Gods and Goddesses, she comes to see, are one. God appears to each of us as we can best understand God. True service to the God who has all and demands nothing comes in serving, not leading, our fellows; this is our sacrifice, and the only one that has any value to an all powerful God-Goddess. Our will is a poor substitute for God's. Love all, harm none; that is the whole of the law.

POWER SHARED: NO DOMINATION IN GOD

Throughout much of Western history—certainly since the time of Constantine, well into the Enlightenment period, and, in some cases, to the present—Christianity has thrived in a culture of domination and supremacy, be it under Roman Catholicism, Protestant versions of Christendom, even Puritan versions of religious liberty. Why is this so? Why have Christians turned God into an omnipotent sovereign "Lord," Jesus into "Christ the King," and the Holy Spirit into an agent who guides only select individuals into eternal, unchanging truth?

The Christian Trinity, properly understood, stands for the exact opposite, a loving, relational entity who flows through all things since the beginning. We fail to understand Jesus and the Holy Spirit if we don't first participate in the eternal dance of mutuality and communion within which they participate. Like the being we call God, Father, or Mother, Jesus and the Spirit dwell in a realm of love, grace, and abundance, not in a realm of domination.

Christians need to let go of their pyramids of power, of their empires, wealth, patriarchy, and control. If Western Christians surrendered their false dualistic models of truth, reality, and relationality to nondualist Trinitarian models, their notions of society, politics, and authority would utterly change—from top-down and outside-in to grass-roots spiritual patterns and norms. Circles, ellipses, and parabolas are far less threatening to individuals and communities based on the wholeness and inclusivity modeled by Jesus.

Unfortunately, it took early Christians less than three centuries, in some cases less than a century, to transform the one who described himself as "gentle and humble in heart" (Matt 11:29)—one described by the early church as having displayed kenosis[12] by humbling himself to the point of death on a cross (Phil 2:8)—into an imperial deity, both in Western (Roman) Christianity and in Eastern (Byzantine) Christianity. When the Roman Empire converted to Christianity, the Greek Zeus (Roman Jupiter) became the Latin *Deus*, the vulnerable, relational, kenotic Jesus became unrecognizable, and the Christian Trinity became imperial, totalitarian, and fearsome.

The Christian Trinity, however, is just the opposite, for, as Jesus taught—in word and through example—God's power is not dominating, threatening, or coercive. Paul, too, was faithful to the original message, telling the Corinthian believers that "when I am weak, then I am strong" (2 Cor 12:10), learning this lesson by revelation from Jesus, who declared for all time the sacred lesson that "power is made perfect in weakness" (2 Cor 12:9), a self-emptying truth Jesus modeled persuasively on the cross.

This, then, is how God creates, and how God rules. God's creative "Let It Be" approach should be ours as well, for all who believe and love God are called to be co-creators in God's eternally unfolding promissory potentiality. "The grace of the Lord Jesus Christ, the love of God, and the communion of the Holy Spirit" (2 Cor 13:13) should be the nondualist and inclusive ecology for all we do and for how we do it, including how we display power, mercy, and justice.

Divine power is shared power, gracious and free. If there is no self-serving domination in the Triune God, how should we, God's children, view power? In her 2018 book *Dare to Heal*, Brené Brown distinguishes between "power over" and "power with." While there is no "power over" in the Trinity, there is empowerment, that is, "power with"—a giving away, sharing, letting-go sort of power, and thus an infinite flow of trust and mutuality. Instead of empowering, self-giving power—in marriage, in culture,

---

12. Kenosis is the concept of willful self-emptying in order to become entirely receptive to the divine will. An aspect of the incarnation of Christ, kenosis involves the relinquishment of divine attributes by Jesus Christ in becoming human.

and in international relations—Christians have traditionally preferred rulers, empires, wars, and domination. This form of human power, modeled in patriarchal, imperial, and ecclesiastical domination systems, is a perversion, a masquerade of divine power. For "in Christ Jesus . . . the only thing that counts is faith working through love" (Gal 5:6). In Jesus, God models power, and it ends up being vulnerable, humble, and self-giving. How different this is from the "rights" that shape the American national identity, with its rights to "life, liberty, and the pursuit of happiness." So much of American history, by contrast to the values espoused by Jesus, consists of groups of individuals protecting themselves and what is theirs with a gun, a flag, or the cloak of racial, class, or gender privilege.

When we take something we possess—our wealth, our power and influence, our comfort and control, our society and institutions, even our identities and abilities—and make them useful to others, we are practicing kenosis, a powerful and creative form of spirituality.

CHAPTER 3

Evangeline Walton's
The Mabinogion Tetralogy

SOME OF THE MOST exciting and fruitful thought in recent theology can be described as a rediscovery of the Perennial Tradition that so many sages and mystics have spoken of in their own ways. This recovery involves the recognition that human beings are part of something greater than that which they can observe or believe in.

Before the Common Era, appearing first with Eastern sages around 800 BCE and coalescing with Jewish prophets and Greek philosophers around 500 BCE, the peoples of the world experienced the emergence of what the German philosopher Karl Jaspers (1883–1969) described as the start of the Axial Age. This phenomenon involved a worldwide emergence of systematic and conceptual thought, using reason and philosophy to process primal notions of participation with nature, others, and the supernatural world, producing what we might call mediated participation.

Among the people called Israel there was a dramatic realization of intimate union and group participation with God. The Israelites came to recognize individually enlightened persons such as Moses and Isaiah, but they went beyond, widening the notion of participation to society as a whole. It is amazing that people in the civilized Western world have forgotten or ignored such Perennial teaching, making salvation all about individual persons going to heaven or hell, which is surely a regression from the collective and even cosmic notion of salvation taught in the Jewish and Christian scriptures.

In his teaching, Jesus offered a renewed vision of the primal holistic teaching. This allowed him to speak of true union and full participation at all levels: with oneself, neighbors, outsiders, enemies, and nature, and through these, union with the Divine. This teaching, often ignored and forgotten by future generations of believers, early Christians called gospel, meaning "good news." It is this gospel, a form of union and participation found in the Perennial Tradition and prior to that in primal traditions, that we explore in this chapter through Evangeline Walton's retelling of the Mabinogion, a tradition we already encountered in Marion Zimmer Bradley's *Mists of Avalon*, only in Walton's case, a tradition more purely Welsh.

The mythological stories comprising the Mabinogion are a masterpiece of medieval European literature. The Mabinogion (the accent is on the antepenult, that is, the third to last syllable, namely, on the first "o") is to Welsh (or Celtic) mythology what the *Poetic Edda* is to the Norse, the *Kalevala* to the Finns, *Beowulf* and the *Nibelungenlied* to the Anglo-Saxons, the *Iliad* and *Odyssey* to the Greeks, the *Aeneid* to Romans, and the Matter of Britain, particularly the Arthurian legends, to the English. Of the eleven traditional Welsh stories, four make up the Mabinogi proper, a body of literature known as the Four Branches. The earliest written manuscripts, dating to the eleventh century, are based on earlier oral sources going back to the settlement of Celtic tribes in Britain, Wales, Scotland, and Ireland during the period of Roman domination. Told and retold by Welsh bards, these stories flourished from the sixth to the fifteenth centuries. The term *mabinogi*, originally meaning "tale of youth" or "tale of a hero," came finally to mean simply "tale" or "story." Thus, a Branch of the Mabinogi is a "portion of the story." While the story, as it appears in the translations of Lady Charlotte Guest in 1834–1849 and more recently in that of Gwyn and Thomas Jones (1949), comprises the loosely connected tales of Pwyll, Branwen, Manawyddan, and Math, most if not all of the branches must originally have circulated independently. The literary "authors" of the Four Branches, by which we mean those who gave them their eventual shape, were likely Christian monks who preserved these stories in somewhat modified terms.

The versions we follow, known as the *Mabinogion Tetralogy*, is that of Evangeline Walton (a pen name used by Evangeline Wilna Ensley; 1907–1996), a Welsh scholar who tells the stories of the Four Branches in bardic style, bringing to life the mythological accounts of real men and women, their exploits set in a spirit-infused age, when belief in many gods and goddesses permeated everyday life, their natural and supernatural realms commingling, interacting, and permeable. As Walton indicates in her published notes, while she felt free to add or subtract details in her sources, she wished to alter nothing found in the Four Branches, save items that seemed anachronistic additions by later "authors." Walton's stories, placed in original settings, reveal a world filled with magic, marvels, and wonders, teeming with strange creatures, bizarre landscapes, and arcane powers.

In the 1960s, after publishing fantasy classics such as J. R. R. Tolkien's *The Lord of the Rings*, Ballantine Books came across the name of Evangeline Walton, known for her first publication, a 1936 book titled *The Virgin and the Swine*, her version of the Fourth Branch of the Mabinogion. The original publisher was defunct, and the title had gone out of print. Despite receiving praise for her novel, the book sold poorly and none of the other novels in the series reached print. Seeking to expand its adult fantasy list, Ballantine Books began a search for the author. No address was available, and inquiries at the Library of Congress indicated that the copyright had not been renewed.

Proceeding with plans for publication under the more suitable title, *The Island of the Mighty*, Ballantine Books produced printed copies, only to discover at the last minute that the copyright had been renewed. They wrote to an address in Tucson, Arizona and received a reply from Walton herself. At that point, the Ballantine staff also learned that Walton had begun a second novel in the Mabinogion series, left unfinished when the first failed to sell. In the early 1970s, the first three novels were published—at first individually as *The Children of Llyr* (1971), followed by *The Song of Rhiannon* (1972) and *Prince of Annwn* (1974)—and eventually in a single volume in 2002.

Who was Evangeline Walton, and what do we know of her life? Born in Indianapolis, Indiana, Walton came from a lively, educated, Quaker family. She suffered respiratory illness as a child, and thus was home-schooled. Her parents separated and divorced in 1924, leaving her in the care of her mother and grandmother, an experience that roused a natural feminism in Walton that appears throughout her writings. In 1946, after the death of her grandmother, Walton and her mother moved to Tucson, Arizona. Her mother died in 1971, but not before she witnessed the start of public recognition for Walton and her works, most written in the 1920s through the early 1950s. She had worked on the Mabinogion tetralogy during the late 1930s and early 1940s, after which she produced books such as *Witch House* (published in 1945), an occult story set in New England, *The Cross and the Sword* (published in 1956), a historical novel set during the Norse conquest of England and the destruction of its Celtic culture, and *The Sword is Forged* (published in 1983), the first of a planned Theseus trilogy never finished.

Upon completing her Mabinogion series, recognition of Walton's immense writing talent followed rapidly. One reviewer noted that her books were not only among the best fantasies of the twentieth century, but also should be viewed as great works of fiction. The editors of *Fantastic Literature* agreed, describing her tetralogy as "a work of genius."

THE MABINOGION TETRALOGY: PLOT AND RESPONSE

Evangeline Walton's recreation of the Mabignon covers the Four Branches, the first being Prince of Annwn, a dramatic, powerful narrative in which Pwyll, Prince of Dyved, encounters Arawn (Death), ruler of Annwn (the Underworld), and undertakes a descent to the Underworld to do battle with the monster Havgan, whom even Death cannot conquer. On his return to the mortal realm, Pwyll meets and woos Rhiannon of the Birds,[1] a beautiful maiden, in a landscape magically transformed to the Bright World of Faery, which the lady proves willing to abandon in order to become Pwyll's bride, at least for a "time." Time in the Bright World is vastly unlike time in the mortal realm. Rhiannon, Pwyll discovers, is the Goddess who reigned in Dyved of old. To win her hand, Pwyll must enter the Bright World and there overcome Gwawl, a rival suitor to whom Rhiannon is betrothed. "We must go through darkness to reach light," Pwyll tells his mortal companions. Pwyll ultimately succeeds by trapping Gwawl in a magic bag that can never be filled, and having him beaten nearly to death in the bag before releasing him, thereby setting the stage for Pwyll and Rhiannon's marriage.

Though Walton's retelling of the account ends here, the First Branch of the Mabinogion ends differently, with an account Walton tells briefly and retrospectively in *The Children of Llyr.*[2] After their marriage, Pwyll and Rhiannon return to Dyved, where they have a son. The baby, however,

---

1. Rhiannon's birds, three in number and white, green, and gold in color, are, like their mother, enchanting in song and demeanor: "they wake the dead and lull the living to sleep." Walton, *Mabinogion*, 50.

2. See Walton, *Mabinogion*, 189–90.

disappears the night after his birth, and the mother, suspected of murdering him, suffers a humiliating punishment. The child, we learn from the First Branch of the Mabinogion account, had been taken by a monster who preys on newborns. The beast had also been raiding the stables of Teyrnon, lord of the kingdom of Gwent, carrying away the latest foal. Caught in the act, the monster is surprised by Teyrnon and his wife, who in rescuing the foal and killing the monster find a child left behind. Teyrnon and his wife name the boy Gwri Golden Hair and raise him as their own, only later to discover his true identity. Rhiannon is released from her ordeal and re-names the boy Pryderi.

Walton's recreation of the Second Branch, titled *The Children of Llyr*, deals with Llyr and his offspring. Llyr is chief among the Old Tribes (that is, Celtic groups understood to be indigenous or ancient), as opposed to the New Tribes (understood as "invaders from beyond the sea," that is, from the [European] mainland). Customary among the Old Tribes is matrilineal rule, meaning rule passes on through a ruler's sister's sons.[3] Llyr rules under Beli, High-King over the Island of the Mighty (Britain). His sister, Penardim, is married to Llyr, through whose male children, according to custom, hereditary rule passes.

The Children of Llyr tells the drama and tragedy of Llyr's five offspring: the giant King Bran (beloved ruler over the Island of the Mighty); Manawyddan, his wise and magically gifted younger brother; their sister Branwen; and half-brothers Nissyen and Evnissyen (antithetical symbols of Good and Evil). Branwen is given in marriage to Matholuch, king of Ireland. Angry that he was not consulted, Evnissyen insults Matholuch by mutilating his horses. Bran placates the Irish king by compensating him with new horses and a magical Cauldron that can restore the dead to life.

The twin brothers, Nissyen and Evnissyen, born of rape, are destined to be the force behind the tragic events that threaten to destroy Bran and his people. Walton uses these twins to philosophize about good and evil. "Change," she notes, "will always bring forth twins . . . Good and Evil."[4] While the twins essentially embody good and evil, morality is not that simple, for it cannot be portrayed dualistically, since "there is good and evil

---

3. In this form of hereditary rule, children are not viewed as descendants of fathers but of mothers. According to this tradition, children are considered gifts made to women by the Mothers (the Goddesses), ancient procreative powers in nature.

4. Walton, *Mabinogion*, 288.

in every man. All men must clear the evil out of themselves, no matter how many lives it takes."[5]

Evnissyen's wicked malice carries the plot to Ireland to witness Branwen's bitter humiliation at the hands of King Matholoch, a weak and pathetic ruler. Of their marriage comes a son, Gwern, whom Matholoch views as a means to unite Ireland with the Island of the Mighty. However, Evnissyen's insult rankles the Irish and Matholoch agrees to Branwen's banishment to the kitchen, where she is shamed and beaten by the head steward. Eventually, Branwen befriends a wounded starling and trains it to deliver a message to Bran, who responds by making war on Matholuch. The fearful Matholuch offers peace and agrees to step aside as king of Ireland in favor of Gwern.

Matholuch builds a house big enough to entertain gigantic Bran, hiding soldiers inside hanging bags, supposedly containing flour. Evnissyen, suspecting treachery, kills the hidden warriors by crushing their heads inside the bags. Later, at the feast, an angry Evnissyen throws Gwern into the fire, precipitating a battle. The Irish use the magic Cauldron to revive their dead. Evnissyen hides among the corpses to have himself thrown in the Cauldron, an act that sends the Cauldron back to the land of the Gods and results in cataclysmic destruction. Only Bran and seven of his followers survive, notably Manawyddan and Pryderi, prince of Dyved. Bran himself is mortally wounded by a poisoned spear, and his living Head is brought back to Britain for burial. Branwen dies on the return voyage, grief-struck from the ruin caused on her account.

The Song of Rhiannon, the Third Branch, is a strong counterpoint to the violence and vengeance of *The Children of Llyr*, from which only Manawyddan and Pryderi, the new Prince of Dyved, survive. Its main themes are the enduring bonds of love and respect between partners, and the dignity of humans, whether noble or humble. The two companions return together to Dyved, where Pryderi is reunited with his wife Kigva and Manawyddan marries Pryderi's mother Rhiannon.

An enchantment falls on Dyved, leaving it a wasteland empty of all domesticated animals and humans, apart from the four protagonists. They support themselves by hunting, then move to the realm of Logres, ruled by Caswallon, son of Beli, a position he won by magic and murder, in violation of the old matrilineal pattern of rule. Giving temporary allegiance to

---

5. Walton, *Mabinogion*, 208. As the concluding phrase indicates, Celtic spirituality, as portrayed by Walton, affirms belief in reincarnation.

Caswallon, Pryderi and his companions make a living by making saddles, shields, and shoes. Their work is of such quality that the local craftsmen cannot compete, and they are driven from town to town.

Finally they return to Dyved and become hunters again. Pryderi and Manawyddan follow a white boar to a mysterious cave on Gorsedd Arberth, the high Mound where kings go to receive vision or encounter death. There, where Pwyll first met Rhiannon, a liminal place to the Bright World of Faery, Pryderi enters, against Manawyddan's advice, and does not return. Rhiannon goes to investigate and she too is trapped therein. The opening disappears, and the two remaining humans are left to survive on their own. They return to Logres but once again are force to leave. When they return to Dyved, they sow three fields of wheat, but the first is destroyed before it can be harvested. When the second field is destroyed under similar circumstances, Manawyddan watches over the third field, only to see it destroyed by mice. He catches one of them, deciding to hang it for theft. However, three strangers appear in succession to offer him gifts if he will spare the mouse. The third stranger, a High Druid, offers to fulfill any wish, whereupon Manawyddan demands the release of Pryderi and Rhiannon and the lifting of the curse from Dyved. The stranger agrees to these terms, revealing himsef as Llwyd, a king in the Underworld and an ally of Gwawl, whom Pryderi's father Pwyll had beaten in order to marry Rhiannon. The mice who destroyed Manawyddan's crops are his attendants, magically transformed, and the one Manawyddan captured is Llwyd's own pregnant wife. The enchantment had been placed on Dyved in vengeance for Gwawl's beating and humiliation.

In *The Island of the Mighty*, Walton's recreation of the Fourth Branch, we reach the conclusion of the epic. This Branch, the longest in the tetralogy, is divided into three Books. The chief protagonists are Gwydion and his roguish brother Gilvaethwy, together with their sister Arianrhod—a gifted sorceress—and their wise father Math the Ancient, ruler of Gwynned in northern Wales. Book I tells of Gwydion's use of illusion to steal pigs from Pryderi, gifts to him from Arawm, King of Annwn (the Underworld) in Faery. The swine are described as a delicacy, a type of meat better than that of cattle and more desirable because of their smaller size. Book I also tells of Gilvaethwy's seduction of the virgin Goewyn. She is the current footholder of Math, whose feet must be held by a virgin at all times except while he is at war. In love with Goewyn, Gilvaethwy persuades Gwydion to trick Math into going to war against Pryderi so Gilvaethwy can have access to her. To end the war, Gwydion and Pryderi engage in single combat, which ends in Pryderi's death. In compensation for her rape, Math marries Goewyn and banishes Gwydion and Gilvaethwy, transforming them into a breeding pair of deer, then pigs, then wolves. After three years they are restored to human form.

Math needs a new foot holder, and Gwydian suggests his sister, Arianrhod, but when Math magically tests her virginity, she gives birth to two sons. The first, Dylan, immediately takes to the sea. The other is raised by Gwydion, but Arianrhod places three curses on her unwanted son, the first two being that he will never have a name or bear arms unless she gives them to him. She also swears he will never have a wife of any race living on earth. Books II deals with Llew's strange upbringing, and Book III with Llew's young adulthood.

Through trickery, Gwydion manages to trick Ariarhod into naming her son Llew Llaw Gyffes (Lew Skillful Hand) and giving him arms. To overturn her third oath, Gwydion and Math make Llew a beautiful wife from flowers, and name her Blodeuwedd ("Flowers"). Blodeuwedd falls in love with Goronwy Pevr, Lord of Penllyn, and they plot to kill Llew. Blodeuwedd tricks Llew into revealing the means by which he can be killed, but when Goronwy attempts to do the deed, Llew escapes, though wounded, transformed into an eagle. Despondent, Gwydion searches for Llew and eventually finds him, transforming him back into human form. He then pursues Blodeuwedd and on apprehending her, turns her into an owl (Blodeuwedd, literally "Flower Face," also means "owl"), a creature of the dark. In compensation for his loss, Llew kills Goronwy in the same manner and place where he was slain, killing him with his spear, thrown so hard that it pierces him through the stone behind which he hides.

POINTS TO PONDER IN *THE MABINOGION TETRALOGY*

To understand Walton's world, seen through the lens of the Four Branches of the Mabinogion, we need some understanding of the Celtic peoples and their religious beliefs. The Celts were a collection of tribes with origins in the upper Danube region of central Europe, including groups known as the Gaels, Gauls, Britons, Irish, and Galatians. Despite their diversity, they shared similar language, religious beliefs, traditions, and cultures. Around 1200 BCE they began spreading throughout western Europe, including to France, Spain, Britain, and Ireland. Galatians settled in Spain and as far east

as Asia Minor, Anatolia, Syria, Egypt, and Babylon. Britons and Gauls settled in present-day France, particularly in the northwestern region known
today as Brittany.

Celtic legacy remains most prominent in Ireland and Great Britain,
where traces of their language and culture are still prominent today. The
Celts were known to the Romans as early as the eighth and seventh centuries BCE, who called them "Galli," meaning barbarians. However, the Celts
were anything but barbarians, for aspects of their culture and language have
survived through the centuries.

By the third century BCE, the Celts controlled much of the European
continent north of the Alps. Beginning with the reign of Julius Caesar in
the first century BCE, the Romans launched a military campaign against
them, killing many and destroying much of their culture in mainland Europe. Caesar's armies attempted an invasion of Britain at this time, but were
unsuccessful, and thus the Celtic people established a homeland there. As
a result, many of their cultural traditions remain evident in present-day
Ireland, Scotland, and Wales.

Following Caesar's death, Romans eventually mounted a successful
attack against the Britons. This incursion effectively pushed the Britons on
the island west to Wales, south to Cornwall, and north to Scotland. When
the Romans built Hadrian's Wall (120 CE) near what today is the border
between England and Scotland, it was partly to protect the conquering Roman settlers from the Celts who had fled north.

Neither the Romans nor the Anglo-Saxons, who replaced the Romans
in fifth-century England, were able successfully to invade Ireland. This en-
abled the Celtic tribes that had settled there—primarily Gaels and Irish—to
survive, and allowed their culture to flourish. When Christianity arrived
in Ireland with Patrick in 432 CE, many Celtic traditions became incorporated into that "new" religion. As some historians claim, Catholicism was
able to take over as the dominant religion in Ireland following the mass
killing of Druids, the religious leaders of the Gaels.

However, even with Christianity's prominence in Ireland, Scotland,
and Wales, traces of Celtic culture remain, including the representation of
the Holy Trinity in the shamrock—Ireland's national symbol—a strong belief in spirits and saints, and a resilient cult of the Virgin Mary (associated
in the minds of many with the Goddess).

Underlying Walton's skillful retelling of the Mabinogion myths is the fundamental theme of great change,[6] involving the conflict between polytheism and monotheism (with spirits and saints filling the gap), between communalism and individualism, and between matriarchy and patriarchy. The latter conflict is central to Walton's sensibility, for she regularly alludes to the beliefs of the Old Tribes, whose women are powerful and free, respected by all and "blessed by the Gods," for only they and not men are the creators of life. The Old Tribes maintained a religious perspective undergirded by matrilineal inheritance, meaning that a male's bloodline is through his sister. The change to patrilineal inheritance became recognized when the growing sophistication of the New Tribes raised the innovative possibility about the male's role in conception. This new thinking brought change, socially, politically, and religiously.

To understand primal cultures, a good place to begin is with their sense of embeddedness. This starts with the tribe, apart from which there is little independent identity. Through the tribe, individuals participate with nature in a unified order. Despite the cultural variety represented by these traditions, three common patterns are evident in their spirituality: (1) the solidarity of human beings with the natural world, (2) the centering of individual human existence in the social community, and (3) the reciprocity of the human spirit with the world of spirits transcending the human. Significantly, each of these holds together elements of reality that have undergone systematic alienation in Western culture.

Ancient religions were almost entirely polytheistic. Prior to the emergence of Christianity and Islam, the only exception was Judaism. Everyone else in the Roman world worshiped many gods, for their gods were not sovereign, omnipotent, or exclusive. Each god had a role, controlling some aspect of human life. There were national gods; gods of localities (each city had its own god); gods of places (such as of rivers, meadows, and forests); gods over every function (such as of one's home, of the pantry, and of the hearth; gods of crops, of healing and rain, of childbirth, and so forth).

---

6. In *The Children of Llyr*, Math counsels that the "old days and old ways are passing. . . . And that is part of the Great Going-Forward." The world grows as a child grows; there can be no stopping it. Tradition has guarded the earth's childhood, he adds. Now humanity must "grow up, and each man find and train the King within himself." Change is good in the end. If it brings evil for a time, that is only like a woman's birth pangs. Change, however, should not occur too quickly, for if so, it may outlast the birth pangs. Walton, *Mabinogion*, 209.

Religion in the ancient world was a way of worshiping these forces, a way of currying favor with benevolent deities while avoiding offending their capricious nature. Worship involved the performance of cultic acts such as performing sacrifices on their behalf and offering prayers as a sign of humility and submission. The root of the word "cultic" in the sense of devotion comes from the Latin phrase *cultus deorum*, meaning "care of the gods." The gods, like humans, had needs, and devotees took care of the gods in order that the gods might take care of their needs. Worship, in this sense, was mutually beneficial. Humans felt the gods' needs could be met through sacrifices, preferably by offering animals or things that were grown, items valuable to humans as well. Sacrifices could be offered in one's home, preferably before one's meals, in the form of a libation poured out or as a burnt offering on a family altar. Larger or more elaborate sacrifices, such as that of animals, were conducted in public temples, many of these places of gathering and worship led by priests and other officials appointed by local authorities to serve as intermediaries with the gods.

What is common to pagan religions is the absence of beliefs. Believing specific things about the gods was not significant to personal religion. What mattered was that the needs of the gods be met through cultic sacrifice and prayer. It was necessary that one believe in the existence of the gods, of course, and in the obligation of sacrifice, but beliefs about specific aspects of the gods, such as their nature, their demands, or what they wanted devotees to believe about them, these were private matters, unessential to worship and practice. Such things might be relevant to mythology—the stories about the gods—or matters for philosophers to discuss or debate, but they were irrelevant to personal religion.

As odd as it might seem to us, ancient polytheistic religions had no beliefs to affirm, theologies to embrace, or creeds to recite. When people went to the temples, they performed sacrifices. They did not recite creeds or confess theological beliefs. As a result, in all religions of the Greco-Roman age, there was no such thing as heresy or orthodoxy, because there was no insistence on right belief or criticism of wrong belief, only an emphasis on the cultic acts necessary to appease the gods. Interestingly, there were no ethical standards associated with these religions. Religions did not establish particular rules of morality. Although the gods were offended by such acts as patricide, they seemed unconcerned with misbehavior such as adultery or cheating on taxes. Such deeds did not disqualify one from worship. Even the gods were known to behave immorally or hypocritically. Such things mattered philosophically, but they were not issues that concerned the gods.

Like other Iron Age Europeans, the early Celts maintained a polytheistic mythology and a specific religious conception. For Celts in close contact with ancient Rome, such as the Gauls and Celtiberians, their mythology did not survive conquest by the Romans, their subsequent conversion to Christianity, and the loss of their Celtic languages. The Celtic peoples who maintained either political or linguistic identities (such as the Gaels in Ireland and Scotland, the Welsh in Wales, and the Celtic Britons of southern Great Britain and Brittany) left vestigial remains of their ancestral mythologies, which were put into written form during the Middle Ages.

Although the Celtic world at its height covered much of western and central Europe, it was not politically unified, nor was there any substantial central source of cultural influence or homogeneity. As a result, there was a great deal of variation in local religious beliefs (although some elements, such as reverence for the god Lugh, appear to have been widespread). Celtic inscriptions to more than three hundred deities, often equated with their Roman counterparts, have survived, but most of them appear to have referred to local or tribal gods, and few were widely worshipped.

Though the Gauls were literate, most of their writings were destroyed by the Romans. Ancient sources also indicate that Celtic priests, the Druids, were forbidden to use writing to record verses of religious significance. In addition, Rome made a concerted effort to break the power of the Druids in areas they controlled. While early Gaels in Ireland and parts of Wales used the Ogham script to record short inscriptions, many Gaelic myths were first recorded by Christian monks, devoid of their original meaning.

While the Irish Celts had a pantheon led by the Dagda, a figure of power armed with a club, the Celts of Ireland and Scotland also worshipped a battle goddess known as the Morrigan. Notable among the goddesses is Brigid, the Dagda's daughter, and the horse goddess. Important elements of British myth appear in the Four Branches of the Mabinogion, especially in figures such as Rhiannon, Teyrnon, Bran, and Arawn (Death king of the Underworld). Other Welsh traditions introduce Mabon ap Mondron ("Divine Son of the Divine Mother").

The cult of the Goddess is a dominant motif in the recovery of women's religious roots. For millennia, humans worshipped female gods, particularly the Mother Goddess, who for many centuries was the chief deity throughout western Asia and Asia Minor. In Celtic mythology, the goddess

Danu (also known as Anu or Dana) was the ancient mother of all the gods and of the Celtic people. She was thought to be both the original goddess and god, an all-encompassing deity who gave birth to everything and everyone. She was regularly associated with Earth, waters, winds, fertility, and wisdom, as well as the patroness of wizards, wells, rivers, prosperity, abundance, and magic. One of the major rivers of central Europe, from whence the Celts originally migrated, is the Danube River, named after her.

In neo-pagan traditions, Danu is revered as the triple goddess, appearing as the maiden, mother, and crone. Is there a fourth face to the divine, as we see in Hindu and Christian theology? If so, pray you never see it! In the Bible, we find the fourth face of God in YHWH, in the "I Am" of God, the unspeakable absolute oneness of God (see Exod 3:14). This is the face of God that, according to Exodus 33:20, no one can see and live. As Rudolph Otto reminds us in *The Idea of the Holy*, spirituality relies upon a deep sense of the "numinous." The holy is *fascinans* (full of wonder and fascination), but also a *mysterium tremendum* (daunting and fearsome). In one account, Danu unites with Bile, the god of light and healing often symbolized by an oak tree. From this union Dagda is born, the chief leader of the Tuatha Dé Danann, the wise or magical folk of Ireland, god-like creatures with supernatural powers.[7] Legend says these skilled warriors and healers later became the fairy folk of Ireland. Danu gifted them shape-shifting power, and they take the forms of leprechauns and fairies to hide from their enemies. According to one legend, Danu's children stay underground and build their own world there. This realm is known as Fairyland, Otherworld, or Summerland, where the pace of time differs from that of our world.

Danu, associated with water, the moon, and the Earth, also has dual qualities, in that she is portrayed as a nurturing mother but also as a strong warrior goddess. In this regard, she also embodies masculine and feminine energies. As a powerful matriarch, she is usually depicted as a beautiful woman surrounded by nature and animals; among the animals associated with the Mother Goddess are fish, horses, and seagulls. In addition, she is associated with the four elements—earth, air, water, and fire—and also depicted with keys, symbols of freedom and liberation as well as knowledge and success.

---

7. In the Mabinogion, this role is performed by figures such as Math, Bran, and Gwydion.

Belief in the Goddess is on the rise in our world today, for many reasons. Among the many lessons we find in ancient Celtic Goddess stories, the following deserve mention:

- *These accounts feature diversity.* Since the Goddess is the embodiment of natural elements and creator of all living things on Earth, she teaches us to embrace diversity, to be tolerant, and to be accepting of different aspects of our personality.

- *These accounts encourage compassion.* From Celtic legends we learn that compassion and love can nurture and raise defeated people back to resilience and self-control.

- *These accounts encourage perseverance.* The Goddess helps people in need. She provides encouragement, persistence, and discernment to recognize our soul's desires, from which come our goals, dreams, and ultimate wisdom.

- *These accounts encourage us to remain open.* The Goddess of rivers and water teaches us that life is ever flowing and changing. Instead of seeking security and stability, we should strive for improvement, learning, knowledge, and spiritual transformation.

Perhaps because the Romans never occupied Ireland and parts of Scotland, the Christianity that developed there retained its connection to the natural world. In his *Listening for the Heartbeat of God: A Celtic Spirituality*, John Philip Newell explains how Pelagius (c. 354–418), an early and much maligned theologian, saw creation as good and a revelation of God's being. Following Augustine's condemnation of Pelagius, much of Christian history wrongly interpreted Pelagius as saying that humans did not need grace to be saved, whereas he was saying that nature was created precisely as a vehicle of grace.

According to Newell, Pelagius was affirming a notion central to Celtic spirituality, namely a strong sense of the goodness of creation. For Pelagius, everywhere in nature "narrow shafts of divine light pierce the veil that separates heaven from earth."[8] In his letters, Pelagius pointed to the animals of the forest, the birds in the sky, the insects in the ground, the trees, flowers, and grass, noting that God's Spirit dwelt in them all. Pelagius recognized the presence of God in all living things; it was this presence that made them beautiful. "If we look with God's eyes," he noted, "nothing on earth

---

8. Van de Weyer, *Letters of Pelagius*, 36.

is ugly."[9] Thus, when our love is directed toward a plant or animal, "we are participating in the fullness of God's love."[10]

In his writings, eco-theologian Thomas Berry (1914–2009) invited his readers to participate in what he called "The Great Work" of our time, which is to carry out the transition from a period of human devastation of the earth to a period of care and support. This call to enter into communion with other beings is deeply spiritual, for it alludes to our capacity for relatedness, for spontaneity in action, and for presence to other beings, aspects central to Celtic spirituality.

9. Van de Weyer, *Letters of Pelagius*, 71.

10. Van de Weyer, *Letters of Pelagius*, 72.

CHAPTER 4

T. S. Eliot's *The Waste Land*

WHEN ELIOT'S MODERNIST POEM, *The Waste Land*, was published in 1922, it received forty-six reviews in the United States, equally divided between positive and negative ones, and twelve reviews in England, ten of them hostile. Two weeks after its publication, John Peale Bishop, an aspiring American poet living in Paris, described Eliot's poem in three words as Immense, Magnificent, and Terrible. To a reader approaching the poem for the first time, those words suggest what lies ahead. For all who read *The Waste Land*, bewilderment and admiration vie with a keen sense of the poem's terrifying power.

Bishop was not alone in sensing the poem's power. An anonymous reviewer in London found *The Waste Land* a poet's vision of modern life: "We have here range, depth, and wonderful expression. What more is necessary to a great poem? This vision is singularly complex and in all its labyrinths utterly sincere. It is the mystery of life that it shows two faces, and we know of no other poet who can more adequately and movingly reveal to us the inextricable tangle of the sordid and the beautiful that makes up life."[1] On the other side of the Atlantic, Burton Rascoe promptly hailed it as "perhaps the finest poem of this generation."

Written in response to personal and cultural failure, the poem is divided into five sections. The first, "The Burial of the Dead," introduces the primary themes of disillusionment and despair. The second, "A Game

---

1. This review, taken from the *Times Literary Supplement*, October 26, 1922, is cited in Rainey, *Annotated Waste Land*, 34.

of Chess," employs vignettes of several characters commenting on those themes experientially. "The Fire Sermon," the third section, explores the decadence of European culture philosophically, juxtaposing images of death and self-denial inspired by Augustinian and Buddhist asceticism. The burning in Augustine is physical and sexual, whereas in the Buddha's "Fire Sermon," the burning is mental and spiritual. The fourth section, "Death by Water," draws from the twenty-sixth canto of Dante's *The Inferno*, in which Ulysses speaks of his death at sea. This section, the lone hold-over from a deleted shipwreck episode, mentions Phlebas, an imaginary Phoenician seaman (see also line 47), with whom Eliot identifies spiritually. The culminating fifth section, "What the Thunder Said," features a water-less landscape—an exposé of humanity's cultural and spiritual failure and judgment—imagery drawn from various sources, including the words of Jesus, Dante, Shakespeare, the Arthurian Grail legends, Hermann Hesse, the philosopher F. H. Bradley, and the "sermon" at the end of the Hindu Brihadaranyaka Upanishad.

When initially published, Eliot's masterpiece appeared in two differ-ent versions, one without notes (in the English journal *Criterion* and the American journal *Dial*), and one in book form, with notes. The longer book format, the version widely read nowadays, came about as a concession to the American publisher Boni and Liveright, who agreed to publish the poem as an independent book, but only if it was enlarged, for the poem alone was far too short to stand as an independent volume, running from twenty-eight to thirty-two pages in length. As originally written, the poem was much longer, but it had suffered severe editorial purging at the hands of Eliot's friend and benefactor, Ezra Pound. The solution, offered by Eliot, was ingenious, and ultimately beneficial to readers, namely, to enlarge the poem by adding notes to the text, resulting in a book of thirty to forty pages in length.

In those notes, now indispensable to understanding the poem's sym-bolism and literary allusions, Eliot indicated that both the title and much of the symbolism originated in his reading of Jessie L. Weston's 1920 book on the Grail legend, *From Ritual to Romance*. Unfortunately, Eliot's notes failed to comment on the poem's epigraph, written in Latin and Greek and undecipherable to average readers.

In the prepublication version of *The Waste Land*, the poem included an epigraph taken from Joseph Conrad's novel *Heart of Darkness*, as the narrator recounts the death of the unscrupulous ivory trader Kurtz, "Did he live his life again in every detail of desire, temptation, and surrender during the supreme moment of complete knowledge? He cried out in a whisper at some image, at some vision—he cried out twice, a cry that was no more than breath—'The horror! The horror!'"

Pound, questioning Conrad's not yet established reputation, prompted Eliot to reconsider. Eliot's eventual choice was significant, quoting the Cumaean Sibyl's words found in *The Satyricon*, a satirical novel written by the Roman writer Petronicus in the first century CE. Translated, the epigraph reads, "For on one occasion I myself saw, with my own eyes, the Cumaean Sibyl hanging in a cage, and when some boys said to her, 'Sibyl, what do you want?' she replied, 'I want to die.'"

Lest we think this to be an ordinary death wish, we need to probe deeper into the Sibyl's context. This account is given by Trimalchio, a wealthy vulgarian vying with dinner guests on who can produce the best tale of wonder. There were as many as ten sibyls in the ancient world, oracles who prophesied at holy sites and whom Greeks and Romans consulted about the future. The most famous was the Cumaean Sibyl, whose oracular cavern was near Naples.

The Cumaean Sibyl figures prominently in Ovid's *Metamorphoses*, the account to which Trimalchio alludes. Promised by Apollo that she could have one wish fulfilled, she chose to live as many years as the grains of sand she could hold in her hand. Her wish was granted, but she failed to choose eternal youth, and so she withered into a creature shrunken small enough to fit into a large bottle. Hence, her desire to die, a wish left ungranted. Death—opening the jar—meant for Eliot not only release from mortality, but a door to immortality.

Eliot's epigraph belongs not to the first segment alone, but to *The Waste Land* as a whole. For Eliot, the Sibyl stands as a guide, not to the metaphysical afterlife, as she does in *The Odyssey* or *The Aeneid*, but to the hell and heaven of the individual soul.

Eliot's poem begins with the well-known phrase, "April is the cruellest month." Spring, like birth, always leads to death, and for some people, like the Sibyl, the trajectory after birth is always downward. As Eliot describes it, human life, full of promise, fails to fulfil its potential, resulting in a social wasteland he describes as "A heap of broken images, where the sun beats, / And the dead tree gives no shelter, the cricket no relief, / And the dry stone no sound of water" (lines 22–24).

Critics often compare Eliot's account of spring with the opening to the prologue to *The Canterbury Tales* by Geoffrey Chaucer, which adopts a more hopeful treatment of spring. Given the themes of disillusionment and despair in *The Waste Land*, and to understand accurately the poem's meaning and message, we need to ask two separate though interrelated questions: (1) is the poem essentially personal (autobiographical), or a commentary about modern life? And given the poem's pessimistic nature, (2) is there any evidence of hope in *The Waste Land*, or is Eliot's confidence in human nature and society hopeless?

Given the poem's fragmented nature, and the poet's fragile emotional state at the time of its writing, the answers are not altogether clear. For that reason, I approach the poem as essentially personal and confessional in nature, viewing this work as a stage in Eliot's religious conversion from sin to salvation, a phase of his spiritual journey from despair to hope. Despite endless fascination and speculation regarding Eliot's imagery in *The Waste Land*, for which ample commentary, interpretation, and explanation appear in print and on the Internet, our focus remains on those two questions.

THE WASTE LAND AS PERSONAL AND CONFESSIONAL COMMENTARY

Reality is fragmented. It comes at us—and through us—in bits and pieces, and it is our task as human beings to process it, arrange it, and organize it into connected and meaningful wholes. This is Eliot's artistry in *The Waste Land*, and our task as readers is to connect the pieces and make sense of the fragmented images.

One of the most interesting of the innovations in *The Waste Land* is the use of quotations from other poems, songs, and religious literature as a regular rhetorical device. Like reading James Joyce's *Portrait* or *Ulysses*, Eliot's stream-of-consciousness technique makes reading his poetry more difficult. Neither author was much concerned with narrative. Events for both were nothing more than vehicles for the expression of complex and extraordinary feelings and states of mind. In their work, events do not move through conflict toward resolution. Instead, they linger in the mind like ghosts, taunting the imagination to extract their full significance. For poetry, this represented a new form, Cubist or Surrealist in nature.

This new literary type—a poetic form in which images representing events, objects, and states of mind are linked not by logical, causal, or chronological progression but by what may be called the associative law of imagination—has much in common with the world of dreams. Like dreams, episodes of *The Waste Land* such as "What the Thunder Said" or the last half of "The Fire Sermon" replicate a free-association structure. Otherwise, the relation of each episode to that which follows is non-sequential. This does not mean that the relationship is random, only that, like a dream, it does not follow, at least on the surface, the norms of logic. The poetic structure holding *The Waste Land* together becomes a fabric of free-associational relationships in which one idea is related to another through a complex of largely unconscious associations. When, in a 1959 interview on "The Art of Poetry," Eliot noted that in writing *The Waste Land* "I wasn't even bothering whether I understood what I was saying," he was providing a clue to the poem's dream-like, stream-of-consciousness compositional nature. Adding to the complexity, the authorized version of *The Waste Land* that we read nowadays is not the original version, but rather a truncated poem radically fragmented by editorial emendation, mostly at the hands of Ezra Pound, to whom Eliot dedicated the work.

In a state of near nervous collapse in late 1921, Eliot took leave from his bank job and went alone to see a psychiatrist in Lausanne, Switzerland. He remained there about six weeks, and it was there that he completed *The Waste Land*. Earlier in the year he had written to Pound that he wished to finish a long poem that was partly written, and after his return from Lausanne he turned over the complete manuscript to Pound for his suggestions. Since we now possess a printed copy of the (or an) original manuscript version, we can see Pound's skill in revising, but also how radically he cut the poem. What transpired is widely recognized as one of the greatest acts of editorial intervention on record. Thinking only of the work's artistic structure, Pound urged Eliot to remove large portions of narrative that comprised the beginnings to parts I, III, and IV of the poem. From part I Pound deleted a fifty-four-line sequence; from part III he removed the lengthy beginning, which ran to eighty-eight lines; and from part IV he slashed away the detailed exposition of the final voyage of Phlebas, another eighty-three lines. He also pruned twenty-seven lines from the central scene in part III, in addition to making another two hundred minor editorial changes, either deleting or questioning isolated words and phrases. Surprisingly, Eliot accepted most of the changes with very little question. However, to counter Pound's deletion of the original beginning to part III, Eliot drafted a ten-line replacement.

In his editing, Pound had no knowledge of the poem's biographical nature, and his revisions further obscured the poem's original intent—perhaps beyond recovery. In addition to enlarging the poem for book publication, we can surmise that Eliot added his notes partly to give back to the poem some of what Pound's revisions had taken away. Eliot eventually came to disavow the notes, saying that his primary intent was to indicate sources for his quotations. Later he stated that his notes had stimulated the wrong kind of interest among the seekers of sources. While giving credit to Jessie Weston's book on the Grail legend for his title, including some fragments in the text on the wounded Fisher King, Eliot regretted "having sent so many enquirers off on a wild goose chase after Tarot cards and the Holy Grail."[2]

To restore the poem's original autobiographical mindset, we need to examine the original title and epigraph. Eliot's first title was "He Do the Police in Different Voices," a line from Dickens's *Our Mutual Friend*. The point implied by this title is that the many voices of the poem all come from one common center, one consciousness, possibly even from a fragmented personality that can act many parts and take many public roles despite lacking a spiritual center. This might help explain the poem's reliance on endless quotations and allusions. However the poem has come to be interpreted, the original title points inward, not outward, in contrast with the eventual title *The Waste Land*, misleading in that it renders the poem's message a comment not on the poet's consciousness but rather on the external world and its decaying civilization. Perhaps Weston's influence regarding the Grail legend was not on the desolation of the kingdom, but on the personal suffering of the Fisher King. In the Grail legend, the land mirrors the condition of its ruler, much as modernity mirrors its leaders, a suffering Eliot embodies as artist. In *The Waste Land*, Eliot describes the sociological stagnation of inauthentic living, when society is bereft of spiritual values, but for him it is a wasteland he embodies, a condition that leaves him wounded and distressed.

What can be said of the title also applies to the original epigraph, a quotation from Conrad's *Heart of Darkness*. What Pound wrote Eliot about that quotation—"I doubt if Conrad is weighty enough to stand the citation"—left Eliot apprehensive, for he did not wish to let the epigraph go. So Eliot replied, "do you mean not use the Conrad quote, or simply not put Conrad's name to it?" Pound's comment indicates he was more concerned

2. Eliot, *Poetry and Poets*, 122.

with the poem's reception, and not with its message, which he seems to have misunderstood.

At the climactic moment in *Heart of Darkness*, as Mr. Kurtz is facing imminent death, he cries out twice "The horror! The horror!" a revulsion erupting, not from a vision of contemporary civilization, but an insight into his inner self. In dropping the Conrad epigraph and substituting the Latin-Greek epigraph from *The Satyricon*, Eliot may have satisfied Pound's desire for a move impressive show of learning, but at the same time he lost a certain sharpness of meaning. The Cumaean Sybil's death wish, while remarkably insightful, is considerably less suggestive than Kurtz's moral self-realization expressed in "The horror! The horror!"

If Eliot had left the poem more nearly in the form submitted to Pound, we might better understand the sequence of characters in the poem, including the hyacinth girl (line 36); Madame Sososstris (line 43); Phlebas, the drowned Phoenician Sailor (lines 46, 312–21); Belladonna (line 49–50); the Hanged Man (line 55); Lil and Albert (lines 139–72); the Fisher King (lines 187–92); and Tiresias (lines 217–56). These represent—to pick up on Eliot's terms referring to his psychic state during his withdrawal to Lausanne for treatment—a man suffering "an aboulie [lack of will] and emotional derangement which has been a lifelong affliction."[3]

Perhaps Eliot's most compelling motive in adding notes to his poem was to restore some element of consciousness it had lost in Pound's revision. In doing so, Eliot needed a still point in his ever flowing poem—something to depart from and return to. Eliot's most significant attempt in this direction was in his footnote on Tiresias, who enters the poem in part III to observe the typist's seduction scene. In his notes on that segment, Eliot wrote, "Tiresias, although a mere spectator and not indeed a 'character,' is yet the most important personage in the poem, uniting all the rest. Just as the one-eyed merchant, seller of currants, melts into the Phoenician sailor, and the latter is not wholly distinct from Ferdinand Prince of Naples, so all the women are one woman, and the two sexes meet in Tiresias."

The story of Tiresias, a legendary blind seer from Thebes, is fascinating. One day, when he saw snakes coupling and struck them with a stick, he was instantly transformed into a woman; seven years later the same thing happened again, and he was turned back into a man. Since he had experienced the body in both sexes, he was asked by Jove and Juno to settle a dispute concerning whether men or women had greater pleasure in making

3. Eliot, *The Waste Land: A Facsimile*, xxii.

love. Tiresias took the side of Jove and answered that women had more pleasure. Juno, angered, blinded him. In compensation, Jove gave him the gift of prophecy and long life. (The story is told in Ovid's *Metamorphoses* 3.316–38; Eliot, in his notes, gives the original Latin for lines 320–38.)

In this respect, we can understand the significance of Madame Sosostris in Eliot's poem. Whether she represents a specific figure in Eliot's life or some literary figure, her role here is to tell the poet's fortune. Entering with her "wicked pack of cards," the first and fundamental card she draws on his behalf is the "drowned Phoenician sailor" (there is no such card in the Tarot deck, but in an autobiographical reading of the text, it stands for Jean Verdenal, Eliot's dead friend). The second card is "Belladonna, the Lady of the Rocks" (again, there is no such card in the Tarot deck, but in an autobiographical reading of the text, "the lady of situations" is Vivienne Haigh-Wood, Eliot's wife). The third card, the "man with the three staves," stands for the poet himself become the Fisher King, suffering the sexual wound (loss of Verdenal?) that has rendered Eliot impotent in his marriage, like the Fisher King of the Grail legend (the man with the three staves and the Wheel are genuine Tarot cards, but the one-eyed merchant is Eliot's invention). These are the cards that fate had dealt Eliot at the time of the writing of *The Waste Land*, and thus Madame Sosotris is telling Eliot what he already knows, summarizing the fate that has brought about his sexual-spiritual paralysis.

Eliot's original title for part II of *The Waste Land* was "In the Cage." Like the change in the poem's epigraph from Conrad to Petronius, the change in the unit title again deflected attention from interior meaning to exterior action. "In the Cage" suggests, in a way that the title "A Game of Chess" does not, the situation of the poet in the opening scene of the section—he is trapped in a loveless marriage, trapped in "memory and desire" (see line 3) that will not let him love a wife he has involuntarily acquired. Like the female protagonist in the Henry James novella *In the Cage*, which influenced Eliot's original title, the speaker in *The Waste Land* is imprisoned in a cage from which there is no discernible exit. Unable to be a participant in the sexual intrigue of the "game," Eliot is resigned to being a spectator (as he is in the second half of "A Game of Chess").

There is no question that Eliot was among the many who were devastated by World War I. He allowed Herman Hesse to speak to this issue in the fragment from Hesse's 1920 volume of essays entitled *Blick ins Chaos* (Glimpse into Chaos) quoted in the notes to *The Waste Land* (lines

366–76), whose translation reads: "Already half of Europe, already at least half of Eastern Europe is on the way to Chaos, driving drunken in sacred folly along the edge of the abyss and, drunken, singing hymn-like songs as Dimitri Karamazov sang. Offended by these songs, the burgher laughs, while the saint and seer listen to them with tears."

Eliot's notes, as we now know, were somewhat diversionary from Eliot's personal, private intent. In 1931, in "Thoughts after Lambeth," Eliot disagreed with the critics who said that *The Waste Land* expressed the "disillusionment of a generation," calling such views "nonsense. I may have expressed for them their own illusion of being disillusioned, but that did not form part of my intention."[4] Later, in a 1959 *Paris Review* interview, Eliot made the astonishing statement, "By the time of the *Four Quartets* [Eliot's later set of poems dealing broadly and hopefully with the theme of salvation as the goal of human life], I couldn't have written in the style of *The Waste Land*. In *The Waste Land*, I wasn't even bothering whether I understood what I was saying."[5] In his 1951 lecture on "Virgil and the Christian World," Eliot made perhaps his most intriguing statement about *The Waste Land* without naming the poem: "A poet may believe that he is expressing only his private experience; his lines may be for him only a means of talking about himself without giving himself away; yet for his readers what he has written may come to be the expression both of their own secret feelings and of the exultation or despair of a generation. He need not know what his poetry will come to mean to others; and a prophet need not understand the meaning of his prophetic utterance."[6]

If *The Waste Land* is not primarily a pessimistic statement about the modern world, what, then, was Eliot's intention, and why did he later disavow conscious knowledge of his message? Could it be that in *The Waste Land* Eliot was "expressing only his private experience . . . a means of talking about himself without giving himself away"? The reason, it seems, is lodged not only in the circumstances that led to his near nervous collapse in Lausanne in 1921, but in what was up to then an ongoing spiritual affliction.

In his *T. S. Eliot's Personal Waste Land*, James Miller speaks of discovering John Peter's articles in the Oxford journal *Essays in Criticism* (July 1952 and April 1969), in which Peter proposed that *The Waste Land* should be interpreted as an autobiographical poem, identifying Joyce's relationship

4. Eliot, *Selected Essays*, 324.

5. Plimpton, *Writers at Work*, 105.

6. Eliot, *Poetry and Poets*, 137.

with a Frenchman named Jean Verdenal as the basis for Phlebas the Phoenician. According to Peter's reading of *The Waste Land*, at some previous time the author had fallen completely—perhaps "irretrievably"—in love. The object of this love was a young man who soon afterwards met his death, it would seem by drowning. This might explain the many images of death in the poem, death "by land" as well as "by water" in parts III through V, including the reference to "white bodies naked on the low damp ground" (line 193) near the beginning of "The Fire Sermon."

Jean Verdenal was a young medical student with whom Eliot had shared an apartment in Paris during his collegiate days. He and Eliot became close friends, but Verdenal died on the field of battle on the shores of Gallipoli in 1915. Eliot's relationship with Verdenal, though mostly mysterious, is heightened by the fact that Eliot posthumously dedicated his first volume of poetry, *Prufrock and Other Observations*, to Verdenal. The front of Eliot's 1920 volume of poems *Ara Vos Prec* has no dedication, but it does contain an epigraph in Italian from Dante's *Purgatorio*, which translated reads, "Now you are able to comprehend the quantity of love / that warms me toward you, / When I forget our emptiness / Treating shades as if they were solid." When the American edition of this collection of poems appeared, also in 1920, there was no epigraph but a dedication identical to that in the *Prufrock* volume. It wasn't until the publication of Eliot's collected poems in 1925 that Eliot brought together his ardent dedication and the name of Jean Verdenal. Apparently, enough time had elapsed since his death for the poet to realize that the focus for affection that this person once provided was irreplaceable. Like other poems, *The Waste Land*, thus, can be read as a meditation upon Eliot's loss, and his stunned and horrified reactions to Verdenal's death, a bleakness extended to the social realm.

At this point, it is worthwhile to review briefly some autobiographical items in Eliot's life. Though he spent most his life in England, Thomas Stearns Eliot (1888–1965) was born in St. Louis, Missouri. The Eliots originally hailed from Somerset in England and settled in America in the late seventeenth century. They began as a Boston family, but Eliot's grandfather, William Greenleaf Eliot, moved to Missouri in 1834 to preach as a Unitarian minister. Trained in philosophy at Harvard, Eliot studied a daunting range of subjects, from Sanskrit and advanced mathematics to Japanese Buddhism and classical Greek. In 1910, at the age of twenty-two, Eliot went to Paris and found living in his *pension* a charming twenty-year-old Frenchman, who was studying medicine and who read and wrote poetry.

The two traveled in Italy and Germany during the summer of 1911, and it is possible that their relationship was renewed in 1914 on Eliot's return to Paris. World War I forced Eliot's departure from Germany to England in 1914, and led to Verdenal's service as medical officer in the French forces. Caught up in the campaign to take the Dardanelles in 1915, he was one of countless young soldiers and medics who were lost in the waters of the Strait and the mud of Gallipoli during and after the landings of April 24, 1915. He was killed on May 2.

Eliot would have heard of Verdenal's death shortly thereafter, and his dismay and anguish may well have impelled him into a hasty civil marriage on June 26, 1915 to Vivienne Haigh-Wood, a marriage encouraged by Ezra Pound. The marriage turned out to be disastrous, apparently so for both partners. Eliot appeared grateful, only some six months after the marriage, when Bertrand Russell, friend of the Eliots and a well-known satyr, took Vivenne off on a seaside holiday alone. In a January 1916 letter, Eliot thanked Russell for taking her away, admitting that Russell handled her "better than I . . . I believe we shall owe her life to you, even." From that point on, Vivienne's mental health began to decline, as did Eliot's ability to write poetry. The critical point was reached in 1921, when Eliot found his only refuge from breakdown was to take leave from his job, consult a psychiatrist, and write the long poem that had been under contemplation for some time. Bernard Bergonzi wrote of Eliot's marriage, "It was to cause him much unhappiness and appears to have reinforced rather than assuaged the sexual anxieties expressed in his early poetry."[7]

Biographers speculate on Eliot's strange marriage, including his irrational fear of sex, something he associated with violence and purely biological urges. The depth of his attachment to Verdenal, coupled with his failed marriage, may help explain sentiments in *The Love Song of J. Alfred Prufrock* and *Portrait of a Lady*, the former a poem about a man who cannot love women, and the latter about a women longing for unrequited friendship and love. A careful reading of these poems led James Miller to conclude that they "show a paralysis of feeling in man-woman relationships, an inability of the speaker to relate profoundly, especially sexually," with his or her counterpart.[8] There is much more that can be said about *Prufrock* and other early Eliot poems, particularly those dedicated to Jean Verdenal. It took a while for Eliot to connect publicly the quotation from

7. Bergonzi, *T. S. Eliot*, 32.
8. Miller, *Personal Waste Land*, 52.

Dante—"Now you are able to comprehend the quantity of love that warms me toward you, / When I forget our emptiness / Treating shades as if they were solid"—with Verdenal, but the two had been firmly linked in Eliot's mind.

In his 1929 essay on Dante, Eliot wrote of the relationship of Dante to Beatrice, finding the meaning not in the "facts" so much as in Dante's reflection of his experience of her. The final cause of all authentic attraction, Eliot believed, "is the attraction towards God." Romantic feelings culminating in "the love of man and woman (or for that matter of man and man) [are] only explained and made reasonable by the higher love, or else [are] simply the coupling of animals."[9]

In late 1917, Eliot wrote to his father, "I have a lot of things to write about if the time ever comes when people will attend to them." If we place this statement alongside Eliot's own experiences we have been examining, we might understand the meaning Jean Verdenal might have had in Eliot's imagination.

The Waste Land, when it finally appeared, opened with the lines, "April is the cruellest month, breeding / Lilacs out of the dead land, mixing / Memory and desire." Lilacs, in Eliot's poetry, suggest sensual allurement, and April brought the cruel reminder of lilacs, as well as Verdenal's departure for war and imminent death. In a brief published statement in 1934, Eliot wrote, "I am willing to admit that my own retrospect is touched by a sentimental sunset, the memory of a friend coming across the Luxembourg Gardens in the late afternoon, waving a branch of lilac, a friend who was later (so far as I could find out) to be mixed with the mud of Gallipoli."[10]

When Eliot wrote *The Waste Land*, his deteriorating relationship with Vivienne may have been caused by multiple factors—the tragic death of Verdenal, estrangement from his family, the death of his father in 1919, sexual neuroses—all of which contributed to immense guilt and anxiety. As he moved away from the Unitarianism of his family background, he flirted with agnosticism under the tutelage of Bertrand Russell, and even considered becoming a Buddhist monk before ultimately converting to Anglo-Catholicism.

In *Broken Images*, a study of *The Waste Land*, Robert Schwarz agrees that behind Phlebas probably hides Jean Verdenal, but lacking definitive evidence, questions Eliot's supposedly homosexual or bisexual inclination.

9. Eliot, *Selected Essays*, 234–35.
10. Eliot, "Commentary," 452.

He argues that Eliot was suffering from solipsism, and it was adherence to solipsism, from which he could see no escape, that led to his religious conversion in 1927.[11] Repeating the axiom that atheists and blasphemers are sometimes closer to God than nominal believers, Schwarz argues that *The Waste Land* represents a major step toward Eliot's conversion, which was not a single event but a process that began early and continued throughout his life. In Schwarz's estimation, it is this struggle with religious conviction, rather than with his sexuality, that helped to epitomize Eliot as a poet and thinker peculiar to the twentieth century.

THE WASTE LAND AS QUEST FOR SIGNIFICANCE

However one characterizes the twentieth century, it was among other things a time of troubled faith in which traditional theology lost much of its persuasiveness, at least for many intellectuals, with nothing yet established as an alternative. For Schwarz, Eliot's message in *The Waste Land* is not so much a quest for God as a search for meaning to existence. That Eliot concerned himself so intensely with this struggle to find significance certainly was a key to his becoming, in the minds of many, the poet par excellence of the twentieth century. However, taking Eliot over the trajectory of his work, leads me to believe that he was not simply a modernist supreme, but one whose work culminates with the *Four Quartets*, a legacy of faith, hope, and love grounded in a personal and sovereign God, and it is this legacy of redemption that qualifies him as one of the greatest religious poets in the English language.[12]

For those who accept Eliot as modernist supreme, it may come as a surprise that his deepest poetic roots lay not in modern existentialism but in the medieval figure of Dante. It was Dante who gave Eliot the unifying vision of a spiritual journey of the soul through which the elements of *The Waste Land* were brought together and made whole. From Dante he learned the allusive method through which to assimilate the personal into the universal. Both Dante and Eliot belong to the ideal order of history that escapes the prison of time and space, leaving behind yet another trail from appearance to reality for future pilgrims of the soul to wonder at and try to follow, past the terror and glory of life to the other side of despair.

11. Schwarz, *Broken Images*, 18.
12. My case for this assessment appears in chapter 6 of *Wading in Water*.

There can be no doubt that Dante was in Eliot's mind as he composed *The Waste Land*. For a number of years he carried a pocket edition of Dante with him. Consider the circumstances under which Dante wrote his *Divine Comedy*. As Dante was exiled from Florence, Eliot was alienated spiritually, ideologically, and politically from Europe and his homeland. Like Dante, Eliot found himself spiritually in circumstances much like those of which Dante wrote: "In the middle of the journey of our life / I came to myself in a dark wood / where the straight way was lost . . . . I cannot rightly retell how I entered there, / so full of sleep was I at that moment / when I abandoned the true way."

It was spiritual crisis for Dante and for Eliot alike, a spiritual crisis precipitated by misfortunes buffeting the soul that led to their literary work. As Dante lamented for the political destiny of Florence, Eliot agonized over the fate of Europe, represented archetypically in the image of London. Whereas in the *Commedia*, despite the allegorical method, the content is well articulated, in *The Waste Land*, partly because of the style and partly because of Eliot's emotional despair, the structure is more like that of a living organism with one thing emerging from another, analogous to dream formation. In *The Waste Land*, Dante's heaven and hell have given way to a timeless metaphysical state, but Eliot, too, comprehends the workings of divine justice.

Eliot's borrowings from Dante are commonly recognized, beginning in "The Fire Sermon" and progressing in "Death by Water," although the parallels are lessened in the final version by the collaborative editing of both Pound and Eliot. "Death by Water" originally commenced with an eighty-four line narrative of a shipwreck off the New England coast, an account inspired by the tale told by Ulysses and recorded in *The Inferno*. In the original writing of *The Waste Land*, the Phlebas episode constituted the entire "Death by Water" segment, a narrative reduced in the end to a mere ten lines. In other words, at the early stage of writing, Dante must have been at the forefront of Eliot's mind.

While Dante is the privileged witness and faithful reporter of the event of his *Commedia*, he is also the central figure of the drama. Like Dante, Eliot is the central figure of *The Waste Land*. While readers can get lost in the arcana of cartomancy (fortune telling by cards) and fertility rites revealed in Sir James Frazer's *Golden Bough* and Jessie Weston's *From Ritual to Romance*, or entangled by Buddhist or Hindu terminology in "What the Thunder Said," it seems clear that Eliot's guide in determining his compositional method—a kind of autobiographical, allegorical approach—was primarily Dante. From Dante, too, came the plan of the poem, as a verbal embodiment or replication of the search for significance. Born into an era of psychological analysis—the era that gave us psychoanalysis, the psychological novel, stream-of-consciousness writing, Dadaism, and Surrealism—Eliot chose to pursue his spiritual quest through a free-associative technique, in which his imagery partakes both dream and mythic elements.

Like other Modernists, Eliot was conscious of the weight and influence of the past. In his essay "Tradition and the Individual Talent," Eliot expressed this obligation to prior writers, claiming that no artist "has his complete meaning alone." In 1927, when he became a British citizen and converted to an Anglican form of Christianity, he consciously and successfully began to pattern his career on the template of Dante's *Divine Comedy*. Much as his mental breakdown—coinciding with the cultural breakdown of post-war Europe—led to *The Waste Land*, his *Ash Wednesday* records his leap of faith to traditional Christianity, while his *Four Quartets*, completed during World War II, describe a deeper plunge into the realm of the spirit. Awarded the Nobel Prize for Literature in 1948, Eliot's *Four Quartets* completed his twentieth-century "divine comedy."

Despite its pessimistic bent, there is hope in *The Waste Land*. Commentators often focus on the closing word "*Shantih*" (also spelled *santi*). In his notes, Eliot calls attention to both its meaning and function. He gives the meaning as the "peace which passeth understanding." In Vedantic thought, *shantih* is the fundamental emotion from which all others spring, just as Brahman is the One from which the Many appearances arise. *Shantih* encompasses all emotions, and as such cannot be conceived; it "passeth understanding." More important, this word closes the Upanishads. A Upanishad is a philosophical treatise attached to the end of a Veda. The Vedas express mystical doctrine in poetic form, and the Upanishads supply commentary that seeks to explore the Vedic content. That is why Upanishadic doctrine is not unified; it contains the opinions of many, and thus, like the Jewish Talmud, is a work of speculation. In the Upanishads, the speculation centers on various aspects of a single problem, including how appearance is related to reality and how the individual self is related to Brahman. Further, the Upanishads were intended to be passed on to initiates about to withdraw into hermitage, where they might meditate upon them in private.

As the Upanishads are not united, so *The Waste Land* is not. It is a poem containing the speculations of Eliot upon his own condition. It was written as Eliot was contemplating withdrawal into a Buddhist monastery. In a sense, it, too, like the Upanishads, was intended for the initiates; few others would be able to understand it.

In addition, both the meaning and the function of the word *shantih* requires one to read it in the subjunctive mode of closing invocation, not entirely dissimilar to the Hebrew *amen*, accordingly translated "May there be peace." And so the peace with which the poem ends is not achieved, but longed for, a peace sought out of anguish. That was Eliot's longing at this phase of life, to find the full significance of silence.

With the publication of *The Waste Land*, it is as though a curtain raises, and Eliot begins describing his political and social views as "reactionary and ultra-conservative." In 1928, a year after his religious conversion (Vivienne did not share his religious devotion; differences of belief and lifestyle led to their permanent separation in 1933),[13] Eliot wrote in a preface to a book of essays that he considered himself "a classicist, a royalist, and an Anglo-Catholic." Having been raised a Unitarian, a religious perspective that rejected key Christian doctrines such as the Trinity and the divinity of Jesus, by the mid-1920s he came to believe that only orthodox Catholic Christianity presented a persuasive solution to the cultural and personal trauma of the post-War world. However, the Roman Catholic Church in England represented what he called a sect, and his loathing of sectarianism and his conviction that the culture and faith of a people should be intertwined led him to the Church of England. That body, he recognized, was also deficient, having an unsatisfactory mixture of Protestantism and Catholicism in its beliefs and practices but being, from the viewpoint of the Catholic Church, not Catholic at all.

Eliot's solution was to align himself with the Anglo-Catholic movement in the Church of England, which saw itself as part of the universal Catholic Church from which it had regrettably separated at the Reformation. Maintaining the validity of its orders and sacraments, Anglo-Catholicism aspired to return in full to Catholic communion, a position rejected by Rome. Initially, or perhaps as a result of his personal trauma due to a failing marriage, Eliot's sense of cultural dissolution in The Great War, his failure to find consolation in philosophy, his study of Eastern religions, and

13. Vivienne's death in 1947 finally freed Eliot from that unhappy segment in his life. Shortly after her death, Eliot began sharing a London apartment with John Hayward, a wheelchair-bound invalid, a younger man who shared Eliot's interest in language and poetry. When in 1957 Eliot married Valerie Fletcher, his separation from Hayward was apparently difficult.

his disillusionment with Unitarianism and Protestantism in all their varieties, led to some of his most distinguished poetry. Like his poetry, Eliot's faith also was shaped by the conviction that both artistry and spirituality emerge from suffering.

CHAPTER 5

Joseph Conrad's *Heart of Darkness*

THOUGH HE DID NOT SPEAK English fluently until his twenties, Joseph Conrad (1857–1924) came to be regarded as a prose stylist who brought a non-English sensibility into English literature. Born in Ukraine (then a part of Russia that had once belonged to Poland) as Jozef Teodor Konrad Korzeniowski, the only child of Polish parents, Teodor and his family moved to Warsaw in 1861, where his father Apollo joined the resistance movement against the Russian empire. Apollo was arrested and in 1862 the family was exiled to Siberia. In 1863, the sentence was commuted and the family settled in northeast Ukraine, where four years later Teodor's mother died of tuberculosis. In 1867 Teodor returned to Poland with Apollo, but two years later Apollo died, leaving Teodor orphaned at the age of eleven.

The youngster was placed in the care of an uncle, but poor health and unsatisfactory schoolwork led to his declaration that he intended to become a sailor. In 1874 the sixteen year old, intellectually precocious but disliking school routine, went to Marseilles, France for a planned merchant-marine career on French merchant ships. By this point, Teodor had absorbed enough history, culture, and literature to be able eventually to develop a distinctive worldview.

After nearly four years in France and on French merchant ships plying the Mediterranean and the Caribbean, Teodor joined the British merchant marine, enlisting in 1878. For the next fifteen years he worked on a variety of ships as crew member, eventually achieving captain's rank. In 1886 he became a naturalized British citizen and changed his name to Joseph

Conrad. His voyages to India, Southeast Asia, and Australia involved him in personal encounters and locations from which he later drew extensively for material for his fiction.

In 1889, when Conrad was thirty-one, he resigned his command of the *Otago* in Australia, for reasons that are not entirely clear, and returned to England. That year, Conrad began writing his first novel, *Almayer's Folly*, and from the very first page he displayed a serious, professional approach to literature, presented in beautiful prose. It became clear that here was an author who should be taken seriously, who used storytelling to both shape and promote his own attitude to art and reality. His experiences at sea and as a world traveler furnished much of his writing, including *Lord Jim, Nostromo, Youth, The Shadow Line,* and *Heart of Darkness.*

In 1890 Conrad was hired by a Belgian company that operated a string of trading stations in the Congo River basin, exporting ivory, rubber, and other local products. Conrad's assignment was to replace a Danish captain who had been murdered after a quarrel with tribesmen. His motives for this venture were mixed; he was out of a job and had spent his savings. Since boyhood he had wanted to journey to the little explored center of Africa, then considered the "dark continent." He spent six months in the Congo, two of them learning the river as first mate of a steamer that traveled upriver as far as the end of navigation at Stanley Falls. There, at the company's inner station, the boat picked up a sick agent named Klein, who died on the return trip—a trip during which Conrad took command of the boat for a few days because of the captain's sickness.

After returning to Kinshasa (then called Leopoldville) and learning that he was not to have charge of the steamer he had been promised, he left for home, ill and disgusted with European imperialism. He came back a changed person, fully cognizant, as T. S. Eliot put it, "of the power and terror of Nature, and the isolation and fallenness of Man."[1] Conrad recorded his journey upriver to Stanley Falls in his *Congo Diary*, which bears witness to the brutalities of the colonial scramble. The Belgian Congo (today's Democratic Republic of the Congo, formerly known as Zaire) was one of the most extreme examples of rampant colonialism in the nineteenth century. Under Leopold II's imperialistic rule for two decades from 1885, the territory was subjected to comprehensive commercial exploitation. Licenses were sold by the Belgian government for the extraction of natural resources, and no remuneration was required for the indigenous people. The manual work of

---

1. Cited in Franklin Walker's introduction to *Heart of Darkness*, xi.

plundering was done, not by Belgians, but by natives of the region. In *Heart of Darkness*, Conrad gives us a glimpse of six such workers, near starvation and chained together at the neck, as they carry out their task.

Feverish sickness and near mental breakdown was one result of the horrors Conrad experienced in the Congo. In 1894, Conrad embarked on his second profession, partly because of poor health, partly due to unavailability of ships, but mostly because he had become so fascinated with writing that he decided on a literary career. *Almayer's Folly*, set on the east coast of Borneo, was published in 1895, followed by *An Outcast of the Islands* (1896), *The Nigger of the "Narcissus,"* (1897), and two novellas, *An Outpost of Progress* (1897) and *Heart of Darkness* (1899), both set in a Congo exploited by colonialism. For much of his first decade as author, Conrad worked in obscurity. By the fall of 1898, he became more settled in his new way of life, ready finally to experiment artistically with private material. *Heart of Darkness* marks the beginning of this next phase of his artistic life. Conrad's earlier narratives were primarily objective, descriptive, and thematically clear; *Heart of Darkness* is more interior, highly psychological, and deeply symbolic.

Although his talent was recognized early on by intellectuals, popular success eluded him until the 1913 publication of *Chance*. Most of his writings were first published in newspapers and magazines, and Conrad often had to request advances from magazine and publishers to survive financially. In 1910 he was awarded an annual government grant, which helped meet his financial need, and in time publishers began purchasing his manuscripts.

Over his lifetime, he published some twenty novels, in addition to dozens of novellas, short stories, and essays. After 1913, he became the subject of more discussion and praise than any other English writer of his time. He had a genius for companionship, including authors and other leading artists. Adverse to public honors, in 1924 Conrad declined British knighthood, having already refused honorary degrees from leading British and American universities. Nevertheless, he possessed hereditary Polish status of nobility, remaining a lifelong Pole at heart.

Conrad was a proponent of artful narration. Like his friend Henry James, Conrad held that how a novelist tells a story is as important as the story itself. Conrad's narrative style and antiheroic characters influenced many authors, including T. S. Eliot, F. Scott Fitzgerald, William Faulkner, Graham Greene, Gabriel García Márquez, and Salman Rushdie.

HEART OF DARKNESS: PLOT AND RESPONSE

Since my first reading of *Heart of Darkness* at the age of sixteen, I recognized the importance of Conrad's novella. I was not fully aware of the
reason, but I knew then its significance lay not only in its colonial or geographical setting, but also in its portrayal of greed, obsession, power, and
alienation stemming from spiritual decay in the human character, a lack of
vision and resolve Conrad labeled "heart of darkness." The influence of this
initial reading led me deeper into Conrad's literary legacy, including *Lord
Jim* and *Nostromo*.

People rarely read *Heart of Darkness* because they want to. It's not that
kind of novel. Instead, they read it because they have to, usually as required
reading in high school or college English courses, or perhaps as required
reading for life. While the plot is straightforward, its meaning, message,
and interpretation are greatly debated.

The novel opens on the mouth of the Thames, gateway to London and
the heart of the British empire. Aboard the *Nellie*, Charles Marlowe tells
fellow travelers how he became captain of a river steamboat for an ivory
trading company in the Belgian Congo. He is inspired by his memories and
by thoughts of the great explorers and mariners, from Sir Francis Drake onward, who have navigated the Thames. Suddenly, Marlow is struck by a different sentiment: "And this also," he says, "has been one of the dark places
of the earth."[2] Unlike most seamen, Marlow is a wanderer, an adventurer,
and unlike most storytellers, Marlow's tales are equally problematic, for "to
him the meaning of an episode was not inside like a kernel but outside,"[3]
its meaning oblique and imprecise. To explain his statement about Britain
once having been "one of the dark places of the earth," Marlow speaks of
a time long ago, when the Romans first conquered this land and found
Britain as a dark and ignorant place. The Romans "were conquerors, and
for that you want only brute force . . . It was just robbery with violence,
aggravated murder on a great scale, and men going at it blind—as is very
proper for those who tackle a darkness."[4] Colonization, like conquest, is
brutal and violent. Like Africa, Britain, too, was once a dark place. In an act
of inversion, Conrad seems to be saying that Britain, as an imperial power,
is still in a sense one of the dark places.

2. Conrad, *Heart of Darkness*, 9.

3. Conrad, *Heart of Darkness*, 9.

4. Conrad, *Heart of Darkness*, 10.

Marlow's story begins in Brussels, but neither that city nor the Congo is mentioned by its geographical name. They are, respectively, the "White City," with allusions to the biblical "whitened sepulcher" metaphor of hypocrisy, and the "heart of darkness," an allusion to the heart shape of the African continent. In a flashback, Marlow makes his way to Africa, taking passage on a French steamer. He sets out for the Congo optimistic of what he will find, but his expectations quickly sour.

From the moment he arrives, he is exposed to the evil of imperialism, witnessing the violence it inflicts upon the African people it exploits. He travels up the Congo River to the Company's Outer Station, where a railroad is being built. Marlow explores a narrow ravine, and is horrified to find himself in a place full of diseased Africans, overworked and dying. Marlow must wait ten days in the Outer Station, where he meets the company's chief accountant, who tells him of a Mr. Kurtz (meaning "short" in German), a colonial agent who is supposedly unmatched in his ability to procure ivory from the continent's interior. According to rumor, Kurtz has fallen ill and apparently gone mad; even worse, he has "gone native," sunk into savagery. To some extent, he has lost that important sense of division between a colonizer and the colonized.

Marlow leaves the Outer Station on a two-hundred-mile trek to the Company's Central Station, run by the Manager, a conspiratorial character and his sidekick, the Brickmaker. There he learns that the steamboat he is supposed to pilot up the Congo had been wrecked and now lies at the bottom of the river. Frustrated, Marlow must wait at the Central Station until his boat is repaired. One night, as Marlow is lying on the deck of his salvaged steamboat, he overhears the Manager and his uncle talking about Kurtz. Marlow concludes that the Manager fears that Kurtz is trying to steal his job. His uncle, however, tells him to have faith in the power of the jungle to "do away" with Kurtz.

Marlow's boat is finally repaired, and he leaves the Central Station (accompanied by the Manager and a crew of Europeans agents Conrad calls "pilgrims," due to their habit of carrying wooden staves, and Africans, whom Conrad shamelessly stereotypes as "cannibals"). As Marlow penetrates deeper into the jungle, it becomes clear that his surroundings impact him psychologically; his journey is not only into a geographical "heart of darkness" but into his own psychic interior—and perhaps into the darkened psychic interior of Western civilization as well. As the steamboat nears the Inner Station, it is attacked by a shower of arrows. Assuming that the same natives who are attacking them have already attacked the Inner Station, Marlow regrets that he will never get to speak to Kurtz. However, when Marlow examines Kurtz's building through a telescope, he notices there is no fence, only a series of posts ornamented with "balls" that Marlow later learns are natives' heads.

A Russian trader and disciple of Kurtz approaches the steamboat and tells Marlow that Kurtz is still alive. He speaks enthusiastically of Kurtz, claiming, "This man has enlarged my mind." Marlow learns from him that the steamboat was attacked because of loyalty by the natives, who idolized Kurtz and did not want him taken away. When Marlow finally reaches Kurtz, he finds him to be wholly mad and corrupted. A manuscript written by a younger Kurtz shows that he was once an ardent idealist, who came to the Congo with the intention of bringing the torch of enlightenment to the natives. The manuscript trails off, however, ending with Kurtz's final, terrible injunction, "Exterminate the brutes!" After exploitation, there will be no further use for the natives; they become expendable, merely vestiges of a primitive past.

The next day, Marlow and his crew leave the Inner Station, taking Kurtz with them. As they travel downriver, Kurtz's health deteriorates. At one point, the steamboat breaks down and Kurtz gives Marlow a packet of letters and a photograph for safekeeping, fearing that the Manager will take them, and Marlow complies. One night Marlow approaches Kurtz, who is lying in the pilothouse on his stretcher "waiting for death." After trying to reassure Kurtz that he is not going to die, Marlow hears Kurtz whisper his final words, "The horror! The horror!" The next day, Kurtz is buried offshore in a muddy hole.

After returning to Europe, Marlow again visits Brussels and finds himself unable to relate to the privileged Europeans around him. A Company official approaches Marlow and asks for the packet of papers that Kurtz had entrusted to him. Marlow refuses, but does give the official a copy of Kurtz's report to The Society for the Suppression of Savage Customs, with Kurtz's chilling postscript ("Exterminate all the brutes!") torn off. Marlow's final duty to Kurtz is to visit the Intended (Kurtz's fiancée) and deliver Kurtz's letter (and her portrait) to her. When he meets the Intended, she is dressed in mourning and still greatly upset by Kurtz's death, but she praises him as the paragon of virtue and achievement she once knew him to be. Marlow lets slip that he was with Kurtz when he died, and the Intended asks him to repeat Kurtz's last words. Marlow cannot bring himself to shatter her illusions with the truth. Instead, he tells her that Kurtz's last word was her name. The Intended states that she "knew" Kurtz would have said such a thing, and Marlow leaves, horrified by his lie yet unable to prevent himself from telling the truth.

At various points in his story to his companions on the *Nellie*, the talkative Marlow interrupts himself, concerned that he is not properly or fully conveying the story. "Do you see him [Kurtz]?" he asks. "Do you see the story? Do you see anything?"[5] Conrad alludes here to the central problem all writers face—indeed all of us face—how to get across our ideas, how to make our material come alive to others. Unlike much realist literature, in *Heart of Darkness*, the straightforward way of telling a story disappears behind an impressionistic screen.

Whose story is this—Marlow's or Kurtz's—and what is the author's intent? Not surprisingly, *Heart of Darkness* has generated a host of interpretations. Is this novella an adventure story, an anatomy of imperialist Europe, or a critique of colonialism? Although the story denounces the greed, exploitation, and inhumanity of European trading interests, it has nonetheless been construed as a racist account of Africa and Africans.

Others have taken a more psychological approach, seeing in Marlow's quest for Kurtz an account of self-discovery, and in Kurtz—whether the Freudian id or the Jungian shadow or simply the outlaw—an exploration of the potential savagery and bestiality within all humans, and therefore a voyage into one's own "dark heart." Philosophically speaking, one might argue that *Heart of Darkness* is about the discovery of nihilism at the core of human achievements, that all projects are ultimately illusory and meaningless.

In *Heart of Darkness*, a constellation of binary images—light/darkness, past/present, civilized/savage, good/evil—informs a way of thinking central to modern Western culture. Oppositional, dualist thinking is so much a part of our everyday lives—male/female, black/white, young/old, rich/poor, happy/sad, like/dislike—that we no longer recognize it as an imposed structure of thought. We tend to naturalize and normalize it, assuming ideational construction, as though these concepts possessed material substance. These pairs do, of course, speak of perceived realities, but these ways of organizing the world conceptually sometimes trap us into assuming that what are essentially metaphorical categories actually describe the real

5. Conrad, *Heart of Darkness*, 30.

world of things, and furthermore, that these categories reflect metaphysical polarities as well.

It is easy to mistake metaphorical ways of thinking for "the real thing." Applied to *Heart of Darkness*, Conrad found in these binary images a powerful tool for a radical and disturbing critique of too-easily assumed cultural norms. Lightness/darkness is the most obvious pair, but illumination/blindness, idea/idol, civilized/savage, conqueror/conquered, vital/dead, and dream/nightmare are others. However we might judge these sets of images, Marlow's narration forces us to see that what are essentially metaphysical categories actually describe things in the real world that exist in relation to one another as an infinitely graduated series of differences, of things constantly at play. Hence, for Conrad, the civilized world is really savage, ideals can become graven idols, faithfulness can be a sham, darkness can be found not only in "the other" but also in ourselves, and service, work, and duty can overcome evil.

HEART OF DARKNESS AS QUEST FOR SOLIDARITY

Central to spirituality is solidarity, by which I mean "wholeness," "unity," "integration," and "acceptance." In this segment, we focus on "solidarity," a term that encompasses the above mentioned aspects of spirituality. But solidarity with what? In the pages that follow, we explore three dimensions of solidarity: with one's self, with others, and, ultimately, with nature—progenitor, mother, and nurturer of us all.

Heart of Darkness was first published in 1899, the same year as Rudyard Kipling's poem "The White Man's Burden." Unlike Conrad's novel, Kipling's poem stands as an example of imperial pride. In it, Kipling laments the suffering of Britain in maintaining imperial domination. In his view, European imperialism stood for benevolence and goodwill; empire was the imposition of a white civilization on a savage world, with no thought of personal gain, of exploitation of natural resources, or of military advantage, and most importantly, with no expectation of reward or gratitude from its beneficiaries. Kipling believed that in its military action and occupation of the Philippines at the end of the nineteenth century, the United States was offering to share the responsibility of empire with Britain. Today, of course, we find this view of imperialism duplicitous and racist.

In *Heart of Darkness*, Conrad unveils the other side of the colonial coin. While Leopold II pursued his Congo interests in the name of philanthropy and anti-slavery, the truth of his imperial presence was that it became his personal territorial possession (rather than that of the Belgian state), a fact recognized by the Berlin Conference of 1885, which arbitrated over European territorial ambitions in Africa (known as the "Scramble for Africa"), dividing the spoils primarily with the aim of averting conflict among the competing European nations.

The Berlin Conference validated Leopold's absolute personal rule over one million square miles of Africa by regulations that guaranteed free trade among European nations and companies there. By 1890, Leopold began treating the Congo as his personal fiefdom, instituting a "labor tax" on natives in the form of forty hours per month of forced labor. Increased production of ivory and rubber was the only priority, physical mutilation and abuse its means of enforcement. Estimates for the decline of the native population during the two decades of Leopold's self-developed "absolute ownership" of the native population range from three to six million. Uninterested in fair trade or benefits for local peoples, he needed Africans only as a cheap labor force. *Heart of Darkness* leaves little doubt about Conrad's verdict on Leopold's rule, but did Conrad go far enough in his indictment of the colonial enterprise?

Despite its enduring popularity, the reputation of *Heart of Darkness* has varied significantly since its publication. In the early 1900s, it was regarded in Britain as a scathing indictment, not of colonialism in general, but of Belgian colonialism. In the post-imperial period (from the mid-1950s), the reputation of *Heart of Darkness* changed dramatically. It became a postcolonial classic, read as an indictment of empire in general. Generations of students in America and Britain read it in this light. Twenty-five years later, the book's reputation changed yet again. In 1975, Nigerian Nobel Prize-winning novelist Chinua Achebe denounced Conrad's novel as racist, noting that Africans exist in this narrative as nameless figures, simply dark like their environment and hardly human. Furthermore, Conrad used words such as *brutal, monstrous, vengeful, implacable, inscrutable, hopeless, accursed, pitiless, dark,* and *evil* constantly and stereotypically in talking about Africa, Achebe averred, qualities easily projected in general to Africans and those of African descent. Why should the suffering inflicted by Europeans on an entire continent and its native peoples be reduced as backdrop for two European males struggling with social and psychological issues? For Achebe, the Eurocentricity of *Heart of Darkness* was itself a form of racism.

While issues such as these are complicated and far beyond the confines of this chapter, we must not forget the cultural and historical context under which this book was written. As a child, Conrad and his family were victims of Russia's colonialist policies toward Poland. As an adolescent, Conrad chose to become a sailor, believing this career would provide him with freedom and choices he had not experienced as a child. Ironically, the profession he thought would release him from the oppression of colonialism often brought him closer to it.

Like the rest of us, Conrad had convictions, beliefs, preferences, and biases, but these did not make him a racist. He was what we might call today a progressive conservative, driven by a high moral code and a profound commitment to egalitarianism. Whether or not we agree on its meaning and message, *Heart of Darkness* is a novel that matters. As such, it has influenced the thinking of millions of people for over a century. A novel such as this, particularly if read in the context of the controversies and the historical situations that surround it, can help create the critical apparatus necessary to understand literature. In *Deep Splendor*, we are not searching for great works of literature that function as pills to be swallowed to obtain a specific effect. Rather, we examine works of literature that open doors and keep us searching long after we have read and discussed them. Kipling's poem "The White Man's Burden" confirmed the prejudices of its time for its readers. *Heart of Darkness* did not do so, for we come away from this novel not knowing quite what to think but nonetheless thinking very hard indeed.

After reading *Heart of Darkness*, readers must decide whose story this is—Marlow's, Kurtz's, or Conrad's—for this novel is constructed like a set of Russian dolls, a series of stories, one embedded within the other. However, as we noted earlier, there is an additional twist, for in this novel the straightforward way of telling a story disappears. The story not only has no center, but its words have little or no contact with reality. In one respect, this is so because the story charts various journeys simultaneously, namely, Kurtz's quest for power—a journey into the potential savagery and bestiality inside every human being, a journey that ends in Kurtz's nervous breakdown and death—and Marlow's quest for Kurtz, a journey into the center of the African continent viewed as the voyage into one's own "heart of darkness."

In *Heart of Darkness*, Marlow uses the unknown, remote, and primitive Africa as a symbol for a malevolent and primeval force found within nature, absorbed into each human soul and inevitably transferred to human society and civilization. Understood thus, the metaphor of darkness found in the title applies to different levels of reality. On one level, it indicates the continent of Africa, shaped like a human heart. On another level, it indicates the Belgian Congo—the geographical heart or center of Africa—and the color of its native inhabitants. On another level, the metaphor refers to the evil practices of the colonizers of the Congo and their sordid exploitation of the natives, and suggests that the real darkness is not in Africa but in Europe, and that its heart is not in the chests of black Africans but in all the whites who engage and benefit from the colonialist enterprise.

There is also a third level to the metaphor, and it is the darkness of pristine nature, itself unknown, remote, and primitive. At the beginning of his own story, Marlow introduces the account of his experience in Africa by philosophizing on the life led by the Roman conquerors of ancient Britain: "Land in a swamp, march through the woods, and in some inland post feel the savagery, the utter savagery, had closed round him—all that mysterious life of the wilderness that stirs in the forest, in the jungles, in the hearts of wild men. There's no initiation either into such mysteries. He has to live in the midst of the incomprehensible which is also detestable. And it has a fascination too, that goes to work upon him. The fascination of the abomination—you know. Imagine the growing regrets, the longing to escape, the powerless disgust, the surrender—the hate."[6]

According to Marlow, the Roman colonizers became psychologically depraved because, being cut off from the norms of civilization, they turned to the lawless jungle. Marlow implies that his trip upriver into the heart of darkest Africa represents a similar experience: "Going up that river was like travelling back to the earliest beginnings of the world, when vegetation rioted on the earth and the big trees were kings. . . . you thought yourself bewitched and cut off from everything you had known once. . . . And this stillness of life did not in the least resemble a peace. It was the stillness of an implacable force brooding over an inscrutable intention. It looked at you with a vengeful aspect."[7]

CONRAD'S SECULAR HUMANISM

In addition to Marlow and Kurtz's stories, *Heart of Darkness*, like all of Conrad's novels, is a story about Conrad's quest for the meaning of life.

6. Conrad, *Heart of Darkness*, 10.

7. Conrad, *Heart of Darkness*, 35–36.

Having read his story and analyzed his metaphor, we return to Conrad with a sense that he, too, looked into the human pit of power and set out to chart what he saw there. Before (and beyond) the economic and the political, what Conrad noticed was the psychic (spiritual, psychological, emotional) strife at hand when the self is subjected to sufficient stress or buffeted by overwhelming obsession. In such instances he revered the "seaman's code," a work ethic that insists on dignified standards and boundaries supplied by concepts such as honor, duty, and restraint; for Conrad, focusing on the task at hand is the only way to hold on to who you are and need to be.

Conrad's aesthetic vision was dominated by the naturalistic despair of the late Victorian worldview, which originated in those developments in nineteenth-century science that combined with industrialism to suggest that the natural world, far from being the eternal setting in which human beings created in God's image could thrive, was merely the temporary and accidental result of purposeless physical processes. In a meaningless, transitory, survival-of-the-fittest universe, there is little apparent reason why individual human beings should have any concern with the lives of others, or even very much concern with their own.

In such a world, humans are aliens; they must create their own order if they can. This was how many Victorians came to think of human destiny. The religion of progress, in Tennyson's words, called on humans to "Move upward, working out the beast / And let the ape and tiger die." However, that was not easy, as Freud was to show, and at much the same time, as Conrad does in *Heart of Darkness*.

Kurtz begins as a representative of the highest aspirations of nineteenth-century individualism; he is an artist, an eloquent political speaker on the liberal side, an economic and social careerist; and his story enacts the most characteristic impulse of Victorian civilization, combining the economic exploitation of Africa with the great moral crusade of bringing light to the backward peoples of the world. But the jungle whispers to Kurtz "things about himself which he did not know, things of which he had no conception till he took counsel with this great solitude."[8] Forgotten and brutal instincts soon lead Kurtz to outdo the other colonial exploiters in sordid rapacity; he enslaves and massacres surrounding tribes, and he ends up being worshipped as a God to whom human sacrifices are offered.

Behind the great nineteenth-century dream was the assumption that humans could be their own God. Conrad's Kurtz thought that "we whites

---

8. Conrad, *Heart of Darkness*, 57.

. . . must necessarily appear to [the savages] in the nature of supernatural beings—we approach them with the might as of a deity."[9] But he ends his report to the International Society for the Suppression of Savage Customs, "Exterminate all the brutes."

Conrad shared with many Victorians their rejection of the religious, social, and intellectual order of the past, but he also rejected the religion of progress with which they had replaced it. This alienation from the prevailing intellectual perspectives both of the past and of his own time naturally did much to color Conrad's picture of his own selfhood and of his role as an author. Alienation, of course, is not the whole story, for Conrad also gives us a sense of a much wider commitment to exemplary ethical, social, and literary attitudes than do other of his great contemporaries. For Conrad, the way out of alienation is through commitment to the process of moral self-discovery. Though he held this approach in common with existentialist thinkers, unlike them, he did not see commitment as a single willed phenomenon occurring in the individual consciousness. For Conrad, it is, rather, an endless process throughout history in which individuals are driven by circumstances into traditional forms of human solidarity; are driven to accept the position that fidelity must govern the individual's relations to the outside world, while his inner self must be controlled by restraint and honor. This conservative and social ethic is certainly different from the existentialist position, for it embodies the values of the most widely shared secular humanist codes of behavior over the ages. For Conrad, however, there was no hope of a sovereign power enthroned in fixed standards of conduct. The way people actually react to the circumstances of their lives seems to be Conrad's only justification for his view of solidarity.

Broadly speaking, most of twentieth-century literature may be said to provide implicit guidance, urging adherence to an ideology either of the future, the past, or of the supernatural world. But Conrad had no belief in liberal reform, or in the politics of the future, and had equally little interest in the utopianism of the past, which can be found in the thought of contemporaries such as Yeats, Joyce, Pound, and Eliot. Nor, finally, did Conrad find any appeal in supernatural transcendence. His objection to Christianity combined a rejection of what he viewed as myth, superstition, and hypocrisy, coupled with what he considered the impracticality of Christian ideals.

Shaped by youthful alienation and his experiences at sea, Conrad the seaman could not commit to any ideology other than individual duty, even

9. Conrad, *Heart of Darkness*, 50.

in cases where fidelity might conflict with truth. In *Heart of Darkness*, Marlow's final act is explicit when he preserves the "great and saving illusion" about the dead Kurtz that is enshrined in the Intended's "mature capacity for fidelity." At that point, Conrad makes practical his notion that, once we have experienced the heart of darkness, we may be driven to the position that, in cases where fidelity is in conflict with truth, it is truth that should be sacrificed.

In Conrad's story, when Marlow finishes his tale, no one moves. The captain finally breaks the silence on a practical note, "We have lost the first of the ebb." The turn of the tide is a reminder of the endless and apparently meaningless circularity of the physical and the human world, caught in the undertow of evolutionary history. This circularity is finally enacted in the fictional setting and the larger meaning of the tale itself, for in the Thames, Marlow discovers that "the tranquil waterway . . . seemed to lead into the heart of an immense darkness."[10]

Such a view, ultimately pessimistic, is one of the few alternatives available to those who deny the reality of the supernatural world. Anthony Hopkins speaks profoundly when he likens being an atheist to living in a closed cell with no windows, for the joy of believing and not knowing far exceeds the joy of believing and knowing. That seems to be the essence of Paul's message in 1 Corinthians 13: in the end, "faith, hope, and love abide, these three; and the greatest of these is love" (13:13). Some people look within and see darkness and despair, others look within and find love. When we look at life solely through humanist eyes, we see others, particularly their faults and limitations, and beyond humanity we see nature—the source of psychological darkness. However, when we look at life through theistic eyes, we see love eternal, and a divine originator who loves unconditionally.

10. Conrad, *Heart of Darkness*, 76.

Chapter 6

J. R. R. Tolkien's *The Lord of the Rings*

THE THEME OF GOOD AND EVIL is central in the writings of the British author J. R. R. Tolkien. Like Conrad's *Heart of Darkness*, Tolkien presents communities of good and evil. In the virtuous groups, sentient creatures, including humans, are guided by humanistic qualities such as justice, prudence, temperance, and fortitude, in addition to duty, loyalty, honor, compassion, and perseverance. In the communities of evil, sentient creatures are directed by vices such as injustice, indiscretion, excess, and intolerance, in addition to greed, cruelty, and selfishness. Unlike Conrad's humanistic ideals, however, Tolkien's heroes are guided by faith, hope, and love, virtues rooted in supernatural realities and ideals.

Set in Middle-earth, a place like earth at some distant time in the past, *The Lord of the Rings* consists of three volumes, written in stages between 1937 and 1939 but not published until the mid-1950s. The three volumes, divided internally into six books, are titled *The Fellowship of the Ring*, *The Two Towers*, and *The Return of the King*. *The Lord of the Rings*, a sequel to Tolkien's *The Hobbit*, is one of the best-selling books of all time, having been reprinted many times and translated into some forty languages.

The series' title refers to the story's main antagonist, the Dark Lord Sauron, an incarnation of evil who is an earlier age created the One Ring to rule over the Rings of Power (Nine Rings for Humans, Seven Rings for Dwarves, and Three Rings for Elves) and further his campaign to conquer all of Middle-earth. In Tolkien's mythology, Sauron is the chief lieutenant of Morgoth, an equivalent of the biblical Satan, or Lucifer, who was originally an angel of high rank who rebelled against God (named Ilúvatar, meaning "Father of All"). Like Morgoth, Sauron also is a fallen angel.[1]

The backstory to *The Hobbit* and *The Lord of the Rings* is told in *The Silmarillion*, a vast unfinished work published posthumously in 1977 and edited by Tolkien's son, Christopher. It chronicles the ancient days that include the First Age of Middle-earth, beginning with creation[2] and concluding with the Great Battle in which Morgoth is overthrown. During the Second Age of Middle-earth, Sauron grows into a new Dark Lord, replacing the banished Morgoth. The story of *The Hobbit* and *The Lord of the Rings* is set during the Third Age of Middle-earth. This age is reckoned from the first defeat of Sauron to the War of the Ring, when Sauron is defeated for a second and final time. This event is narrated in *The Lord of the Rings*, when Sauron's defeat marks the start of the Fourth Age of Middle-earth, which begins the age of human dominance and the virtual fading of the Elves and hobbits (distant relation of humans). Much of the history of the Third Age concerns the human kingdoms of Arnor and Gondor, as well as a region known as the Shire, home of the hobbits.

The plot of *The Lord of the Rings* requires acquaintance with *The Hobbit*, an account in which a peace-loving middle-aged hobbit named Bilbo Baggins accompanies a party of thirteen Dwarves on a quest to recapture their long lost treasure, which is jealously guarded by a dragon named Smaug. The Dwarves employ Bilbo as their burglar, at the recommendation of the wizard Gandalf. On the slopes of the Orc infested Misty Mountains[3]

---

1. In Tolkien's mythology, Melkor (or Margoth, as the Elves later named him), the greatest of God's archangels, wished to become equal with God, disrupting the beauty and harmony of God's created order.

2. In Tolkien's epics, perceptively described as "theological thrillers," Ilúvatar (God) is indirectly present but never named; rather, the cosmos, as the entire story, reflects God's graces. In Tolkien's story, Ilúvatar first created the Ainur, the archangels, giving to each a portion of his wisdom and knowledge, and together, they sang the universe into existence. Ilúvatar declared a theme, then commanded his archangels to "make in harmony together a Great Music." This creating song was to last until the "end of days," when God would create an even greater theme. However, due to Melkor's rebellion, Ilúvatar secretly and uniquely created Elves and humans; hence, the music of the Ainur had no part in their making.

3. The Orcs (the name means "demons"), violent by nature, are a race bred by Morgoth purposely for his evil, and hence have no moral choice. Because Morgoth is incapable of creating life, it seems that he made use of captured Elves that he tortured for his genetic engineering. In the Second and Third Ages, Sauron used Orcs in his service. As elves symbolize what is high and noble in human life, Orcs represent what is base, twisted, insensitive, and cruel.

Bilbo is knocked unconscious and left behind in the darkness. Reviving, he discovers a ring lying beside him in the tunnel. It is this ruling Ring that forms the subject of *The Lord of the Rings*, but Bilbo fails to understand its purpose, discovering only its magical property of invisibility at this stage. After putting the Ring in his pocket, Bilbo comes across a subterranean lake where Gollum dwells, a horrid shriveled once-hobbit creature corrupted by long centuries guarding yet possessed by the One Ring. His life has been preserved over centuries by the Ring he gained through murder and that he calls "my precious," believing it his by right.

After defeat of Smaug and the Battle of the Five Armies, in which the forces of evil are dominant, the noble eagles—symbols of providence—intervene and save the day. Bilbo and Gandalf journey back to the peaceful Shire. Bilbo, seeing the results of greed, refuses his share of the Dwarves treasure, though he returns with the Ring, which shapes the events recorded in *The Lord of the Rings*.

The ensuing trilogy begins with the return of Gandalf to the Shire, for he is now aware that the Ring found by Bilbo is in fact the One Ring controlling the Rings of Power. Frodo, inheritor of the Ring, flees from the Shire with Sam, Merry, and Pippin, fellow hobbits. On their trail are the Black Riders sent from Mordor, a region possessed by Sauron. With the help of the Ranger, Aragorn, they succeed in reaching the security of Rivendell, a stronghold of the Elves. There, at a great council, it is decided that the Ring must be destroyed, and that Frodo should be the Ring-bearer. The Company of the Ring is also chosen to help him on the perilous quest. The Ring can only be destroyed where it was forged, in the Mountain of Fire at Mount Doom, located at the heart of Mordor.

At some point, Frodo and Sam part from the rest of the Company, with the creature Gollum on their trail, seeking back his lost Ring. Finding the main entrance to Mordor impassable, Frodo accepts Gollum's offer to lead them to a secret entrance. After many perils, the two make their way to Mount Doom. At the final moment, Frodo cannot throw the Ring into the fire. Gollum bites off the ring finger, but falls to his death with the Ring. The quest ends with the disintegration of Mordor and the final defeat of Sauron, who cannot survive without the revitalizing power of the Ring. The story ends with the gradual healing of the land, preparing the way for the Fourth Age of Middle-earth. The hobbits return to the Shire and the human Aragorn, a symbol of the wise, righteous Christian king, marries the

Elf-maiden Arwen and is crowned king of the old northern and southern kingdoms.

Given the mythological magnitude of Tolkien's writings, we wonder what kind of person inspired such magnificence. John Ronald Reuel Tolkien (1892–1973) was born in South Africa of English parents. After his father's death in 1896, his family moved to a rural part of England, living in countryside like the Shire. His mother died in 1904, leaving Tolkien and his siblings orphaned. Brought up Roman Catholic, at his mother's death Tolkien came under the guardianship of Father Francis Morgan, who continued the youngster's strict Catholic upbringing.

From his mother and Father Morgan, Tolkien acquired a love for philology, especially of Germanic languages, and he became a gifted linguist, influenced by German, Celtic, Finnish, and Greek language and mythology, all of which influenced his literary and professional career. At Exeter College, Oxford, he initially studied classics, but changed to honors in English language, devoting his career to expanding the field and its reputation.

After graduating from Oxford in 1915, he saw bitter action in World War I, losing all but one of his friends in the war. Contracting "trench fever" at the Battle of the Somme, in November 1916 he was invalided to England. Deemed medically unfit for general service, Tolkien spent the remainder of the war alternating between hospitals and garrison duties. During the war years he began working on *The Silmarillion*, constructing the general plot, several major episodes, and most of its legendary cycle before 1930.

In 1918 he was demobilized and left the army. His first civilian job was working on the *Oxford English Dictionary*. Two years later, he accepted a teaching position in English language at the University of Leeds, where he produced *A Middle English Vocabulary* and a definitive edition of the late fourteenth-century chivalric romance, *Sir Gwain and the Green Knight*, one of the best-known Arthurian legends. In addition, he undertook a translation of *Beowulf*, which he finished in 1926. In a famous lecture on *Beowulf* in 1936, he argued against misreading the work merely as fantastical literature, claiming its anonymous author was addressing human nature in general. In 1925, Tolkien returned to Oxford as Professor of Anglo-Saxon,[4] a position he held until 1945, when he was appointed Merton Professor of English Language and Literature, a position he held until his retirement in

---

4. At this time, Tolkien's sub-specialty was the literature and language of Mercian, an Anglo-Saxon dialect. Over his lifetime, Tolkien's love of philology led him to invent languages such as Elvish, aspects he incorporated in his writings.

1959. During these years, he was a close friend of C. S. Lewis and a member with him of the informal literary discussion group the Inklings, being influential in Lewis's conversion from agnosticism to Anglican Christianity.

During his retirement years, Tolkien received steadily increasing public attention and literary fame, being nominated for the Nobel Prize in Literature in 1961. When asked to rank the influences on his writings, he stated that his Catholic faith was most important. This being so, it is clear that Tolkien's *The Lord of the Rings* must be understood as a specifically Christian myth. Rendering the Catholic Church highest honor for its devotion to the Eucharist, Tolkien's traditionalist stance led him to oppose many of the liturgical changes implemented in the 1960s following the Second Vatican Council, especially the use of the vernacular for the liturgy. In his final days, he continued to make his liturgical responses in Latin, ignoring the use of English by his fellow congregants.

Tolkien never expected his stories to become popular. By sheer accident, *The Hobbit*, which he had written solely for his children, came in 1936 to the attention of a publisher, who persuaded him to submit it for publication. Its popularity led Tolkien to produce the epic novel *The Lord of the Rings* as its sequel. Despite incongruities between elements of *The Hobbit* and *The Lord of the Rings*, both works were set against the background of *The Silmarillion*. Tolkien originally intended *The Lord of the Rings* to be a children's tale, but it quickly attracted an older audience. *The Lord of the Rings* became immensely popular in the 1960s and thereafter, ranking among the most popular works of fiction in the twentieth century. In a 2003 survey by the BBC, *The Lord of the Rings* was voted the audience's "Best Loved Novel," enhancing Tolkien's reputation as the "father" of modern fantasy literature.

THE PROBLEM OF EVIL: ITS NATURE, SOURCE, AND SOLUTION

The theme of evil is fundamental to spirituality, for evil is prevalent in human culture. Were it not for evil, there would be no religion, little philosophy, and far less great literature. The big questions of our time, I believe, can be understood in terms of how we view and respond to the fact of evil in our world. The reality of evil is central to spirituality, literature, and the arts, but what is evil, and is there an antidote, solution, or answer?

When we examine actual evil around us, we detect three kinds: moral evil, pain, and natural evil. *Moral evil* is found only in human life and society because only humans are capable of moral choices. While Christian teaching makes humans wholly accountable for moral evil, we need to avoid two possible misunderstandings. On the one hand, Christianity does not teach that single persons are responsible for all the evil in their lives and for nothing else. None of us lives in isolation. We are all bound together and interrelated on numerous levels. Whatever we do, whether for good or evil, influences the people around us and those who will come after us, much as we are influenced by our neighbors and those who came before us.

On the other hand, we must not so exaggerate the social solidarity that we place the entire responsibility for the evil in our world upon our ancestors. Ezekiel dealt with people who blamed their ancestors for the political disaster that had overtaken Jerusalem, insisting that they should bear their own share of the blame: "What do you mean by repeating this proverb concerning the land of Israel, 'The parents have eaten sour grapes, and the children's teeth are set on edge'? As I live, says the Lord God, this proverb shall no more be used by you in Israel . . . ; it is only the person who sins that shall die" (Ezek 18:2–4).

This attitude of irresponsibility is carried to an extreme if we say that all the evil in human life is due to the sin of our first ancestor, Adam. The story of Genesis 3 was not intended to be read as history. A study of Hebrew names in Genesis 3 indicates that we are dealing here with myth—a story that is true of any person at any period of history. The story of Adam is the story of every person—your story and mine. It is true that in the history of Christian thought the story of the Garden of Eden has often been misinterpreted to mean that all human beings are sinners because they inherit the taint of Adam and Eve's "original sin." But that idea is now discredited, and if Christians use the phrase "original sin" today, they mean by it that we are all affected by the sinister accumulation of wrong. There are then two kinds of moral evil: the weakness of human nature, for which we are not personally responsible, though we suffer from it daily; and the actual wrong choices we make when we have the opportunity to choose otherwise.

The *problem of pain* is more complicated, a subject we dare approach only with hesitation. It is easy to say that suffering is a discipline that ennobles the character, but not so easy to endure that discipline when we experience it directly. We can however call attention to three facts that will make plain the real problem. First, the capacity to feel pain is one of our most valuable forms of self-protection. It is a warning of danger from without and of disease from within. Secondly, while humans cannot be held responsible for disease germs, a vast amount of the suffering and sorrow cause by disease would be eliminated if it were not for human ignorance, folly, and vice. Thirdly, in a world where people break moral laws, it is better that they should suffer directly for their own sin. Laws that may be broken with impunity are not laws but chaos.

The real problem is not the existence of pain but its distribution, for its impact seems disproportionate to human character and behavior. Questions regarding the fairness of life and the justice of God surface whenever tragedy strikes, in every age and place across the globe. If everyone suffered exactly in proportion to his or her deserts, our sense of justice would be satisfied. However, as long as we think of pain in terms of justice, it will remain a mystery. Justice is not the final truth of the universe. Most of us receive more benefits that we deserve, sharing one another's joys and triumphs, and many of our sins go unpunished. When it comes to suffering and pain, most important is not what happens to us but how we respond. Though not always welcome, pain has proven to be a great mentor, valuable for its transformative potential.

The third kind of evil, *natural evil*, includes such things as earthquakes, tidal waves, and hurricanes. A great deal of distress is caused by natural disasters of this kind, but it is nevertheless doubtful whether we ought to call them evil. Would a world without such calamities really be better than the world we know? In order to answer this question we must ask, "Better for what?" If you think that the purpose of life is comfort and security, then an earthquake must be considered an evil. If you think that the purpose of life is the training of character, then surely it is well that humans should live in a world that presents opportunities for heroism and vitality. That people die suddenly and in large numbers is a tragedy, but such catastrophes should not obscure our judgment. For we must all die eventually, and while dying today in one's forties is a calamity, to have done so in earlier centuries meant one had lived a long life.

A major issue with the problem of evil is its source. In antiquity, the simplest religious explanation was to attribute evil to the actions of the gods. They seemed capricious, and if humans were to survive, they needed to appease the deities. Eventually, more complex answers arose. Some treated evil as illusory; others envisioned it as cosmic, attributing equal status to evil and good. Some acknowledged its presence within the rhythm of nature and simply learned to cope, while others limited it to human deci-sion-making and behavior. Whatever its nature, evil affects humans where they live and must be understood on that level.

Evil is real, particularly for those who believe in God. When theists examine their world, disfigured with cruelty, disease, vice, and injustice, the reality of evil initially provides them with a conundrum, forcing them to choose between the power and the goodness of God. Either God detests evil but cannot do anything about it, in which case God is good but not almighty, or else God could put a stop to evil but wills not to, in which case God is almighty but not good. Taking seriously the reality of cosmic evil and human suffering, theologians have constructed elaborate intellectual arguments (known as theodicies) to defend God's existence or goodness. Modern unbelievers, examining the same world, declare evil's presence temporary, an aberration to be eliminated through progress, whether cul-tural, scientific, educational, or technological.

The problem of evil arises for the believer out of the meeting of three beliefs: that God is good, that God is almighty, and that evil is real. We may avoid the dilemma of the Christian by denying any one of these proposi-tions. For example, a denial of the omnipotence of God leads to dualism, the belief that the good principle behind the universe is eternally at war with an independent principle of evil. This belief—associated historically initially with Mani (216–274) and Manichaeism—was devised to explain the origin of evil, and initially it might seem to be a most satisfactory ex-planation. However, this explanation is profoundly inadequate. For if evil is one of the two ultimate realities of the universe, then it is as natural as good; it has as much right to be there as good has. However, as soon as we regard evil as natural, we cannot consider it as an intruder in the universe that ought not to be there at all.

If, on the other hand, we deny the goodness of God, we lapse into pantheism, which says that everything that exists is a manifestation of God, and that things seem to be evil only because we see them from the wrong point of view. If we could only take God's view of the world, we would see that all things fit into a perfect pattern. However, if one believes that from the point of eternity murder, rape, fraud, and treason are but facsimiles of fidelity, chastity, honesty, and heroism, one has denied that evil is really evil.

One of the most attractive and persuasive Christian theodicies was devised in North Africa by medieval theologian Augustine, bishop of Hip-po. By the fourth century, the problems raised by the existence of evil and suffering had become a theological embarrassment to Christians living in a pagan world. Manichaeism, a form of Gnosticism that fascinated Augustine as a young adult, had no difficulty in accounting for the existence of evil. Viewing the cosmos as essentially evil, the Manicheans explained its origin in the fundamentally evil nature of matter. The entire purpose of salvation was to redeem humanity from the evil material world, and transfer it to a spiritual realm that was uncontaminated by matter.

Augustine could not accept this explanation. It might offer a convenient solution to the problem of evil, yet it was incompatible with the biblical worldview. For Augustine, creation and redemption were the work of the same God. It was therefore impossible to ascribe the existence of evil to creation, for this merely transferred blame to God. For Augustine, God created the world good, meaning that it was free from the contamination of evil. So where did evil originate? Augustine's fundamental insight was that evil is a direct consequence of the misuse of human freedom. God created humanity with the freedom to choose good or evil. Sadly, humanity chose evil. As a result, the world is contaminated by evil.

Augustine's solution, known as the doctrine of privation, explains evil as human rebellion, as a turning away from God. As in the world of physics, where cold is defined as "the absence of heat," so in the world of theology, evil is defined as "the absence of good." Avoiding the trap of dualism, which views evil as eternal or matter as evil, Augustine argued that evil originated in human disobedience, in an act of the will. Evil arose historically as something good gone bad.

As Augustine himself realized, however, this explanation did not fully resolve the problem. For how could humans choose evil if there was no evil to choose? Evil had to be an option within the world if it were to be accessible to human choice. Augustine therefore located the origin of evil in satanic temptation, by which Satan lured Adam and Eve away from obedience to their creator. In this way, he argued, God could not be regarded as being responsible for evil. This explanation, however, still did not resolve the problem. For where did Satan come from if God created the world good? Augustine traced the origin of evil back another step, arguing that Satan, originally created good, is a fallen angel, who rebelled against God and thus spread that rebellion to the world. But how, Augustine's critics asked, could a good angel turn out to be so bad? How are we to account for Satan's original fall? The problem had simply been pushed back a step.

Augustine's explanation, though not fully adequate, continues to persuade. Evil is real, but it exists only through the perversion of that which was created good. Evil derives not only its existence but also its power from the good that it distorts. A small evil results from the corruption of a small good, and a great evil results from the corruption of a great good. If a person of weak intellect and reduced ability goes wrong, he can be a petty nuisance to society, but he cannot be a master criminal. But when a person of fine intellect and great ability goes wrong, he can affect the course of world history. Furthermore, we understand evil only by contrasting it with the good that it perverts. We recognize disease as an evil by contrasting it with health, and vice by contrasting it with virtue. One who cheats is a bad person because he ought to play fair. A mass murderer violates the moral law found in nature, which compels humans to preserve life, because he ought to treat others with dignity and compassion. In that single word "ought" is the justification for the whole Christian approach to evil.

We can now see more clearly the fundamental weakness of dualism as an answer to the problem of evil. For dualism attempts to make evil independent of goodness. But an eternal power of evil is unthinkable, for evil is essentially destructive, and utter evil would be utter destruction. Evil is a parasite that lives only by preying upon the good. To this point, we have been dealing with evil theoretically, but the problem with this approach is that if we find a reason for its existence, it ceases to be evil. The only safe way to deal with evil is not to explain it but to defeat it.

When we examine evil and its effects, we wonder what God is doing about the evil in the world. When it comes to moral evil, we recognize that God has granted freedom to human beings, and that humans cannot be compelled to be good without taking away their freedom. Yet we cannot rest content with a theory that leaves God's purpose thwarted and God's world defiled by sin. If there were no more to be said, we could hardly avoid the feeling that God would have done better not to have made the world at all than to have created a tragic failure.

The final answer of the Christian to the problem of evil is that God has done something, that in Christ God has defeated sin and death. The Christian gospel is that Christ has broken the hold of sin on human life and society, that he has shown how evil things may be redeemed and used for a good purpose, that he has taken the thorns of life and worn them as a crown of glory, and that he has transformed death from an enemy into a friend.

In the biblical book of Revelation, Christians are given a solution to cosmic evil. A series of visions in 12:1–14:20 form the central axis of the book and the core of its argument. Chapters 12–13 pull away the curtain that hides the transcendent world from ordinary sight and offer a behind-the-scenes view of the powers of evil at work in the present, while chapter 14 presents a behind-the-scenes view of the victory of God in salvation and judgment. This unit introduces some of the most dramatic images in the entire book. The four depictions of evil include Satan—the great dragon hurled from the sky to prowl the earth—and Satan's cronies, consisting of a seven-headed beast from the sea, a cunning beast from the land, and Babylon the harlot. A key to this segment is the announcement of the heavenly chorus in 11:18 that the time has come to destroy the destroyers of the earth. If God is the Creator and God's will for the world is life, then God must defeat those forces that threaten life.

The second half of Revelation is dominated by the struggle against these agents of evil. Following the plot, one discovers that John systematically introduces four depictions of imperial evil, only to defeat them—in reverse order. The harlot is first to be destroyed, when the seven-headed beast turns against her (17:16). Then the two beasts are defeated, when Christ overpowers them with the sword (the word) that comes from his mouth (19:19–20). Only Satan is left, temporarily banished from earth to the abyss below only to be hurled into the lake of fire (20:10). The second half of Revelation is the story of the defeat of these agents of evil.

In dealing with the reality of evil, the Bible relies on two traditions, the prophetic and the apocalyptic. According to the apocalyptic mindset, evil is so great that humans cannot eliminate it. Only God can do so. Unlike the apocalyptic tradition, which viewed evil cosmically and demonically, the prophetic tradition spoke of good and evil largely in human terms. The New Testament builds upon both traditions, as does the book of Revelation. The call to Revelation's audience to "conquer" is fundamental to the structure and theme of the book (see 2:7, 11, 17, 28; 3:5, 12, 21; and 21:7). It demands the readers' active participation in the divine war against evil.

THE NATURE OF EVIL IN TOLKIEN'S *THE LORD OF THE RINGS*

Those who read Tolkien's saga are struck by its all-encompassing struggle between the forces of good and evil. Throughout his life, Tolkien believed strongly in the reality of evil. In his understanding, evil manifests itself in two possible ways—predominantly as a physical entity, evident during pre-history or in myth, and secondarily in historical events such as in the trenches of World War I or in the Soviet gulags.

By placing evil in the background of *The Lord of the Rings*, Tolkien created an evil that was derivative and perverse. It was also ominous, for it seems to be everywhere, pervading the entire landscape of Middle-earth, surrounding the Fellowship of the Ring on all sides. Even the birds and mountains seem corrupted, watching and informing on every movement of the Fellowship.

Throughout *The Lord of the Rings*, evil appears both in direct and indirect forms. It is all the more terrifying because the story is told from the hobbits' perspective, that is, from the common person's point of view. Human history, in Tolkien's view, is one constant defeat, with victory only at the end, and even then attained only by divine intervention. Though Tolkien admitted that the various crises of his lifetime helped shape his mythology, his works are not allegorical. The enemy is not Nazism, Communism, secularism, humanism, or any other ideology. Rather, his storyline is about the perpetual struggle between metaphysical good and evil, compounded by the corrupting intoxication of power. The twentieth century may have been notable for the amount of bloodshed and horror it witnessed, but evil has always been, and always would be, present in an unredeemed world. As Tolkien wrote in 1937, "A safe fairy-land is untrue to all worlds."[5]

Comments such as these make us wonder, in his understanding of evil, is Tolkien a dualist? The magnitude of evil in his writings suggest that he is, but to answer the question, we need to distinguish between the Manichaean and Augustinian views of evil. One has an objective understanding of evil, the other a subjective understanding. The Manichean view sees evil as objective, meaning it is part of the very nature of the universe, whereas the Augustinian sees evil as a negation of good, neither independently nor ontologically real. For Augustine, God pronounced all creation good.

Tolkien's fertile imagination creates many embodiments of evil, including dragons, Orcs,[6] werewolves, and trolls, as well as Morgoth and his servant Sauron. In addition, there is the ever-present symbol of the Ring borne by Frodo, an objective reality with a power of its own, which can and

5. Carpenter, *Letters*, 105.

6. Orcs, as Tolkien originally conceived them, are Elves corrupted by Morgoth and Sauron.

must be resisted. The Ring also appeals subjectively to a person's weakness, and evil is possible to creatures capable of creativity and free will.

As a monotheist, Tolkien's portrayal of the objective reality of evil through the Ring is not Manichaean. Such a view sees evil as part of the very nature of the universe, and that is not Tolkien's belief. In *The Lord of the Rings*, Tolkien speaks through Elrond, an immortal Elf whose life spans the three ages of Middle-earth, to indicate that God makes nothing evil; rather, all that God makes is good. As Elrond states at his Council, "Nothing is evil in the beginning." Even Morgoth, the satanic figure in Tolkien's mythology, was created out of pure goodness and unadulterated love. Indeed, Ilúvatar gave Morgoth more gifts than any other being. Nevertheless, Morgoth craved more. After his rebellion, even greater power was not enough. Rather, to corrupt or destroy anything new or good became his chief desire.

The theme of "the fall" is central to Tolkien's understanding of evil, serving as one of the most significant concerns of his stories. In biblical mythology, humans are responsible for their sin, but such sin has its origin in satanic rebellion and temptation. However, almost without exception, sin is connected with pride and with the desire by humans to question their creaturely status. Sometimes it is angelic pride, sometimes individual pride, and sometimes it is the pride of an entire race, as with humanity in general.

In Tolkien's epics, a character's use of magic is a sign of the presence of evil. Unlike most fantasy writers, who use magic to represent primal spirituality or primeval power, either drawn from the character's inherent spirituality of from the character's spiritual counterpart or alter ego, Tolkien's Catholicism led him to believe that magic in the sense of power is evil. In his mythology, the ultimate symbol of magic is the One Ring of Power, forged by Sauron in Mount Doom, and into which Sauron poured much of his spirit and will. At one level, the One Ring represents the desire to control others. At a more fundamental level, the Ring represents sin itself, especially the first sin, as recorded in Genesis: "you will be like God" (3:5). Like Plato's Ring of Gyges, the Ring renders the wearer invisible, giving power commensurate to one's estate. To Gollum, it is his "precious"; to Frodo, it is his "cross to bear." Nevertheless, whoever wears it becomes slowly consumed, habituated to evil, chaos, and vice rather than to goodness, decorum, and virtue. The more one uses it, the more one succumbs to its dark power.

In Tolkien's Augustinian spirituality, those consumed by power ultimately become imprisoned by it. Like dominoes, when humans fall under evil's corrupting spell, they also fall under an even greater power and spell. In Tolkien's Middle-earth, all secondary evils—whether corrupt trees, spiders, Orcs, or wizards such as Saruman—seem to be controlled, or at least to be heavily influenced by the will of Sauron, himself controlled by Morgoth. Tolkien's perspective reverses Aristotle's metaphysical notion of love, order, and the Prime Mover's motivations and actions. Aristotle argued that the Prime Mover threw forth divine love and called it back to its source. Tolkien presents the diabolical Morgoth as the mirror image of Divine Love, a grotesque evil calling all evil back to himself in his stronghold at Mordor. As Gandalf recognizes, for goodness to triumph, free will is required. Unlike Sauron and Saruman, who succumb to corruption and greed voluntarily, Gandalf chooses to have the Ring destroyed.

Tolkien is a monotheist, not a dualist; hence, his mythology is more biblical and Augustinian than Manichaean, in the sense that his view of the creation actually rejects a cosmic dualism of good and evil. Because of his theology of Middle-earth, Tolkien is able to portray evil as utterly real, without falling into cosmic dualism. Evil is real, but it originated in the fall from grace of Morgoth, and is not inherent to the universe as such. For Tolkien, the study of evil necessarily involves the use and misuse of creativity and free will.

THE BEAUTY OF ORDINARY LIFE

In *The Lord of the Rings*, Frodo carries the One Ring into the heart of hell (Mordor). While the Ring influences him emotionally and spiritually, often to the breaking point, Frodo continues in his role of "suffering servant," heading toward Mordor to fulfill his specific purpose. Though he grows weary, he remains faithful to his task almost to the end. Only in the final moments of his quest does he falter, as the burden of the Ring—representing the power of temptation that makes people sin—becomes too great. However, due to unexpected circumstances, prompted by Gollum's desperate move to steal the Ring, it is destroyed in the fire of Mount Doom.

In Frodo's shadow is the ever faithful Sam Gamgee, perhaps the true hero of *The Lord of the Rings*, for he displays what for Tolkien is humanity's greatest virtue—loyalty. Like Jesus's "beloved disciple" John, Sam plays the character of St. John the Evangelist to Frodo's Jesus. Like John, Sam remains faithful to Frodo throughout their journey. And like John, who stood at the foot of the cross, Sam stands with Frodo at Mount Doom. In the end, the quest to Mount Doom is as much about Sam as it is about Frodo the priest, Gandalf the prophet, or Aragorn the king. Undoubtedly, Sam—a true believer who understands the beauty of ordinary life—would rather have stayed at home in his Shire garden and farm than walk into the heart of Hell itself. However, he feels called to a divine task, and he accepts his duty, as all believers must, following Frodo with pure loyalty and without question or complaint. The destruction of the Ring represents the victory of Christ's companions over evil.

CHAPTER 7

J. K. Rowling's *Harry Potter Heptalogy*

IN 1997, JOANNE ROWLING, better known by her pen name J. K. Rowling, published the first of her *Harry Potter* series of seven fantasy novels. The series chronicles the lives of a young wizard, Harry Potter, and his friends Hermione Granger and Ron Weasley, all of whom are students at Hogwarts School of Witchcraft and Wizardry. The narrative concerns Harry's struggle against Lord Voldemort, a dark wizard who intends to become immortal, overthrow the wizard governing body known as the Ministry of Magic, and subjugate all wizards and Muggles (non-magical people). If we consider Tolkien's *The Lord of the Rings* trilogy a great hit, the *Harry Potter* series far surpassed it in popularity and success, to date having sold more than five hundred million copies.

Born and raised in England, Rowling worked as a researcher and bilingual secretary for Amnesty International in 1990 when she conceived the idea for the *Harry Potter* series. Her first book in the series was *Harry Potter and the Philosopher's Stone*, followed by six sequels, progressively darker in tone as Harry and his friends grew older; the last, *Harry Potter and the Deathly Hallows*, was published in 2007. From obscurity and poverty, Rowling progressed to become the first billionaire author, wealth she has shared with multiple charities, including her own charity, Lumos. She later became president of the charity Gingerbread (originally One Parent Families), while becoming an outspoken advocate of transgender people and their civil rights.

A fan of Jane Austen, Charles Dickens, C. S. Lewis, and Tolkien, she earned a degree in French and Classics at the University of Exeter in 1986. In 1990, during a lengthy train trip, she conceived the idea of a young boy attending a school of wizardry. The following year she moved to Portugal to teach English as a second language. After a brief marriage that resulted in the birth of a daughter, Rowling and her daughter moved to Edinburgh, Scotland. Still unpublished and now unemployed, Rowling was diagnosed with clinical depression. Her depression inspired the characters known as Dementors, soul-sucking creatures she introduced in her third book. After multiple rejections, her first book was published in 1997. Four months later, the book won the first of many awards, including the British award for Children's Book of the Year. Following her fourth book, she was named Author of the Year in the British Book Awards.

Despite accusations by religious groups and individuals for the perceived promotion of witchcraft in her books, Rowling has publicly states that she identifies as a Christian, stating she believes "in God, not magic." Admitting her struggle with religious doubt, she calls herself a person of faith with firm belief in an afterlife.

THE *HARRY POTTER* SERIES: PLOT AND RESPONSE

The central character in the series is Harry Potter, a boy who lives in the fictional town of Little Whinging, Surrey with his aunt, uncle, and cousin—the Dursleys—and discovers at the age of eleven that he is a wizard, though he lives in the ordinary world of non-magical people known as Muggles. The wizarding world exists parallel to the Muggle world, only hidden and in secrecy. Harry's magical ability is inborn, and children with such abilities are invited to attend exclusive magic schools that teach the necessary skills to succeed in the wizarding world.

Harry becomes a student at Hogwarts School of Witchcraft and Wizardry, a wizarding academy that educates teenagers on their magical development for seven years, from age eleven to seventeen, and it is here where most of the events in the series take place. As Harry develops through his adolescence, he learns to overcome the problems that face him: magical, social, and emotional, including ordinary teenage challenges such as friendships, infatuation, romantic relationships, schoolwork, anxiety, depression, stress, and the greater test of preparing himself for the wizarding confrontation that lies ahead. Each novel in the series chronicles one year in Harry's life.

When the first novel, *Harry Potter and the Philosopher's Stone*, opens, it is apparent that some significant event has taken place in the wizarding world. The full background to this event and Harry's past is revealed gradually throughout the series. After the introductory chapter, the book leaps forward to a time shortly before Harry's eleventh birthday, when his magical background begins to be revealed.

Despite Harry's aunt and uncle's desire to keep Harry ignorant about his abilities, their efforts are in vain. Harry meets Hagrid, a half-giant who is also his first contact with the wizarding world. As Keeper of Keys and Grounds at Hogwarts, Hagrid is able to disclose some of Harry's history. Harry learns that, as an infant, he witnessed his parents' murder by the power-obsessed dark wizard Lord Voldemort (commonly known by the magical community as He-Who-Must-Not-Be-Named), who subsequently attempted to kill Harry as well. Instead, the unexpected happened: Harry survived with only a lightening-shaped scar on his forehead, and Voldemort disappeared soon afterwards, gravely weakened by his own rebounding curse.

As inadvertent savior from Voldemort's reign of terror, Harry has become a living legend in the wizarding world. However, at the orders of the venerable wizard Albus Dumbledore, the orphaned Harry had been placed in the home of his unpleasant Muggle relatives, the Dursleys, who have kept him safe but treated him poorly, including confining him to a cupboard without meals and treating him as their servant.

With Hagrid's help, Harry undertakes his first year of study at Hogwarts. As Harry begins to explore the magical world, the reader is introduced to many of the primary locations used throughout the series. Harry meets most of the main characters and gains his two closest friends: Ron Weasley, a fun-loving member of an ancient, large, happy, but poor wizarding family, and Hermione Granger, a gifted, bright, and hardworking witch of non-magical parentage. Harry also encounters the school's potions master, Severus Snape, who displays a conspicuously deep and abiding dislike for him, the rich brat Draco Malfoy, with whom he quickly makes enemies, and the Defense Against the Dark Arts teacher, Quirinus Quirrell, who later turns out to be allied with Lord Voldemort. Harry also discovers a talent of flying on broomsticks and is recruited for his house's Quidditch team, a sport in the wizarding world where players fly on broomsticks. The first book concludes with Harry's second confrontation with Lord Voldemort, who, in his quest to regain a body, yearns to gain the power of the Philosopher's Stone, a substance that bestows everlasting life and turns any metal into pure gold.

The series continues with *Harry Potter and the Chamber of Secrets*, describing Harry's second year at Hogwarts. He and his friends investigate a fifty-year-old mystery that appears uncannily related to recent sinister events at the school. Ron's younger sister, Ginny Weasley, enrolls in her first year at Hogwarts, and finds an old notebook in her belongings that turns out to be the diary of a previous student, Tom Marvolo Riddle, written during World War II. Riddle is later revealed to be Voldemort's younger self, who is bent on ridding the school of "mudbloods," a derogatory term describing wizards and witches of non-magical parentage. The memory of Tom Riddle resides inside of the diary and when Ginny begins to confide in the diary, Voldemort is able to possess her.

Through the diary, Ginny acts on Voldemort's orders and unconsciously opens the "Chamber of Secrets," unleashing an ancient monster, later revealed to be a basilisk, which begins attacking students at Hogwarts. It kills those who make direct eye contact with it and petrifies those who look at it indirectly. The book also introduces a new Defense Against the Dark Arts teacher, Gilderoy Lockhart, a cheerful, conceited wizard who later turns out to be a fraud. Harry discovers that prejudice exists in the Wizarding World through delving into the school's history, and learns that Voldemort's reign of terror was often directed at wizards and witches who were descended from Muggles.

Harry also learns that his ability to speak the snake language Parseltongue is rare and often associated with the Dark Arts. When Hermione is attacked and petrified, Harry and Ron finally piece together the puzzles and unlock the Chamber of Secrets, with Harry destroying the diary for good and saving Ginny, and, as they learn later, also destroying a part of Voldemort's soul. The end of the book reveals Lucius Malfoy, Draco's father and rival of Ron and Ginny's father, to be the culprit who slipped the book into Ginny's belongings.

The third novel, *Harry Potter and the Prisoner of Azkaban*, follows Harry in his third year of magical education. It is the only book in the series that does not feature Lord Voldemort in any form. Instead, Harry must deal with the knowledge that he has been targeted by Sirius Black, his father's best friend, and, according to the Wizarding World, an escaped mass murderer who assisted in the murder of Harry's parents. As Harry struggles with his reaction to the dementors—dark creatures with the power to devour a human soul and feed on despair—which are ostensibly protecting the school, he reaches out to Remus Lupin, a Defense Against the Dark Arts teacher who is eventually revealed to be a werewolf. Lupin teaches Harry defensive measures that are well above the level of magic generally executed by people his age. Harry comes to know that both Lupin and Black were best friends of his father and that Black was framed by their fourth friend, Peter Pettigrew, who had been hiding as Ron's pet rat, Scabbers. In this book, a recurring theme throughout the series is emphasized—in every book there is a new Defense Against the Dark Arts teacher, none of whom lasts more than one school year.

During Harry's fourth year of school (detailed in *Harry Potter and the Goblet of Fire*), Harry is unwillingly entered as a participant in the Triwizard Tournament, a dangerous yet exciting contest where three "champions," one from each participating school, must compete with each other in three tasks in order to win the Triwizard Cup. This year, Harry must compete against a witch and a wizard "champion" from overseas schools, as well as another Hogwarts student, causing Harry's friends to distance themselves from him.

Harry is guided through the tournament by their new Defense Against the Dark Arts professor, Alastor "Mad-Eye" Moody, who turns out to be an impostor—one of Voldemort's supporters named Barty Crouch, Jr. in disguise, who secretly entered Harry's name into the tournament. The point at which the mystery is unraveled marks the series' shift from foreboding and uncertainty into open conflict. Voldemort's plan to have Crouch use the tournament to bring Harry to Voldemort succeeds. Although Harry manages to escape, Cedric Diggory, the other Hogwarts champion in the tournament, is killed by Peter Pettigrew and Voldemort re-enters the Wizarding World with a physical body.

In the fifth book, *Harry Potter and the Order of the Phoenix*, Harry must confront the newly resurfaced Voldemort. In response to Voldemort's reappearance, Dumbledore re-activates the Order of the Phoenix, a secret society that works from Sirius Black's dark family home to defeat Voldemort's minions and protect Voldemort's targets, especially Harry. Despite Harry's description of Voldemort's recent activities, the Minister of Magic and many others in the magical world refuse to believe that Voldemort has returned. In an attempt to counter and eventually discredit Dumbledore, the Ministry appoints Dolores Umbridge as the High Inquisitor of Hogwarts and the new Defense Against the Dark Arts teacher. She transforms the school into a dictatorial regime and refuses to allow the students to learn ways to defend themselves against dark magic.

Hermione and Ron form "Dumbledore's Army," a secret study group in which Harry agrees to teach his classmates the higher-level skills of Defense Against the Dark Arts that he has learned from his previous encounters with Dark wizards. Through those lessons, Harry begins to develop a crush on the popular and attractive Cho Chang. Juggling schoolwork, Umbridge's incessant and persistent efforts to land him in trouble, and the defensive lessons, Harry receives disturbing dreams about a dark corridor in the Ministry of Magic, followed by a burning desire to learn more. An important prophecy concerning Harry and Lord Voldemort is then revealed, and Harry discovers that he and Voldemort have a painful connection, allowing Harry to view some of Voldemort's actions telepathically. In the novel's climax, Harry is tricked into seeing Sirius tortured and races to the Ministry of Magic, where he and his friends face off against Voldemort's followers (nicknamed Death Eaters). Although the timely arrival of members of the Order of the Phoenix saves the teenagers' lives, Sirius Black is killed in the conflict.

In the sixth book, *Harry Potter and the Half-Blood Prince*, Voldemort begins waging open warfare. Harry and his friends are relatively protected from that danger at Hogwarts. They are subject to all the difficulties of adolescence—Harry eventually begins dating Ginny and Hermione starts to develop romantic feelings towards Ron. Near the beginning of the novel, Harry is given an old potions textbook filled with annotations and recommendations signed by a mysterious writer titled "the Half-Blood Prince." This book is a source of scholastic success and great recognition from their new potions master, Horace Slughorn, but because of the potency of the spells that are written in it, becomes a source of concern.

With war drawing near, Harry takes private lessons with Dumbledore, who shows him various memories concerning the early life of Voldemort in a device called a Pensieve. These reveal that in order to preserve his life, Voldemort has split his soul into pieces, used to create a series of Horcruxes—evil enchanted items hidden in various locations, one of which was the diary destroyed in the second book. Draco, who has joined with the Death Eaters, attempts to attack Dumbledore upon his return from collecting a

Horcrux, and the book culminates in the killing of Dumbledore by Professor Snape, the titular Half-Blood Prince.

Harry Potter and the Deathly Hallows, the last original novel in the series, begins directly after the events of the sixth book. Lord Voldemort has completed his ascension to power and gained control of the Ministry of Magic. Harry, Ron and Hermione drop out of school so that they can find and destroy Voldemort's remaining Horcruxes. To ensure their own safety as well as that of their family and friends, they are forced to isolate themselves. A ghoul pretends to be Ron ill with a contagious disease, Harry and the Dursleys separate, and Hermione wipes her parents' memories and sends them abroad.

As the trio searches for the Horcruxes, they learn details about an ancient prophecy of the Deathly Hallows, three legendary items that when united under one Keeper, would supposedly allow that person to be the Master of Death. Harry discovers his Invisibility Cloak to be one of those items, and Voldemort to be searching for another—the Elder Wand—the most powerful wand in history. At the end of the book, Harry and his friends learn about Dumbledore's past, as well as Snape's true motives (he had worked on Dumbledore's behalf since the murder of Harry's mother). Eventually, Voldemort kills Snape out of paranoia.

The book culminates in the Battle of Hogwarts. Harry, Ron and Hermione, in conjunction with members of the Order of the Phoenix and many of the teachers and students, defend Hogwarts from Voldemort, his Death Eaters, and various dangerous magical creatures. Several major characters are killed in the first wave of the battle, including Remus Lupin and Fred Weasley, Ron's older brother. After learning that he himself is a Horcrux, Harry surrenders himself to Voldemort in the Forbidden Forest, where Voldemort casts a killing curse at him. The defenders of Hogwarts do not surrender after learning of Harry's presumed death, but continue to fight on. Harry awakens and faces Voldemort, whose Horcruxes have all been destroyed. In the final battle, Voldemort's killing curse rebounds off Harry's defensive spell, killing Voldemort.

GOOD AND EVIL IN THE *HARRY POTTER* SERIES

The *Harry Potter* books are widely read as morally uplifting novels about the conflict of good and evil, including loyalty and standing up for friends. However, Rowling's *Harry Potter* series does not present the unequivocal triumph of good over evil. Rather, it features the struggle to transcend the apocalyptic dualism that promotes conflict between good and evil. Furthermore, the story promotes an alternative to traditional apocalyptic morality by starring characters who do not fit neatly into binary categories of good and evil. In an article available online, "Ending Dualism at Hogwarts," Ariana Tobias argues that the *Harry Potter* books retell and revise the apocalyptic myth of the biblical book of Revelation to deliver a clear non-dualist moral message. According to Tobias, Rowling's books provide a postmodern critique of, and an alternative to, the binary apocalyptic moral system ingrained in modern-day American society.[1]

The book of Revelation, central to traditional Christian cosmology, is written to provide a sense of cosmic order, to reassure early groups of persecuted Christians that God has a master plan and will eventually deliver faithful believers from suffering and uncertainty. In Revelation, the binary nature of the myth—good versus evil, the saved versus the damned—maintains loyalty by establishing order. By so doing, Revelation rejects any notion of a middle ground between these extremes. Doing so would invite uncertainty and ambiguity. Thus, the rigidly dualistic morality of Revelation creates a hierarchical value system that limits identities to classification in one of only two potential categories, and then upholds one as ideal and the other as evil.

The overwhelming popularity of the *Harry Potter* series ignited a debate within the American Christian community between religious fundamentalists, who believe the story is subversive and unchristian, and more moderate Christians, who point out biblical symbolism in the series and the triumph of Christian values like faith, love, redemption, and the victory of good over evil. On the one hand, Richard Abanes, author of *Harry Potter and the Bible: The Menace Behind the Magick*, argues that the *Harry Potter* series contains "spiritually dangerous material that could ultimately lead youth down the road to occultism" by promoting "unbiblical values and unethical behavior."[2] Alternatively, in *God, the Devil, and Harry Potter: A Christian Minister's Defense of the Beloved Novels*, John Killinger notes parallels between *Harry Potter* and the New Testament in an attempt to prove that, ultimately, "the master plot, the one underlying the entire novel, is the

---

1. Tobias, "Ending Dualism at Hogwarts," §1.

2. Abanes, *Harry Potter and the Bible*, 6.

critical struggle between good and evil" with Harry as a stand-in for Christ and the evil wizard Voldemort representing Satan.[3]

While the significance of good and evil is central to Rowling's intent, opponents of her work focus on elements of black magic, paganism, and unethical behavior. While it is hard to argue consistently for evidence of Christian morality in the *Harry Potter* books, particularly when contrasting Rowling's secular approach with Tolkien's devout Christian perspective, certain characters in Rowling's novels, such as Dumbledore, Professor Snape, and Sirius Black (Harry's godfather) are morally complex. One-dimensional characters, by definition, cannot be morally ambiguous, and Rowling's capacity to create multi-dimensional character clearly distinguishes her from Tolkien. Ambiguity—moral, theological, literary—is part of life, and in that respect, Rowling's artistry is a threat to fundamentalist views of morality. Even the moderate Killinger wishes to present characters as ultimately destined to be either good or evil, although he acknowledges that throughout the *Harry Potter* story, "good sometimes looks like evil . . . and evil often masquerades as good."[4]

In the final pages of his book, Killinger concedes that the message of the *Harry Potter* series is to "accept life on its own terms—the evil with the good," but then needs to admit, "This is the one point at which the Christian vision sticks and can go no further, but must finally remain dualistic; it recognizes that evil cannot entirely be absorbed by good. The devil and his angels must be cast into the lake of everlasting fire, for they will never repent."[5]

Unlike Tolkien and the book of Revelation, Rowling does not simply present the unequivocal triumph of good over evil. Instead, she features a struggle to transcend the apocalyptic dualism that promotes conflict between good and evil. Furthermore, Rowling promotes an alternative to traditional apocalyptic morality by creating characters who do not fit neatly into the binary categories of good or evil. As we saw in Conrad's writings, organizing the world conceptually sometimes traps us into assuming that what are essentially metaphorical categories reflect metaphysical polarities as well. None of us approaches *The Lord of the Rings* literally, as though it captures reality faithfully. Likewise, in reading Rowling, we should not mistake metaphorical ways of thinking for "the real thing." Unlike Tolkien,

3. Killinger, *God, the Devil, and Harry Potter*, 38.

4. Killinger, *God, the Devil, and Harry Potter*, 40.

5. Killinger, *God, the Devil, and Harry Potter*, 185–86.

Rowling's *Harry Potter* series retains the traditional apocalyptic narrative structure while subverting the dualistic apocalyptic paradigm.

John Granger, a self-identified "traditional Christian" who home-schooled his seven children "to keep them on course with biblical values and virtue," wrote *Looking for God in Harry Potter* to explore how the story's themes and narrative reveal "a profoundly Christian meaning at the core of the series."[6] While Granger goes too far in claiming, "The gospel has rarely, if ever, been smuggled into the heart and mind of readers so successfully and profoundly,"[7] the evidence he provides in this book and in other writings makes a strong case that the series is "loaded with specific Christian symbolism and meaning from the author's faith and literary traditions."[8]

The *Harry Potter* tale, heavy with Christian symbolism and with connections to the New Testament, is more than a secular story. Without explicitly mentioning God or other traditional theological elements, it may not be a Christian story, clearly not traditionally Christian like Tim LaHaye and Jerry Jenkins's fundamentalist *Left Behind* series. Nevertheless, fantasy novels like *The Chronicles of Narnia* and *The Lord of the Rings* are now accepted as staples of Christian literature. Though Rowling's books may never fall into the category of traditional Cristian children's tales, they function, like Lewis's wardrobe, as a very real means of entrance into Narnia.

At the end of every *Harry Potter* book, a conversation takes place between Harry and Dumbledore, the headmaster of Hogwarts. Without fail, Dumbledore divulges vital information that reveals the bigger picture behind Harry's personal experiences throughout the school year. After a while, the annual interview is predictable. The fact that Harry never knows all of the facts requires readers to doubt the validity, or at least the scope, of any "truth" Harry presents as certain and complete.

In the first four books of the series, Dumbledore is portrayed as powerful, infallible, and all-knowing. Harry knows Dumbledore as the greatest sorcerer in the world, whose awesome powers rival those of He-Who-Must-Not-Be-Named (Voldemort) at the height of his strength. When Voldemort returns at the end of the fourth book, Harry fully expects Dumbledore to be the savior of the wizarding world. However, throughout the fifth, six, and seventh books, this vision of Dumbledore is systematically destroyed. Harry gradually loses faith in Dumbledore as he learns about

6. Granger, *Looking for God*, xix.

7. Granger, *Looking for God*, 108.

8. Granger, *The Deathly Hallows Lectures*, 115.

the more unsavory details of his past. In their annual chat at the end of the fifth book, Harry blames Dumbledore for Sirius's death, and Dumbledore admits to having made mistakes. For the first time, Dumbledore is neither all-knowing nor all powerful, and Harry realizes that it is his task, not Dumbledore's, to defeat Voldemort. In the sixth book, Harry watches Dumbledore die, leaving no doubt about his mentor's mortality. The illusion of Dumbledore's god-like invincibility is shattered. In the final book, Dumbledore actually takes on qualities of an evil or Antichrist figure, as we learn that in his youth, he was ambitious, power hungry, and committed to "cleansing" the world of Muggles and Muggle-borns (witches or wizards from non-magical families)—the very qualities for which Voldemort is famous. At first, Harry refuses to believe Dumbledore could ever be evil, but eventually the evidence against Dumbledore is overwhelming. As a deity figure, Dumbledore resists classification within a binary moral paradigm.

At the end, Hogwarts comes under attack by Death Eaters (Voldemort's attacking army), and Harry's world begins to implode. As Death Eaters breach the walls of the Hogwarts castle, the death toll mounts, and it becomes clear the students and teachers defending the school have no hope of victory. Harry comes to believe that he must sacrifice himself to save the wizarding world. Harry and Voldemort clearly represent good and evil, but Rowling avoids the dualism of the Revelation myth by creating morally ambiguous characters on both sides of the war between Harry and Voldemort. Like Conrad in *Heart of Darkness*, Rowling creates a spectrum of good and evil, instead of two separate and opposing groups, and does not claim to offer any kind of permanent truth about the nature of good and evil. Her judgments are not cross-cultural or universal, unlike in the book of Revelation, where there is no escape from final judgment by an all-knowing God.

An exchange takes place at the end of the final *Harry Potter* book when Harry meets his (dead) mentor in a dream-like state following Voldemort's attempt to kill him. "Tell me one last thing," Harry asks. "Is this real, or has this been happening inside my head?" Harry presents Dumbledore with a binary choice, as though "real" and "happening inside my head" are mutually exclusive: Dumbledore smiles knowingly and responds, "Of course it is happening inside your head, Harry, but why on earth should that mean that it is not real?" Dumbledore's response reveals that he thinks Harry has created a false dichotomy. There is another option to account for his either/or perspective, unity between what is real and what we imagine. When Dumbledore casts aside Harry's dichotomy and replaces it with an option that blurs the distinction between two extremes, Rowling is presenting an alternative to the prevailing dualistic mindset.

As we have seen, Rowling's characters are carefully crafted so very few can be easily classified using a binary paradigm. Harry, the hero, is a powerful wizard, but he was raised in the Muggle world; his mother was Muggle born. His best friend Ron's family are purebloods, but considered traitors for their tolerance of Muggles and Muggle-borns. Harry's other best friend, Hermione, despite being the "cleverest witch of her age," is Muggle-born. Harry's allies also include the half-giant Hagrid, a werewolf, a Squib (someone from a magical family born without magic), and others who blur the lines between the magical and non-magical binary and the human and magical creature binary paradigms.

Harry feels anguish each time a character proves to be more than he or she seems. He is devastated when he discovers that his father, whom he idolizes as a martyr and about whom he has never heard anything but praise, was a bully as a teenager. Likewise, he learns that his godfather, Sirius Black, who fought against Voldemort and rejected Voldemort's prejudice against Muggles, mistreated his house-elf. For Harry, Sirius's sacrificial death means he could never have been anything but completely good. It is impossible for him to reconcile Sirius's good and bad traits; he can only see his godfather, like his father and Dumbledore, as one or the other.

Perhaps the most ambiguous of Rowling's character is Severus Snape, Harry's Potions professor. At eleven years old, Harry decides that because Snape picks on him for apparently no good reason, he must be evil. For the following six books, nothing can convince him Snape is actually working to protect him. Harry suspects Snape of helping Voldemort in every scheme, even after Dumbledore repeatedly assures him that he trusts Snape completely.

After Sirius's death, Harry uses his righteous indignation to demand that Dumbledore give him a good explanation for Snape's behavior. Even though it comes at the cost of powerful allies like Snape and Dumbledore, seeing the world in black and white makes Harry's life far simpler and his emotions easier to handle. It isn't until the end that Harry finally matures spiritually to the point where he can lose his dualistic crutch and appreciate shades of grey.

The dream-like conversation Harry has with the deceased Dumbledore just before the final battle sets in motion the events that enable Harry's move beyond binary morality. Harry's eventual acceptance of Snape's true loyalty and Dumbledore's transformation from devil to god to neither one nor the other would have been impossible within a binary framework. The fact that Snape could be Harry's ally and that Dumbledore could embody all three identities forces readers to consider the complex and shaded possibilities they are now able to entertain about the nature of evil. By inviting the reader to share Harry's transcendence of the binary moral paradigm, Rowling "satisfies the need we all feel for meaning that is not moralizing and for virtue that is heroic and uniting rather than divisive."[9] In an epilogue, written nineteen years after the events in the last chapter of *The Deathly Hallows*, Rowling reveals that Harry named his middle child Albus Severus, giving him both Dumbledore and Snape's first names.

Using *Harry Potter* to teach about morality in a non-dualistic way can help our society achieve democratic goals and move us beyond insistence on absolute morality, theologically justified patriarchy, and apocalyptically pre-ordained historical timelines with imminent endings.

9. Granger, *Understanding Harry Potter*, 236.

CHAPTER 8

C.S. LEWIS's *The Screwtape Letters* and *The Great Divorce*

THIS CHAPTER CONTINUES OUR discussion of good and evil, an element pervasive in great literature and central to the authors we have explored thus far. The topic is examined through the eyes of the British author Clive Staples Lewis (1898–1963), best known for his works of fiction, especially *The Screwtape Letters* and *The Chronicles of Narnia*, and for non-fiction Christian apologetic works such as *Mere Christianity*, *Miracles*, and *The Problem of Pain*.

In addition to writing more than thirty books, Lewis held academic positions in England at Oxford University (1925–1954) and Cambridge University (1954–1963). Baptized in the Church of Ireland, he fell into atheism during adolescence. Largely through the influence of J. R. R. Tolkien and other friends, he converted to Anglicanism in 1931. Lewis's faith profoundly affected his literary work, and his wartime radio broadcasts on the subject of Christianity brought him wide acclaim.

Among his many books, novellas, and essays, Lewis wrote several works on heaven and hell. His short book *The Screwtape Letters*, one of his most popular works, consists of thirty-one letters of advice from senior demon Screwtape to his nephew Wormwood (named after a fallen star in the book of Revelation) on the best ways to tempt a young male adult (known only as "the Patient") and secure his damnation.

Another short volume, *The Great Divorce*, is a novella in which a few residents of hell take a bus ride to heaven, where people who dwell there meet them. Lewis's proposition is that these visitors can stay in heaven if they choose, in which case they can call the name of their previous residence "purgatory" instead of "hell." However, most visitors do not find heaven appealing, willingly returning instead to hell.[1]

THE SCREWTAPE LETTERS: PLOT AND THEMES

In 1942, C. S. Lewis published *The Screwtape Letters*, his satirical book of theological fiction which, while fictional, creates a plot and characters to address Christian theological issues, primarily dealing with spiritual temptation and resistance to it. In a brief preface, Lewis states he discovered the bundle of Screwtape's letters somewhere, but will not say where. Screwtape is a devil, he warns the reader, and Screwtape's version of events, therefore, should not be taken as the truth. Then the letters begin. As a trainee, Wormwood is an inexperienced devil, though he has gone to a training college to help prepare him to tempt humans into sin. Screwtape complains, however, that this college has taught Wormwood nothing because of its incompetent director, Slubgob.

By the second letter, readers learn that the Patient has converted to Christianity and has begun going to church, for which Wormwood is chastised. A striking contrast is formed between Wormwood and Screwtape during the rest of the book, wherein Wormwood is depicted as anxious to tempt his patient into extravagantly wicked and deplorable sins, often recklessly, while Screwtape takes a more subtle approach, as in letter 12, wherein he remarks, "the safest road to hell is the gradual one—the gentle slope, soft underfoot, without sudden turnings, without milestones, without signposts."[2]

The Patient, likely in his mid-thirties, still lives with and takes care of his aging mother, a difficult and demanding woman. Screwtape advises Wormwood to make the Patient think that being Christian is an internal, spiritual thing rather than an external way of being in the world. After the Patient prays, Wormwood should make him fight with his mother about insignificant details regarding the house and chores. Over the course of these early letters, the dynamic between Screwtape and Wormwood begins to take shape. Wormwood keeps himself invisible as he follows the Patient around on earth. He essentially whispers in the Patient's ear, encouraging

1. Lewis, *Great Divorce*, 67.
2. Lewis, *Screwtape Letters*, 56.

the Patient to experience negative emotions and to pursue unhealthy distractions. Unlike Wormwood, Screwtape is an experienced tempter. He has already won souls for Hell. This has earned him, it seems, a mid-management position in Hell's vast "Lowerarchy"—a devilish corporation that determines how best to organize Hell's temptation strategies on earth.

With his own views on theology, Lewis goes on to describe and discuss sex, love, pride, gluttony, and war in successive letters. At one point, Lewis, a university scholar, suggests that even intellectuals are not impervious to the influence of temptation, especially during complacent acceptance of the "Historical Point of View," a perspective concerned only with secular facts, not spiritual truth.[3]

After World War II begins, the Patient worries about whether he will be drafted. Screwtape advises Wormwood to exploit the Patient's uncertainty, and soon, there is a period of relative inactivity during the war. During this time, Patient makes new, unnamed friends. These friends, however, are not Christians. They are skeptical and worldly. Screwtape advises Wormwood to make the Patient a hypocrite. The Patient should think he is better than his fellow, humble churchgoers because he has such smart and sophisticated friends, and he should think he is better than his friends because he, unlike them, is a Christian. As a result of the negative influence of these friends on the Patient, Wormwood, initially, seems to be doing a good job winning over the Patient's soul. Soon, however, after reading a book and going on a walk by an old mill (two solitary pleasures Wormwood should not have allowed), the Patient experiences a reawakening of his faith. This reawakening amounts to a second conversion, and, during it, the Enemy—God—forms a barrier of grace around the Patient that appears to Wormwood as a noxious fog.

After the Patient's second conversion, Screwtape advises Wormwood to tempt the Patient with sexual pleasures. Screwtape instructs Wormwood to make a list of all the young women in the Patient's neighborhood that would prove to be bad marriages matches for the Patient. But the Patient falls in love with "the Woman," a Christian girl who achieves a tremendously positive influence on the Patient's life. Screwtape hates the Woman. During this time, Wormwood reports Screwtape to Hell's secret police because Screwtape writes that the Enemy (God) really loves humans. In Hell, this claim is heresy. It contradicts Hell's essential teaching that the Enemy's love is a lie that the Enemy uses to mask self-interest. Wormwood

3. Lewis, *Screwtape Letters*, 128.

continues to make poor progress with the Patient and, during an episode of intense anger, Screwtape transforms into a giant centipede, mimicking a similar transformation in book 10 of *Paradise Lost*, wherein demons are changed into snakes.

World War II, meanwhile, grows active again. The Germans begin to drop bombs on the Patient's unnamed hometown. The Patient's unspecified duties place him in harm's way, and he soon begins to fear for his life. Screwtape advises Wormwood to exploit the Patient's cowardice, but not to the extent that the Patient prays for help with it. During one bombing, the Patient acts according to his duty. Because he is afraid, however, the Patient feels himself to be a coward. This is bad news for Wormwood, Screwtape says. It keeps the Patient humble. Screwtape warns Wormwood that the Patient's soul is prepared for Heaven, and he advises Wormwood to keep the Patient alive as long as possible. That way, Wormwood can use the Patient's whole life to tempt him away from the Enemy and into sin. However, the Patient dies while courageously performing air-raid duties, and his soul is taken into Heaven.

Hearing of the Patient's exemplary courage and modesty in his first raid, Screwtape begins letter 30 by threatening his nephew, "Bring us back food, or be food yourself."[4] While the food reference may be seen as an inversion of the Eucharist, Screwtape concludes the final letter by saying he is ravenous at the prospect of eating Wormwood alive—eat or be eaten, that is the hellish menu. Because of his failure, Wormwood must take the Patient's place. Wormwood begs Screwtape for mercy, but Screwtape laughs, saying there is no mercy in Hell.

The Screwtape Letters is predicated on an eternal struggle between the forces of good and evil. These forces are represented by the opposing camps of Heaven and Hell, God and Satan, angels and devils. These letters are presented with the expectation that readers have a basic understanding of Christian beliefs, such as the story of the Fall. The story does not occur in the Bible, but in it, Satan (then called Lucifer) and a group of angelic followers rises up against God. God, who is all-powerful, casts them out of Heaven and into eternal damnation. As a consequence of being banished from Heaven, Satan and his forces strive to "win" souls to their cause by tempting them away from God and virtue, and into vice and sin. The struggle between Heaven and Hell that began with Satan's uprising plays out as a competition for human souls. Though God is all-powerful, he

4. Lewis, *Screwtape Letters*, 141.

allows humans to make their own decisions. Devils like Wormwood and Screwtape try to trick humans into making the wrong ones.

In letter 25, Screwtape complains that the Patient's love interest, the Woman, and her family are *merely* Christian. They practice basic Christian principles without turning their belief in God and Christian teachings into a fashion statement. Screwtape advises Wormwood to use the Woman's family's political interests to corrupt the Patient. Instead of being merely Christian, the Patient might start to practice "Christianity And." Wormwood should make the Patient interested in movements like, for example, Christianity and the War, Christianity and Vegetarianism, Christianity and Animal Abuse. This model of Christianity, in which Christian teachings become a sideshow for fashionable political agendas, is a way for Hell to corrupt the positive influence of Christian teachings on people's lives, a way to make Christians less Christian. Lewis uses Screwtape's position to criticize the political trends of his day. He argues that Christianity is about the simple practice of virtue, justice, and Jesus' teachings in the gospels.

Mere Christianity is also the title of one of Lewis's apologetic works, a book based on the radio talks he gave from 1942 through 1944, during World War II. These talks were written and delivered shortly after *The Screwtape Letters* appeared between May and November of 1941 in the Anglican newspaper *The Guardian*. *Mere Christianity* is, to a large extent, an expansion of themes Lewis began to explore in *The Screwtape Letters*. Practicing "mere" Christianity doesn't just mean avoiding political specification and fashionable trends. It also means steering clear of divisions within Christianity, like the split between Protestant groups and the Catholic Church and divisive issues such as differences in rites and beliefs associated with the sacraments. In *The Screwtape Letters*, Lewis implies that such distinctions are only a distraction from the true call of Christianity—the call to live rightly.

The Seven Deadly Sins—Lust, Pride, Gluttony, Greed, Sloth, Envy, and Wrath—play a prominent role in Screwtape's advice to Wormwood. Not all of these Sins are mentioned by name within the letters, but elements of each can be found in them. Of the seven, pride, lust, and gluttony are the most discussed. In Christian teaching, the Seven Deadly Sins are the root of all the other vices, so it makes sense that, in order to promote vice in the Patient, Screwtape would guide Wormwood to succumb to these temptations.

Despite their theological differences and in appreciation for their ongoing friendship, Lewis dedicated *Screwtape* to Tolkien, inscribing in the copy he gave to his friend, "In token of payment of a great debt." Lewis was indebted to Tolkien literarily and spiritually, though not, apparently as much ecclesiastically or theologically. Surprisingly, Lewis's dedication angered Tolkien, who considered Lewis's work a hazardous experiment. How could Lewis have delved so deeply into the arts of "the Enemy," as Tolkien commonly referred to evil? Clearly, Tolkien disapproved of such ventures, even when undertaken by an authentic Christian like Lewis. For Tolkien, the devil was too powerful for a human to trifle with or to write much about. As Tolkien wrote in *The Lord of the Rings*, even to mimic evil could lead to an irrevocable alteration of a virtuous person's understanding of the world. Evil, for Tolkien, was real and perilous—a perversion and mocking of God's creation. The topic itself seemed contentious among the Inklings, the literary study group central to Tolkien and Lewis. For Tolkien, Lewis was acting too much like fantasy writer Charles Williams, whom Tolkien considered a "witch doctor."

Religion proved both a unifier and a point of contention between Lewis and Tolkien. Lewis had been raised as a strong Irish Protestant. From an early age, he had heard much from his relatives about the wickedness of Roman Catholics. His maternal grandfather, a preacher, regularly chastised Catholics as evil. As a child, Lewis took his faith seriously, finding nothing attractive in Catholicism. During his teenage years, however, Lewis lost his faith, replacing it with pure rationalism. Tolkien played a fundamental role in bringing Lewis back to Christianity, not to Catholic Christianity, however, but to Anglican Christianity.

Though the Inklings never officially disbanded until Lewis's death in 1963, after 1949, the members began to meet less frequently, strained in part by changes in Tolkien and Lewis's friendship. While theological differences played the most significant role in the decline of their friendship, other issues intruded as well. Tolkien resented Lewis's strong and quick friendship with Charles Williams, which began in 1940. Tolkien also seemed perturbed by Lewis's significant borrowing of Tolkien's ideas and private mythology for his novels. In the late 1950s, Tolkien disapproved of Lewis's decision to marry a divorced woman, Joy Gresham, an act forbidden in the Roman Catholic Church. In addition, Tolkien openly rejected Lewis's children's fiction, especially the Narnia tales, which he felt took mythology to extreme lengths. Finally, Lewis's "mere Christianity" became a source of annoyance to Tolkien, which he saw as an attempt to reduce faith to commonplace rationality.

Despite their differences, Tolkien helped to secure Lewis a prestigious chair at Cambridge, and Lewis nominated Tolkien for the Nobel Prize in Literature. It was also Lewis who encouraged Tolkien's publisher to accept *The Hobbit*, and it was Lewis who encouraged the writing and publication of *The Lord of the Rings*. Lewis's death hit Tolkien hard. "This feels like an axe-blow near the roots," Tolkien wrote his daughter. "Very sad that we should have been so separated in the last years; but our time of close communion endured in memory for both of us."[5]

THE GREAT DIVORCE: PLOT AND THEMES

Despite being known as an apologist for traditional or evangelical Christianity, Lewis is less dualistic than conservatives such as J. R. R. Tolkien, but not as nondualistic as one might think, for as he notes in his preface to *The Great Divorce*, "Evil can be undone, but it cannot 'develop' into good. Time does not heal it. . . . It is still 'either-or.'"[6] However, Lewis concludes his preface affirming uncertainty in eschatological matters: "The last thing I wish is to arouse factual curiosity about the details of the after-world."[7]

Lewis first published *The Great Divorce* as a serial in *The Guardian* in 1944 and 1945, and soon thereafter in book form. The novel arose out of Lewis's interest in the nature of spiritual choices, and it is based on a dream or vision of his in which he reflects on the Christian conceptions of heaven and hell.[8] The title was a play on William Blake's poem *The Marriage of Heaven and Hell*, with Lewis implying that no such marriage is possible. Despite maintaining a dualism between good and evil—heaven and hell— Lewis entertains an intriguing semi-dualistic (or semi-nondualistic) option in the following prefatory remark: "But what, you ask of earth? Earth, I think, will not be found by anyone to be in the end a very distinct place. I think earth, if chosen instead of Heaven, will turn out to have been, all along, only a region in Hell: and earth, if put second to Heaven, to have been from the beginning a part of Heaven itself."[9] While Tolkien might

5. Carpenter, *Letters*, 341.

6. Lewis, *Great Divorce*, 6.

7. Lewis, *Great Divorce*, 8.

8. In Lewis's conception, Hell is urban and Heaven rural.

9. Lewis, *Great Divorce*, 7; in the text, George MacDonald, the narrator's guide in Heaven, tells Lewis: "perhaps ye had better not call this country Heaven. Not *Deep Heaven*, ye understand . . . Ye can call it the Valley of the Shadow of Life. . . . Both good

have found nebulous theology such as this perplexing, others might find it fascinating.

The idea for allowing damned spirits a "holiday" in Heaven was suggested to Lewis by his reading of the seventeenth century Anglican poet Jeremy Taylor, who introduced him to the ancient Catholic notion of *refrigerium*—that the damned are given occasional repose from the torments of Hell by being granted "days off" in other places, understood generally as an excursion to Paradise.

In *The Great Divorce*, the narrator inexplicably finds himself in a grim and joyless city, the "grey town," where it rains continuously, even indoors, this place is either Hell or Purgatory, depending on whether or not one remains there. The narrator eventually finds a bus stop for those who desire an excursion to some other place (the destination later turns out to be the foothills of Heaven). He waits in line for the bus and listens to the arguments between his fellow passengers. As they await the bus's arrival, many of the passengers quit the line in disgust before the bus pulls up. When it arrives, the bus is driven by the figure of Jesus Christ, who we learn later is the only One great enough to descend safely to Hell. Once the few remaining passengers have boarded, the bus flies upward, off the pavement into the grey, rainy sky.

The ascending bus breaks out of the rain clouds into a clear, pre-dawn sky, and as it rises, its occupants bodies change from being normal and solid into being transparent, faint, and vapor-like. When the bus reaches its destination, the passengers—including the narrator—are gradually revealed to be ghosts. Although the country they enter is the most beautiful they have ever seen, every feature of the landscape, including streams of water and blades of grass, is unyieldingly solid compared to themselves. It causes them immense pain to walk on the grass, whose blades pierce their shadowy feet, and even a single leaf is far too heavy for any to lift.

Shining figures, men and women whom they have known on earth, come to meet them and to urge them to repent and walk into Heaven proper. As the ghosts travel onward and upward the shining figures promise that they will become more solid and thus feel less and less discomfort. These figures, called "spirits" to distinguish them from the ghosts, offer to help them journey toward the mountains and the sunrise.

---

and evil, when they are full grown, become retrospective. Not only this valley but all this earthly past will have been Heaven to those who are saved. Not only the twilight in [Purgatory/Hell], but all their life on earth too, will then be seen by the damned to have been Hell." Lewis, *Great Divorce*, 67.

However, almost all of the ghosts choose to return to the grey town instead, giving various reasons and excuses. Much of the interest of the book lies in the recognition it awakens of the plausibility and familiarity—and the thinness and self-deception—of the excuses that the ghosts refuse to abandon, even though to do so would bring them to "reality" and "joy forevermore." For example, an artist refuses to remain in Heaven, arguing that he must preserve the reputation of his school of painting; a bitter cynic predicts that Heaven is a trick; a bully ("Big Man") is offended that people he believes beneath him are there; a nagging wife is angry that she will not be allowed to dominate her husband in Heaven. By contrast, one man corrupted on earth by lust, which rides on his ghost in the form of an ugly lizard, permits an angel to kill the lizard and becomes a little more solid, and journeys onward.

The narrator, an author when alive, is met by the writer George Mac-Donald. The narrator hails MacDonald as his mentor, just as Dante did when first meeting Virgil in the *Divine Comedy*, and MacDonald becomes the narrator's guide in his journey, as Virgil became Dante's. MacDonald explains that it is possible for a soul to choose to remain in Heaven despite having been in the grey town; for such souls, the goodness of Heaven will work backwards into their lives, turning even their worst sorrows into joy, and changing their experience on earth to an extension of Heaven. Conversely, the evil of Hell works so that if a soul remains in, or returns to, the grey town, even any remembered happiness from life on earth will lose its meaning, and the soul's experience on earth would retrospectively become Hell.

Before continuing with the plot, we must say a word about George MacDonald. MacDonald's appeal, for Lewis, was in the holiness of his imagination. His sermons, essays and novels were a great support to Lewis throughout his Christian life, and Lewis testified constantly to the spiritual nourishment he drew from them. Not surprising, Lewis makes MacDonald his teacher in *The Great Divorce*, a figure of spiritual authority like Virgil or Beatrice in Dante's *Divine Comedy* (a text upon which Lewis frequently drew for heavenly inspiration) to guide and support him in his journey through Heaven and in his quest to understand it.

In *The Great Divorce*, MacDonald has the narrator crouch down to look at a tiny crack in the soil they are standing on, and tells him that the bus came up through a crack no bigger than that, which contained the vast grey town, which is actually minuscule to the point of being invisible compared with the immensity of Heaven and reality. In answer to the narrator's question about the truth of his experience, MacDonald confirms that when he writes about it "Make it plain that it was but a dream."[10] Toward the end, the narrator expresses the terror and agony of remaining a ghost in the advent of full daybreak in Heaven, comparing the weight of the sunlight on a ghost as like having large blocks fall on one's body (at this point falling books awaken him).

The theme of the dream parallels *The Pilgrim's Progress*, in which the protagonist dreams of judgment day in the House of the Interpreter. The use of chess imagery as well as the correspondence of dream elements to elements in the narrator's waking life is reminiscent of *Alice's Adventures in Wonderland* and *Through the Looking-Glass*. *The Great Divorce* ends with the narrator awakening from his dream of Heaven into the unpleasant reality of wartime Britain, in conscious imitation of *The Pilgrim's Progress*, the last sentence of which is, "So I awoke, and behold: It was a Dream."

As noted in our preface, Lewis favored a medieval model of reality, but he viewed no model of reality as final. The realization that human models are not sacrosanct and that myths are part of a greater story pervades Lewis's fiction. His Narnian stories include talking animals—a concept from the preliterary human imagination—and the stories in his space trilogy are based on the concept of different models for truth in other worlds. Some of Lewis's imaginative models are disturbing to those who cannot see their own models as replaceable.

In *The Great Divorce*, Lewis pictures Hell as a grey city with free bus service to the bright, cool, mountain landscape of Heaven. Yet there is, for him, no "marriage of heaven and hell." Lewis shows in this dream vision that their divorce is made inevitable by human choice between good and evil on earth. In his preface, Lewis reminds readers that his model, true in his opinion, should not be taken literally: "I beg readers to remember that this is a fantasy. . . . The transmortal conditions are solely an imaginative supposal: they are not even a guess or a speculation at what may actually await us."[11]

The same problem sometimes arises with Lewis's Narnia stories. Readers recognize the creation of Narnia through the Lion's song as a model based on Genesis. They understand Aslan's self-sacrifice as a model of the Christian atonement. Yet some balk at the acceptance of Emeth, the

---

10. Lewis, *Great Divorce*, 127.

11. Lewis, *Great Divorce*, 7–8.

follower of the false god Tash, into the everlasting Narnia at the climax of *The Last Battle*. In Lewis's conception, good and evil—heaven and hell—are both true, models of reality embodied by Aslan and Tash. The truths are absolute, but the models are relative.

BELIEF IN THE AFTERLIFE

As biblical scholars remind us, the habit of thinking individualistically as opposed to corporately in the Bible is rather late, as are the ideas of heaven and the afterlife. The book of Daniel, composed during a precarious time in Jewish history, less than two centuries before the birth of Christianity, emphasizes God's providential role in history. Daniel is one of the few books in the Hebrew Bible that can be reliably dated. The book is said to set forth the theology of the Maccabean revolution and to represent the manifesto of the Hasidim. The book's final form, especially the second half, can be dated to the period 167–164 BCE, when the Seleucid tyrant Antiochus IV Epiphanes ruled the Jewish homeland. While the author of the book of Daniel remains unknown, he belonged to the resistance movement called the Hasidim ("faithful ones"), a group of nonconformists who resisted the Seleucid policy of Hellenization, a coercive policy that forced Jews to compromise or abandon key distinctives such as monotheism, the Sabbath, circumcision, purity codes, kosher food laws, and the sacrificial system.

In Daniel 12, those who resist the enforced Seleucid program of Hellenization are called "the wise." It is they who are promised a glorious and eternal future: "Many of those who sleep in the dust of the earth shall awake, some to everlasting life, and some to shame and everlasting contempt" (Dan 12:2). Here, according to some scholars, we have the first explicit biblical reference to resurrection. Further confirmation of second- and first-century Jewish belief in a corporeal resurrection comes from the apocryphal book of 2 Maccabees, written in Greek in the decades following the Maccabean revolt (167–163 BCE). The story of the extreme torture and martyrdom of seven brothers in chapter 7 presupposes a resurrection of the body and even a reassembling of dismembered limbs, while the passage in 12:43–44 assumes on the basis of resurrection that prayers for the dead are efficacious (see also 1 Cor 15:29). The Maccabean material clearly grew out of the need for justice. If young Jewish people died as martyrs rather than compromise their faith, then surely God must reward them.

Earlier biblical references to the afterlife, including the notoriously difficult passage in Job 19:26–27 and the undateable Isaiah 26:19, are unclear in the original Hebrew version and cannot support the later doctrinal meaning imposed on them by Christian translators. Two passages found in the book of Ecclesiastes also should be mentioned. The remark about the possibility of an afterlife inserted in Ecclesiastes 3:21 should not be interpreted out of context, since it is prefaced by the clearer meaning of the preceding verse: "All go to one place; all are from the dust, and all turn to dust again." Another passage, Ecclesiastes 12:7, suggests that the human breath or "spirit" returns to God, but this verse is simply affirming the viewpoint of Genesis 2:7, in which human life and death are said to be dependent upon the breath of God, which returns at death to God, from whence it came.

By the start of the Christian era, Jews disagreed on eschatological beliefs, with the Sadducees holding the older belief that there is no afterlife and consequently no resurrection and the Pharisees accepting the newer belief that there is an afterlife as well as a resurrection. Belief in rewards and punishments became significant in rabbinic Judaism, which emerged in the aftermath of the destruction of the temple in 70 CE. The apostle Paul, called "the second founder of Christianity" for his theological influence on earliest Christianity, was a Pharisee before his conversion. Through him, the key doctrinal beliefs of the Pharisees became central to Christianity, including their doctrine of the afterlife.

It is important to keep in mind that the New Testament remains ambiguous about life after death. While the idea of Jesus' resurrection is central to Christianity, its meaning is debated within the New Testament. As Paul writes in 1 Corinthians 15:50, "flesh and blood cannot inherit the kingdom of God, nor does the perishable inherit the imperishable." And Paul did not address the notion of hell. As scholars now note, most of the images of fire and torment in the afterlife come from the gospel of Matthew and the book of Revelation. As notions of heaven and hell evolved over time in the Christian tradition, related concepts and adjustments were added, including such notions as purgatory, limbo, and child limbo. Since all sins were not considered equal, time sentences and other forms of plea-bargaining entered the equation.

In his *Divine Comedy*, Dante Alighieri gives poetic expression to medieval Christian beliefs concerning the afterlife. Describing a journey through Inferno (hell), Purgatorio (purgatory), and Paradiso (heaven), the poem makes substantial use of the leading themes of Christian theology and spirituality, culminating with heaven, the ultimate goal of the Christian life. Dante portrays the geography of hell as consisting of nine successive levels, each circle exponentially greater in torture and pain. The first circle, populated with virtuous non-Christians such as Aristotle, Seneca, and Virgil, is a place called "limbo," seen as a kind of "ante-hell," where no pain is experienced. Dante's work, written during an age when society and human life were precarious and under constant threat, helped establish medieval perceptions of the afterlife.

During the Enlightenment, many if not all Christian doctrines came under intense scrutiny. Enlightenment thinkers viewed belief in the afterlife as superstition and wish fulfillment, a projection of human longing for rewards and retribution. They particularly attacked the idea of eternal punishment, since it seemed to serve no useful purpose. The twentieth century, however, saw a rediscovery of eschatology. Though the doctrine's revival can be attributed to a number of factors, it was primarily due to a general collapse in confidence concerning human goodness and human civilization. World War I, especially traumatic, was followed by the Great Depression and the terrors of Nazism, leading to the Holocaust and the threat of nuclear war. These events and related concerns raised doubts among Christians concerning the credibility of the liberal humanist vision and led to renewed stress on their eschatological beliefs, characterized by apocalyptic solutions focused on the rapture of believers to heaven and the punishment of unbelievers in hell.

Despite the residue of apocalypticism in twenty-first-century America, exacerbated in part by the global war against terrorism and other ongoing threats to our well-being, it is hard to imagine that any reflective person today believes in a literal doctrine of hell. It should be obvious by now that all traditional images of the afterlife, including heaven and hell, are born of fertile human minds.

Is there life after death? We cannot know for sure. While most biblical passages on this topic represent the early believers' apocalyptic hope, one passage rings true for me, keeping open the door to the afterlife: "No eye has seen, nor ear heard, nor the human heart conceived, what God has prepared for those who love him" (1 Cor 2:9).

RETHINKING HEAVEN

While boundaries exist between heaven and earth, future and present, deity and humanity, and good and evil, there is dynamism to boundaries in the Bible. Boundaries do not fix limits beyond which it is impossible to pass. Rather they locate the place where transformations occur, allowing a flow across planes, eras, social categories, or moral values.

In the book of Revelation, "heaven" is the starting point for all revelation. John is taken into God's throne room so that he can see "behind the scenes" and understand how things fit together. "And there in heaven a door stood open" (4:1); this perspective is vital to the message of Revelation. John's cosmological perspective should be interpreted spiritually, not spatially. Going to "heaven," in John's vision, is less about cosmic geography and more about the place where God chooses to reveal himself, the place where heavenly realities are made plain. Heaven offers a divine perspective concerning events on earth, a new way of seeing that is beyond the control of earthly rulers. Heaven is the deeper dimension that offers God's perspective on what happens on earth.

We should not, however, restrict "heaven" to the spiritual dimension of reality, for it represents more than that. What John sees in heaven is not simply divine perspective. Heaven represents what is right and good and proper. When Jesus tells his followers to pray, "Your kingdom come . . . on earth as it is in heaven" (Matt 6:10), he understands "heaven" not as a future destination for humans but as God's dimension of everyday reality. Heaven is in charge; heaven takes the lead; heaven represents what ought to be happening on earth. Every moment of each day is a unique point of contact with the divine. The eternal now is God's great gift to humanity. As Elizabeth Barrett Browning wrote:

> Earth's crammed with heaven,
> And every common bush afire with God;
> And he who sees it takes off his shoes—
> The rest sit round it and pluck blackberries.[12]

In his fictional story, *A New Kind of Christian*, Brian McLaren writes about a young man name Dan striking up a friendship with an older, former pastor who mentors him into a larger, more generous and loving Christianity. The pastor leads Dan through a thought experiment concerning heaven. Imagine that you have just died and passed through the doorway

12. *Aurora Leigh*, Book VII, line 820.

of death. And you enter heaven. And it is a place where no one argues, no one fights, no one hates, and no one complains—not because they aren't allowed to but because they don't want to, because they accept and love one another completely. Think about how would you feel entering that place.

Then the pastor asks Dan to imagine someone who walked beside him through the doorway of death. That person had lived his life cramped by hatred and fear, tight in guilt and greed, ingrown in selfishness and lust. He had spent every day of his life being ungrateful, complaining and blaming others, and he had become an expert at lying and cheating and using others. Now, how would that person feel in heaven? Could it be that the light that seems beautiful to you would seem blinding to him? Could the love, trust, openness, and acceptance that welcomes you seem to him disgusting, weak, terrifying, insipid, or repulsive?

Maybe it's not that there are two places beyond the door of death: heaven and hell. "Sometimes I wonder," the pastor tells Dan, "if hell is just what heaven feels like for those who haven't learned in this life what this life is intended to teach. I believe with all my heart that God is not willing for even one person to miss out on the joy and glories of heaven. . . . We are becoming on this side of the door of death the kind of people we will be on the other side."[13]

In the gospels, Jesus teaches that we will face consequences for the choices we make in our lifetimes, but they are never for the sake of punishment. Instead, they are a manifestation of God's redemptive and healing love, which will ultimately prevail.

13. McLaren, *New Kind of Christian*, 90–91.

CHAPTER 9

Nathaniel Hawthorne's
The House of the Seven Gables

THE PERIOD CENTERING ON 1850 stands out as one of the glorious ages in the history of the novel, both in England and in the United States. The span of three or four years around 1850 encompasses the Brontë sisters' *Wuthering Heights* and *Jayne Eyre*, William Thackeray's *Vanity Fair*, Elizabeth Gaskell's first novel, *Mary Barton*, and Charles Dickens's first carefully structured works, including *Dombey and Son, David Copperfield*, and *Bleak House*. During this concentration of creative energy, an equally significant fictional achievement occurred in North America. This short span encompassed the most fertile conjunction of large vision and formal craft that the American novel was to experience for at least several decades, for it featured the production of the major work of Nathaniel Hawthorne and Herman Melville. The central moment of this great period was even more compressed in time in America than in England, for in the span of two years we see the appearance of *The Scarlet Letter* in 1850 through *The House of the Seven Gables* and *Moby-Dick* in 1851.

These two golden ages seem to be parallel but not causally related phenomena. Hawthorne read new English novels faithfully, and Melville sporadically, but the work of their English contemporaries was of relatively little importance to them as a direct influence. The example that most helped Melville to clarify his ambitions for the novel was that of Hawthorne's work, and the friendship of the two authors as neighbors during these crucial years can be seen as symbolic of their self-contained revolution.

The remarkable outpouring of complex novels by Hawthorne and Melville arose in large part out of previous literary endeavors, shorter and less profound in conception. By 1850, Hawthorne had been writing tales and sketches for twenty years, and, after having been for so long, as he says, "the obscurest man of letters in America," he began to win a significant measure of recognition for his work. However, there are indications that he had come to find these sorts of productions increasingly unsatisfactory. In "The Custom House," a largely autobiographical sketch added to the preface of *The Scarlet Letter*, he imagines the scorn of his Puritan ancestors for his achievement as "a writer of storybooks." Similarly, the felt presence of eight generations of religious clerics recorded in "The Old Manse," again makes him feel ashamed of his "idle stories." Under their shadow, he resolves to achieve a novel—a large and serious work of art that by way of a profound theme should be true to the human heart.

Nathaniel Hawthorne (1804–1860) was born in Salem, Massachusetts, from old New England stock. His great great grandfather was a judge during the Salem witchcraft trials of 1692 and 1693. For several generations, Hawthorne's paternal ancestors took to the sea, while the family declined in wealth and social importance. His father, Captain Hathorne (Nathaniel added the "w" to the spelling of the family name after he graduated from college) died at Surinam, when his son was four years old.

Nathaniel was brought up in the households of his mother's family in Salem and in the backcountry of Maine. He attended Bowdoin College, and upon his graduation in 1825, he determined to become a writer of fiction. For more than a decade, he devoted himself to learning his craft, living at home, reading, writing, and destroying many of his productions, but sending some of his stories to magazines, which were published anonymously. After some ventures in editing undertaken to support himself—the many stories he published in these years brought him little income—and after a brief period of employment in the Boston Custom House and a short period in 1841 as a member of the experimental socialist community at Brook Farm, Hawthorne married, at the age of thirty-eight, Sophia Peabody. Several years living in the Old Manse in Concord (Emerson's ancestral home, which for three years, he rented from Emerson) brought him into contact with Emerson and Thoreau.

Later, back in Salem, he was employed in the Salem Custom House until, losing his job for political reasons, he tried to devote himself wholly to literature. He wrote *The Scarlet Letter* quickly, following soon after with *The House of the Seven Gables, The Blithedale Romance,* and other works. In Lenox, in the Berkshires, he formed his most significant literary friendship when he became a neighbor of Herman Melville, then at work on *Moby-Dick,* which Melville dedicated to Hawthorne. Hawthorne then spent seven years in England, where he tried to solve his financial problems by serving as United States Consul in Liverpool, and in Italy, adding steadily to his notebooks but unable to do any creative work until, at the end of his stay, he wrote *The Marble Faun.* Returning to Concord in 1860, he died after four unhappy years, during which, working against failing health and flagging creative energies, he tried to bring to satisfactory conclusions several late romances which he left unfinished at his death.

When, in the preface to *The House of the Seven Gables,* Hawthorne defines his purpose as a writer of "romances," his first care is to distinguish the (Gothic) romance from the traditional novel. Hawthorne claims that novels adhere closely to everyday circumstances, whereas romances give the writer more freedom to present another version of truth, which could be enhanced with aspects that transcend reality. Hawthorne tells us that the story told in *The House of the Seven Gables* is actually something of a mix between the two genres, but that it is primarily a romance. Hawthorne also states that his book exemplifies the moral that the sins of one generation will be passed on to future generations; he expresses his hope that he has not made the story too heavy-handed or moralistic. He concludes with a disclaimer that readers should not make too many associations between the places and characters in the story and any possible real-life counterparts.

When he made his now famous distinction between the novel and the romance, he was not intending to assign "truth" to the novel and mere "fantasy" or escapist dreaming to the romance. He was distinguishing between "fact" (with which the novel deals) and "truth" (which is the traditional province of the romance), and at the same time he was suggesting an orientation in which "fact" is external and "truth" internal.

The Romantic artist creates, Hawthorne thought, by transforming fact into symbol—that is, by transforming fact into *meaningful* fact, and by discarding facts believed to be meaningless. Such artists are at liberty to manipulate their materials, to shape them freely into meaningful patterns, so long as the artist does not violate the "truth of the human heart."

Hawthorne felt that he could best pursue his desired truth by looking within and exercising a kind of imaginative sympathy in both his subject and his method. In a suggestive metaphor in another of his prefaces—that to *The Snow-Image and Other Twice-Told Tales* in 1851—he defined his role as artist as that of a person burrowing into the depths of human nature by the light of observation.

Once we read his definition of a novel, as opposed to a romance, we get the feeling that Hawthorne was groping toward a conception of fiction that is more unique than he realized. Others before him had wondered where to place fiction among the several kinds of literature, but Hawthorne's emphasis on fiction as an art form, his insistence that it be tested by laws appropriate to its mode of existence rather than to its accuracy as a document, clearly establishes a sound critical principle for distinguishing the novel from a romance. Most important to Hawthorne's distinction between a romance and a novel was his life-long insistence that the kind of truth that he wanted to portray was the "truth of the human heart," and that the best way to portray this was by using the strategy of indirection. The "truth" that he hoped to conceive was of a different order from the truth conveyed by ordinary didactic fiction, by philosophy, or by the symbolism of the exact sciences. It is a truth that can be expressed only in the images of the imagination, and as Hawthorne himself thought, this truth could not be "grasped" except in such images. The most striking way in which Hawthorne's work foreshadows all modern fiction lies in the mythic and poetic aspects of his novel.

In addition to his theory of fiction, in the preface Hawthorne also tells us the subject of *The House of the Seven Gables*. The theme, he says, is that wrong and retribution, as well as sin and suffering, are carried on through generations. He further announces that he will observe how the wrong-doing of one generation lives into successive generations until it finally becomes a "pure and uncontrollable mischief." In an even more serious tone, he adds that he hopes that this work might warn mankind against accumulating "ill-gotten gold, or real estate," and bequeathing them to later, innocent generations. In Hawthorne's view, the romance provides texts for sermons on the sins of pride and avarice and on the possibility of changeability through transformation.

The novel, on the other hand, presents us with the "legendary mist" of the distant past, intermingling with the memories of the recent past, especially in the minds of the house of the seven gables' inhabitants. Hawthorne combines his conviction about the continuum of history and about the interdependence of person and place into a complex idea of an identity extended in time, in space, and through its own layered awareness. Within that identity, the past intrudes on the present as the subconscious intrudes on the conscious. In this sense, *The House of the Seven Gables* presents the old Pyncheon house, haunted by the guilt of the founder and the ghost of his victim.

THE HOUSE OF THE SEVEN GABLES: PLOT AND RESPONSE

Hawthorne published his first work in 1828, the novel *Fanshawe*, which he later tried to suppress as inferior to his established books. He published several short stories in periodicals, which he collected in 1837 as *Twice-Told Tales*. He published his four major novels between 1850 and 1860, including his most famous works, *The Scarlet Letter* and *The House of the Seven Gables*. His first successful novel, *The Scarlet Letter*, set in seventeenth-century Puritan New England, is about a young woman who becomes pregnant after having an affair and is ostracized by her community. The book explores the themes of sin, guilt, and legalism. Considered Hawthorne's masterpiece, this was one of the first mass-produced books in America. Published in 1850; the first printing of 2,500 copies sold out in ten days. The book was well received by critics and is still considered one of the best novels ever published.

The House of the Seven Gables, published in 1851, outsold *The Scarlet Letter*. Set in the 1850s, the novel is about an old New England family and their ancestral home. The house was inspired by the Turner-Ingersoll Mansion in Salem. In Hawthorne's time, it was used by Hawthorne's cousin, Susanna Ingersoll, and Hawthorne visited it often. Although the novel is set in the nineteenth century, it features flashbacks to the seventeenth century, and is about the cursed old mansion and how its dark past still haunts the current inhabitants. The theme of the book centers around guilt, retribution, and atonement, and the story involves the supernatural and witchcraft.

According to the literary critic Harold Bloom, the novel explores how material and spiritual power affects individuals and drives them to try to dominate others, which is a recurring theme in many of Hawthorne's novels. Henry James declared *The House of the Seven Gables* "the closest approach we are likely to have to the Great American Novel," while Hawthorne's friend Henry Wadsworth Longfellow called it "a weird, wild book, like all [Hawthorne] writes."

The story begins in the mid-1600s, when the farmer Matthew Maule builds a small house next to a lovely, clear spring in what will become a small, well-to-do Massachusetts town. A local landowner named Colonel Pyncheon, who wants the land for himself, accuses Maule of witchcraft at a time of mass hysteria against witches. Maule is convicted and hanged, but, before he dies, he warns that God will give Pyncheon blood to drink.[1] Undaunted by this curse, Colonel Pyncheon builds a house with seven gables, triangular points on a house that run from the roof's center to its edge. Maule's own son helps design and build the house, and on the day of its opening, a great feast is held. When Colonel Pyncheon fails to greet his distinguished guests, they charge into one of his rooms, only to find him sitting dead at his desk. Blood coats his beard and his shirt. There is no evidence of foul play, but no one knows how he died. His portrait remains in the house as a symbol of its dark past and the weight of the curse upon the spirit of its inhabitants. According to legend, the picture is magically built into the house's walls, and if it should be removed, the entire edifice would collapse in ruin.

Future generations of the Pyncheon family continue to occupy the house over the next century and a half, but they are never able to claim one of the dead Colonel's final acquisitions, a large tract of land in Maine. Generations of the family are raised thinking the land is rightfully theirs, and they make unsuccessful attempts to obtain it. The area where the Pyncheon house was built falls out of fashion. Thirty years before the novel is set, a wealthy Pyncheon is murdered, seemingly by one of his nephews, a Pyncheon named Clifford. The killer is convicted and jailed, but the dead man's other nephew, the prominent man known as Judge Pyncheon, is successful and builds a large house just outside of town. Hepzibah, the sister of the jailed Pyncheon, continues to live alone in the house of the seven gables.

The Maules, on the other hand, have not had such a clear descent through history. Many of them have no knowledge of Matthew Maule or his curse on Colonel Pyncheon, and some are not even aware that they are of Maule descent. Nevertheless, many retain the Maules' characteristic alienating reserve, and some are believed by townspeople to have inherited mysterious powers from their ancestor.

1. The curse is believed to have been inspired by the passage in Revelation 16:6.

In chapter 2, readers are introduced to Hepzibah Pyncheon, the current resident of the old mansion, who becomes an embodiment of all the misery narrated in the previous chapter. An unmarried woman with a permanent scowl brought on by nearsightedness, Hepzibah demonstrates the ruin and shame of the life of a fallen aristocrat. Dignified but desperately poor, she decides to open a shop in a side room to support her brother Clifford, who has completed a thirty-year sentence for murder. She refuses all assistance from her wealthy but unpleasant cousin, Judge Jaffrey Pyncheon. A distant relative, lively and attractive Phoebe, arrives and quickly becomes invaluable, charming customers and rousing Clifford from depression. A delicate romance grows between Phoebe and the mysterious attic lodger Holgrave, who is writing a history of the Pyncheon family and practices an early form of photography known as daguerreotype.

Holgrave and Phoebe spend much time together, tending the garden and feeding the house chickens, a once-mighty breed whose former glory is compared to that of the Pyncheons. Holgrave explains his radical politics, which revolve around the principle that each generation should tear down the work of those before it, and asks Phoebe about Clifford and his past.

Holgrave also tells Phoebe the story of Alice Pyncheon. A hundred years before, Alice's father, Gervayse Pyncheon, summoned the young grandson of the older Matthew Maule, a carpenter also named Matthew Maule. Gervayse believed that since the younger Matthew Maule's father built the Pyncheon house, the young man might know where to find the missing deed to the Pyncheon land. The Pyncheons had searched thoroughly for the missing document, even digging up the grave of the first Matthew Maule to look for it, but had been unable to find it. The younger Matthew Maule, although bitter at the Pyncheons' mistreatment of his family, agrees to help in exchange for the house of the seven gables and the land on which it stands. He summons the spirits of his father, grandfather, and old Colonel Pyncheon by hypnotizing Gervayse's young daughter, Alice, intending to use her as a medium. The two Maule spirits prevent Colonel Pyncheon's ghost from telling Gervayse and the younger Matthew where the deed is, so the carpenter cancels the deal. He is elated to find that Alice has remained under his spell, and torments her in cruel and petty ways. On his wedding night, the young Maule forces Alice to serve his new bride. When Alice awakens from her trance, she rushes home through the snow, catches pneumonia, and dies. Maule is devastated by what he has done.

This story functions as the romantic centerpiece of the novel, combining wizardry, spirits, and the tragic death of a young innocent. The chapter may be said to encapsulate the whole of *The House of the Seven Gables* in exaggerated form, as it is a tale of relative realism laced with a strong dose of the fantastic. Holgrave, who has written this story, becomes representative of the author, and readers, in turn, are cast as the captive, hypnotized audience. This representation of storytelling is not particularly cheerful or even tongue-in-cheek. Instead, storytelling is represented as a sort of dark art, capable of giving its practitioners enormous power.

As Holgrave finishes his story, he realizes he has hypnotized Phoebe, but his integrity prevents him from abusing his power, and he wakes her from her trance. While Phoebe is making a visit to her home in the country, Judge Pyncheon returns to the house of the seven gables, desperate to find information about the large tract of land in Maine rumored to belong to the family. He forces Hepzibah to fetch Clifford, saying he will put Clifford in an asylum if Hepzibah does not retrieve him. The Judge explains that Clifford knows the location of their late uncle's inheritance. Hepzibah cannot find Clifford in his room, but when she comes back downstairs she finds her brother pointing gleefully to the slumped figure of Judge Pyncheon, mysteriously dead while sitting in Colonel Pyncheon's chair. Worried that Clifford will be blamed for the murder, Hepzibah and Clifford flee.

The next day, when Phoebe returns, only Holgrave is home. He shows her a daguerreotype of the dead Judge and tells her that the curse has been lifted. Holgrave also tells Phoebe he loves her, and she admits to loving him in return. Although the neighbors become suspicious, Hepzibah and Clifford return before the body is discovered. Clifford is not suspected in the Judge's death, and it is rumored that the Judge himself framed Clifford for the crime for which he served thirty years in prison.

The Judge would be saddened could he know the circumstances that followed his death. Unbeknownst to him, his son has died of cholera in Europe, and his inheritance now goes to Clifford, who decides to move to the Judge's lavish estate with Hepzibah, Phoebe, and—the novel sarcastically notes—that sworn enemy of wealth, Holgrave. Phoebe teases Holgrave when he remarks with regret that the new house is built of impermanent wood rather than permanent stone, and he acknowledges with a melancholy smile that he is rapidly becoming a conservative. He finds his new views "especially unpardonable in this dwelling of so much hereditary misfortune," standing beneath the stern gaze of the portrait of

Colonel Pyncheon, who "rendered himself [for] so long the Evil Destiny of his race." Clifford remarks that the portrait has always made him think of great wealth, and Holgrave responds by pushing a hidden spring that knocks the portrait to the floor, revealing an ancient parchment entitling the Pyncheons to the giant tract of land in Maine. Holgrave adds that he knows about the spring because he is a Maule, and that the parchment was hidden by the older Matthew Maule's son when he built the house. Like other hidden objects in Hawthorne's fiction, the deed is evidence of past evil persisting into the present. However, the land in Maine is now settled by others, rendering worthless the ancient Indian deed. Together, Holgrave and the remaining Pyncheons depart for the Judge's country estate, leaving the house of the seven gables to deteriorate further, effectively ending the curse of the Pyncheons.

POINTS TO PONDER IN *THE HOUSE OF THE SEVEN GABLES*

Nathaniel Hawthorne's *The House of the Seven Gables* is a classic Gothic novel. Set against a New England mansion, the story charts the fortunes and misfortunes of the Pyncheon family as its members navigate complex spiritual terrain such as guilt and forgiveness, the meaning of home, and the sometimes-thin line between the physical world and the supernatural.

Hawthorne's novel is rich in symbolic passages. One of its most explicit symbols is Maule's Well, the cheerful spring whose waters turn brackish after Maule's death and the arrival of the Pyncheons, a very literal illustration of the land's deep corruption. It is indicative that the Maule rather than the Pyncheon well should be the one spouting dirty water, as Maule's curse will prove to be tied to the ill-gotten land rather than to the Pyncheon family itself. Pyncheons who leave the house appear to be the least affected by the curse, some not at all. The murder of old Jaffrey Pyncheon by his nephew is also irrevocably tied to the house of seven gables. After the crime, Judge Pyncheon moves away and soon becomes happy, prosperous, and successful, although his return to the house of seven gables in later chapters will signify his downfall.

From the start, Hawthorne describes the old house as if it were human—almost evil—its "meditative look" suggesting "that it had secrets to keep, and an eventful history to moralize upon." The old Pyncheon mansion contains the collective consciousness of a single family; it is a sort of domesticated American version of a European Gothic castle, the old and haunted house permeating the minds of its aging inhabitants.

Clifford thinks of himself and Hepzibah as ghosts doomed to haunt their accursed house. Hawthorne, however, says that they have protracted their own anguish. Their hearts have been dungeons, and each person has become his or her own jailer; the house is a larger equivalent of that dungeon. Both Clifford and Hepzibah, like Roderick and Madeline Usher in Poe's short story *The Fall of the House of Usher*, face a future that is also, strangely enough, the past, for they can only become, in a manner of speaking, what they already are. Prisoners of time, they are equally prisoners of space, that space expanded into an entire house and its environs.

The orientation of the house signifies its place midway between two civilizations. It faces the commerce of the street on the west, while to the rear is an old garden. The darkness of the old Pyncheon house is impressive and significant. Within its depths are shadowy emblems of the past, each representing evil geniuses of the Pyncheon family. The ancestral chair is a reminder not only of the old Colonel but also of susceptibility to Maule's curse. The portrait and the map of what is referred to as the "Eastern claim" are dimly visible tokens of the Colonel's inflexible sternness and greed. None of the objects can be distinguished very clearly in the darkness, but the novel shows that they have an inescapable reality. Clearly, their burden weighs heavily upon the present inhabitants of the house. Hepzibah's unbending and decadent gentility is matched by the stiff chairs, and her persistent frown echoes the dark front of the house as it faces the sunny street. Any warmth that might be within her is masked by her gruff exterior. Clifford's undisciplined sensibility and faded beauty remind us of Gervayse and his daughter. The long intervening years and Clifford's unjust punishment have weakened and coarsened any of the positive traits of his ancestors.

Hawthorne's writing centers on New England, his works generally critical of Puritan beliefs and morality. His fiction, considered Romantic in nature, features the dark side of life. His themes center on the inherent evil and sin of humanity, and his works often have moral messages and psychological complexity. In composing *The Scarlet Letter* and *The House of the Seven Gables*, Hawthorne seems purposely to gather together the themes—historical, moral, psychological—that gave his earlier shorter works their distinct identity, and then, by integrating them and projecting them onto a larger canvas, he manages to eclipse his earlier achievements by further realizing their subject's interest and potential. For example, he had explored the restrictiveness of Puritanism in tales like *The Maypole of Merry Mount* and *Endicott and the Red Cross*, and the self-destructive operations of concealed guilt and the obsession with sin portrayed in *Roger Malvin's Burial* and *Young Goodman Brown*.

Few novels realize their own potential as completely as does *The Scarlet Letter*. Nevertheless, toward the end of "The Custom House," its prefatory essay, he declares this book too stern and somber, its characters incapable of escaping from their own self-divisions and defeats, however magnificently they may live through their suffering. Uncomfortable with the starkness of his own tragic vision, Hawthorne writes a second tale of guilt and sorrow, but this time, that tale ends with a vision of expiation and renewal. Like Shakespeare's romances, *The House of the Seven Gables* includes and transcends tragedy.

In Colonel Pyncheon and descendants such as Judge Pyncheon, Hawthorne depicts the stolid unimaginativeness of New England's Puritans, who first settled in Massachusetts in the 1600s, founding colonies that concentrated on biblical teachings, enacting a mission to live providentially according to God's will. However, this mindset led to hypocrisy, inflexible standards, vindictive policies, and moralistic behavior. In New England, this ethos was eventually swallowed up by commercialism and greed. To paraphrase G. K. Chesterton, the Puritans took Christian wine and turned it into Calvinist vinegar.[2]

Hawthorne personalized the connection between Salem and the Puritans in his writings. His family originally settled in Salem, and Hawthorne became a direct descendent of several notable ancestors. In "the Custom House," he describes his ancestors as severe Puritans decked out in black robes, laying harsh judgment upon people who strayed from their faith. When discussing his ancestors, Hawthorne is both reverent and irreverent, jokingly wondering how a free spirit such as himself could have descended from such lineage.

As a person of youth and vigor, Hawthorne felt at odds with the Puritan nature of his society. He seems to have felt a deep resentment for the strict fidelity to rules and values that would brand the artist as decadent or unproductive in a commercialized world and considered his ambition to write as frivolous and even as sinful. The militant moral vigor with which

---

2. A devout Roman Catholic, Chesterton's original wording refers to the Reformation and its aftermath, which he calls "the second fermentation" of Christian vintage, "when the wine of Catholicism turned into the vinegar of Calvinism." Chesterton, *Everlasting Man*, 264.

the Puritans imposed their values on others survives in Colonel Pyncheon, only that energy has become purely selfish. The overbearing masculine aggressiveness that rumor records in his sexual life is the private version of the grasping greed he exhibits in his public life. By treating others in this way, the Colonel transforms them into reverse images of himself. Thus, the Maules, who at first are simple ordinary settlers, after their dispossession become associated with occultic magic and manipulators of the subconscious. Rendering the Maules as inhuman as himself, Colonel Pyncheon commits them to the logic of vengeance, so that their power becomes no longer creative but destructive.

The cyclical struggle of the Pyncheon spirit and the Maule spirit is extended by Holgrave's macabre tale of Alice Pyncheon, the central myth of *The House of the Seven Gables*. Holgrave's diatribe in chapter 12 enables Hawthorne to transform the old mansion into a metaphor for society. When Holgrave touts some of the Transcendentalist ideas to which Hawthorne had been exposed, he stresses the importance of renewal, arguing that society is based on the views of "Dead Men"—a chilling way of arguing that New England culture is based on stale ideas. Thus, the only way for those haunted by the past is to leave the Pyncheon homestead. In that moment, the story of the old house seems to stand for our own inability to deal with the problems around us and within us, and our unwillingness even to try. In this way, Hawthorne uses the romance device of a hereditary curse to suggest why public life takes the shape it does. Holgrave's myth permits him to supplement his record of contemporary society with a kind of psychohistory of New England. Furthermore, the myth gives his book its moral center as well, for it is the myth's depiction of the dialectic of assertion and retribution that clarifies the ultimate value of love as a refusal to victimize others.

In his writings, Hawthorne both condemns and admires Puritanism. Lest we think him contradictory, there must be a reasonable explanation for his ambivalence. The answer is found in our modern understanding of Puritanism, generally limited to a narrow Calvinist theology based on predestination and universal depravity. Puritanism, however, cannot be treated adequately unless we understand that it involves two other dimensions: Puritanism as a way of life, and Puritanism as a patriotic feature in the early struggle for political liberty in America.

While Hawthorne was never shy in expressing his gratitude to the Puritans for their early political struggle for liberty, particularly in demanding liberty of conscience and freedom in law from their British rulers, he always felt that the religious system of Puritanism was cold, hard, and confined. He seems to praise the attitude of individual believers, but not the system of belief. While personally affirming the doctrines of providence and original sin in his writings, he consistently deplores the sin of pride, in his mind a natural consequence of those who would exclude much of the human race in the same way that predestination arbitrarily elects some to salvation and others to damnation.

The tendency that Hawthorne had for calling unpleasant things "Puritanical" indicates that he rejected Puritanism as a way of life. In *Young Goodman Brown*, the devil bears "no slight similitude, both in garb and manner, to some grave divine of the New England churches."[3] In his prefatory essay, "The Old Manse," he describes the manse's study as black, "made still blacker by the grim prints of ministers that hung around. These worthies looked strangely like bad angels, or, at least, like men who had wrestled so continually and so sternly with the devil, that somewhat of his sooty fierceness had been imparted to their own visages."[4]

This was, in essence, Hawthorne's chief complaint against Puritanism as a way of life: it was gloomy, joyless, and rigid. In the Puritan way of life, religion and law were closely related. The law itself was severe, and severely carried out, as Hawthorne makes clear in *The Scarlet Letter*. He never questions the need for civil law, but he clearly criticizes the Puritan method of conferring it. Such a life, he says, is "sinister to the intellect and sinister to the heart."[5] While Hawthorne gives us an unparalleled study of the spirituality of his ancestors, it is a study filled with anxiety and horror.

The liberal philosopher John Stuart Mill, writing about the same time as Hawthorne, wrote about the threat posed by social conformity in his famous book, *On Liberty*. Alexis de Tocqueville wrote about the problem as well. It was a serious challenge in nineteenth-century America, and it is again in the twenty-first century. In an October 2021 article in *The Atlantic*, staff writer Anne Applebaum speaks of "The New Puritans." Unlike the Puritan ethos of old, with its strict conformism, narrowmindedness, and hypocrisy, contemporary Americans function under a legal system that provides a right to self-defense, a statute of limitations, and presumes innocence for the accused. However, there exists today something called

3. Hawthorne, *Tales and Sketches*, 286.

4. Hawthorne, *Tales and Sketches*, 1124–25.

5. Hawthorne, *Tales and Sketches*, 1038.

"cancel culture," a mindset thriving in social media fashioned by those who, irritated by nuance and ambiguity, favor rigid ideologies, immediate verdicts, and obligatory blame. The values of this "new Puritanism" have come to dominate many American cultural institutions, including universities, newsmagazines, foundations, and even museums. Instead of hearing evidence and witnesses, these groups make judgments behind closed doors. As freedom-loving Americans know, the notion of forced conformity underlies totalitarian movements such as Nazi and Soviet rule, but also theocratic regimes. In America today, we don't have that kind of state coercion, but similar mindsets are thriving and proliferating, producing similar outcomes.

In addition to Puritanism, another point to ponder regards Hawthorne's protofeminist depiction of women. Critics often view Hawthorne's use of female characters such as *The Scarlet Letter*'s Hester Prynne as foreshadowing the self-reliance and responsibility that led to women's suffrage and reproductive emancipation. Aside from Hester, the women of Hawthorne's other novels are more fully realized than his male characters. This observation is equally true of his short stories, in which lead female characters serve as allegorical figures, such as Rappaccini's Daughter and Young Goodman Brown's wife Faith Brown. In *Drowne's Wooden Image*, it is a woman who "first created the artist who afterwards created her image."[6]

Critics often speak of the lack of plot in *The House of the Seven Gables*. The first fourteen chapters (well over half of the book) amble along so slowly and undirectedly that the book almost seems to lack plot. The appearance of plotlessness is reinforced by Hawthorne's technique of cutting away from the action to analyze his characters. We know, for instance, what Phoebe's essence is: she represents good (in contrast to Colonel Pyncheon's and Judge Pyncheon's evil), the actual, freedom from the past. physical and mental health, and practicality. Her vital purity embodies a redemptive potential. She is also an exorcist, exorcizing the gloom and learning from the past while growing into a new being.

Through Phoebe's personal development, the deterministic Pyncheon cycle can be reversed. The tale of Alice Pyncheon defines the importance of the relationship between Holgrave and Phoebe, for their love represents the potential that releases them from the pattern of domination and psychic revenge that the tale illustrates. Because Hawthorne's characters exist within a

6. Hawthorne, *Tales and Sketches*, 942.

larger patter of conflict, when one of them changes the pattern of his or her life, it changes the shape of the whole pattern.

In committing to a double source of inspiration—the fiction of realism and the fiction of romance—Hawthorne indicates that healthy spirituality combines both approaches: one grounded in reality, the other soaring in mystery. His double exposures invite us as readers to join him and his characters in a self-conscious attempt to make sense of our own story. They make us see our experience—ancestral and individual—as substantial and meaningful, as determined by a prolonged past but also as present and free, and thus they leave us with the task of forging for ourselves, on the basis of our clear understanding of the choices involved, the future we think most appropriate.

CHAPTER 10

Herman Melville's *Moby-Dick*

WHENEVER WE HEAR the name Herman Melville (1819–1891), the title that comes at once to mind is *Moby-Dick*. By common consent, the book is Melville's masterpiece. While most Americans are familiar with the story, which involves the hunt for a great white whale, few have actually read the book, unless required to do so in high school or college. Considered by some critics to be the greatest American writer of his time, Melville has not always been highly regarded.

Melville's first book, *Typee* (1846), a narrative of his captivity among cannibals in the Marquesas, made him an overnight celebrity but also an enemy to religious conservatives. Missionaries resented his contrast of attractive pagan life in the Marquesas with the conditions of Hawaiian natives, who, in Melville's mind, had been "evangelized into beasts of burden." Melville's first book and its sequel, *Omoo* (1847), gave him financial success. Once Melville began writing, minor novels and a collection of short stories emerged, many in rapid succession. However, as his books became more learned, formally intricate, and socially critical, book sales declined. Following his last novel, *The Confidence-Man* (1857), Melville withdrew from public authorship and took a job as a minor customs official. He died in relative obscurity with most of his books out of print, his later stories and poems either privately circulated or unread. His novella *Billy Budd* was left unfinished at his death, but was published posthumously in 1924.

The centenary of his birth in 1919 coincided with a renewed interest in his writings known as the Melville revival, during which time his works were republished in multiple editions and his work experienced a significant critical reassessment. Thousands of literary scholars and journalists became engaged with his writings, primarily with *Moby-Dick* (1851), accepted now as a classic, with Captain Ahab and the White Whale familiar fixtures in popular culture. Starting in the mid-1930s, the Yale University scholar Stanley Thomas Williams supervised more than a dozen dissertations on Melville, many of them focused on psychology. In 1945, the Melville Society was founded, a non-profit organization dedicated to the study of Melville's life and works. Between 1969 and 2003, it published 125 issues of *Melville Society Extracts*, and beginning in 1999, it has published *Leviathan: A Journal of Melville Studies*, currently three issues a year.

Attempts to account for Melville's fall and rise are mixed with answers to still other questions, such as, Is Melville overrated? Which of the many voices in his fiction express his own beliefs? Are his adventures taken from eyewitness accounts or plagiarized travel narratives and other literary sources? Given the demands of the publishing industry, to what extent was he ever in control of his material? What exactly were his relations with Hawthorne? How can we explain his rediscovery in 1919 and the reassessments that followed? These and other related questions, largely academic in nature, need not concern us here, but they are fascinating and important.

Viewing his work chronologically, *Moby-Dick* occupies an appropriately central position: five books lead up to it and five lead away from it. While the original manuscript has not survived, Melville originally described it to his English publisher as "a romance of adventure." However, over time he radically transformed his initial plan, conceiving what Andrew Delbanco described in 2005 as "the most ambitious book ever conceived by an American writer."[1] On October, 1851, the book was published as *The Whale* in England in three volumes, and on November 14, in a single volume as *Moby-Dick*. Melville dedicated his book to Hawthorne: "In token of my admiration for his genius, this book is inscribed to Nathaniel Hawthorne." In December, Hawthorne noted his own view of the book in a letter to his literary colleague Evert Duyckinck: "What a book Melville has written! It gives me an idea of much greater power than his preceding ones."

The book's reputation as a "Great American Novel" was established only in the twentieth century, during the Melville revival. William Faulkner said he wished he had written the book, and D. H. Lawrence called it "one of the strangest and most wonderful books in the world" and "the greatest

1. Delbanco, *Melville*, 124.

book of the sea ever written." In 1922, the distinguished cultural historian Carl Van Doren described *Moby-Dick* as "the greatest book that has yet been written in America."

Before we examine the book's plot and its major themes, some additional biographical information may be beneficial. Melville was born in New York City, the third child of a prosperous merchant whose death in 1832 left the family in financial straits. Having an unhappy childhood and an unsettled early adulthood, at the age of twenty Melville took to the sea as a common sailor on a merchant ship and then on the whaling vessel *Acushnet*, which he deserted in the Marquesas Islands. Upon his return from Polynesia, Melville regaled his family and friends with his adventurous tales and experiences, which they urged him to put into writing. The success of these travel adventures gave him the financial success in 1847 to marry Elizabeth Shaw, the only daughter of Lemuel Shaw, Chief Justice of the Supreme Judicial Court of Massachusetts.

Continuing his writing career, Melville modeled successive books on genres then popular with readers, combining elements of the picaresque novel, the travelogue, the sentimental novel, and the Gothic thriller, but these books were not well received. In 1850, Melville borrowed money from his father-in-law to purchase a 160-acre farm in Pittsfield, Massachusetts, only a few miles from Hawthorne's home. Despite being fifteen years apart in age and temperamentally quite different, Melville and Hawthorne began reading one another's works, with Melville writing, "I feel this Hawthorne has dropped germanous seeds into my soul."

Melville began writing *Moby-Dick* in February 1850, and finished eighteen months later, a year longer than he had anticipated. Melville drew on his experience as a common sailor from 1841 to 1844, including several years on whalers, and on wide reading in whaling literature. He modeled the white whale on the notoriously hard-to-catch albino whale Mocha Dick, and the book's ending is based on the sinking of the whaleship *Essex* in 1820. The detailed and realistic descriptions of whale hunting and of extracting whale oil, as well as life aboard ship among a culturally diverse crew, are mixed with exploration of class and social status, good and evil, and the existence of God. In addition to narrative prose, Melville used styles and literary devices ranging from songs, poetry, and catalogs to Shakespearean stage directions, soliloquies, and asides. In August 1850, with the manuscript perhaps half finished, he met Hawthorne and was deeply moved by his *Mosses from an Old Manse*, which he compared to

Shakespeare in its cosmic ambitions. This encounter may have inspired him to revise and expand *Moby-Dick*, which he dedicated to Hawthorne.

Moby-Dick, published to mixed review, was a commercial failure, and was out of print by the time of Melville's death in 1891. After writing *Moby-Dick*, Melville had high hopes that his next book would please the public and restore his finances. In 1851, he told his British publisher that his new book, *Pierre; or, The Ambiguities*, was calculated to have wide appeal with elements of romance and mystery. In fact, *Pierre* was heavily psychological, and difficult in style. It was not well received, one newspaper publishing a harsh attack headlined "HERMAN MELVILLE CRAZY."

From 1853 to 1856, Melville published short fiction in magazines. In 1857 he published his last work of prose, *The Confidence-Man*. He moved back to New York City in 1863 to take a position as customs inspector. From that point, he focused his creative powers on poetry, publishing his poetic reflection on moral questions of the American Civil War in 1866. At his death, he left several works unpublished.

MOBY-DICK: PLOT AND RESPONSE

Ishmael, the narrator, announces his intent to leave Manhattan Island to board a whaling vessel. He had made several voyages as a sailor, but none as a whaler. He travels from Manhattan to New Bedford, Massachusetts, where he spends the weekend in a whalers' inn. Since the inn is full when he arrives, he must share a bed with a harpooner from the South Pacific named Queequeg. At first repulsed by Queequeg's strange habits and tattooed appearance, Ishmael eventually comes to appreciate the man's generosity and kind spirit, and the two decide to seek work on a whaling vessel together. On Sunday morning, Ishmael and Queequeg attend Father Mapple's chapel, where they hear a sermon on Jonah before taking a ferry to Nantucket, the traditional capital of the whaling industry, with one hundred ships as opposed to about twenty in New Bedford and Fairhaven.

At Nantucket, Ishmael signs up with the Quaker ship-owners Bildad and Peleg for a voyage on their whaler *Pequod*. From them he learns of the ship's mysterious captain, Ahab, who is still recovering from losing his leg in an encounter with Moby Dick. The following morning, the owners hire Queequeg. As the sailors prepare to board their vessel, a man named Elijah prophesies a dire fate should Ishmael and Queequeg join Ahab. The *Pequod* leaves Nantucket on Christmas Day, with a crew made up of men from different countries and races.

Soon the ship is in warmer waters, and Ahab makes his first appearance on deck, balancing on his prosthetic leg, made from a whale's jaw. He announces his desire to pursue and kill Moby Dick, the legendary white whale that took his leg, because he sees the whale as the embodiment of evil. Ahab nails a gold doubloon to the mast and declares that it will be the prize for the first man to sight the whale. Ahab discusses cetology (the study of the history and zoological classification of the whale) and describes the crewmembers, including the chief mate Starbuck, the second mate Stubb, and the third mate Flask.

As the ship heads toward the southern tip of Africa, whales are sighted and unsuccessfully hunted. During the hunt, a group of men, none of whom anyone on the ship's crew had seen before on the voyage, emerges from the hold. The men's leader is an exotic-looking man named Fedallah. These men constitute Ahab's private harpoon crew, smuggled aboard in defiance of Bildad and Peleg. Ahab hopes that their skills and Fedallah's prophetic abilities will help him in his hunt for Moby Dick.

The *Pequod* rounds Africa and enters the Indian Ocean. A few whales are successfully caught and processed for their oil. From time to time, the ship encounters other whaling vessels, making nine sea-encounters, or "gams," with other ships, defined as a social meeting of two or more whaling vessels, in which the two captains remain on one ship and the chief mates on the other. This series of nine meetings has both a structural and a symbolic significance, important in several ways. In addition to providing a structural element, the meetings plot the "rising curve" of Ahab's monomaniacal need to capture and kill the White Whale. Furthermore, in contrast to Ahab, Ishmael interprets the significance of each encounter individually, each ship functioning as a scroll that the narrator unrolls and reads. Finally, each encounter provides both concrete and symbolic ways of thinking about the significance of and ultimate encounter with the White Whale. To this point, Melville indicates that Moby Dick represents the forces of nature, known and unknown, that provoke both awe and fear in human beings. However, it is apparent that no one in the story, not even Ishmael, fully comprehends Moby Dick, which at the end is as much "the ungraspable phantom of life" as is the image in the water he describes in the beginning. The whiteness of the whale, for example, suggests nature in its totality, including human nature.

At the first "gam," Ahab hails the *Goney* to ask whether they have seen the White Whale, but the trumpet through which her captain tries to speak falls into the sea before he can answer. In the second "gam," with the *Town-Ho*, a concealed story of a "judgment of God" is revealed, about a defiant sailor named Steelkilt who, in an attempt to mutiny, struck a sadistic officer named Radney. However, when that officer led the chase for Moby Dick, he fell from the boat and was killed by the whale.

The *Pequod* next encounters the *Jeroboam*, which not only lost its chief mate to Moby Dick, but also is now plagued by an epidemic. The ship carries Gabriel, a crazed prophet who predicts doom for anyone who threatens Moby Dick. His predictions seem to carry some weight, as those aboard his ship who have hunted the whale have met disaster. The *Pequod* next gams with the *Jungfrau* from Bremen. Both ships sight whales simultaneously, with the Pequod winning the contest. The Pequod's next gam is with the French whaler *Bouton de Rose*, whose crew is ignorant of the germs in the gut of the diseased whale in their possession. Days later, an encounter with a harpooned whale prompts Pip, the Pequod's black cabin boy, to jump from the whaleboat. The whale must be cut loose, because Pip has become entangled in the harpoon line. Fearful for their lives, the whalers leave Pip alone in the immense sea, and by the time he is picked up, he has gone insane.

Soon after, the Pequod meets the *Samuel Enderby* of London, captained by Boomer, who lost an arm in an encounter with Moby Dick. The two captains discuss the whale; Boomer, happy simply to have survived his encounter, cannot understand Ahab's lust for vengeance. Leaving the *Samuel Enderby*, Ahab wrenches his ivory leg and orders the carpenter to fashion him another. Starbuck informs Ahab of oil leakage in the hold. Reluctantly, Ahab orders the harpooners to inspect the casks. Queequeg, sweating all day below deck, develops a chill and soon is feverish. Anticipating death, Queequeg has the ship's carpenter make him a coffin. He recovers, however, and the coffin eventually becomes the *Pequod*'s replacement life buoy.

Ahab orders a harpoon forged in the expectation that he will soon encounter Moby Dick. He baptizes the harpoon with the blood of the *Pequod*'s three harpooners. The *Pequod* gams next with the *Bachelor*, a Nantucket ship heading home full of sperm oil. Every now and then, the *Pequod* lowers its whaleboats with success. On one of those nights in the whaleboat, Fedallah prophesies that neither hearse nor coffin can be Ahab's; that before he dies, Ahab must see two hearses, one not made by mortal hands and the other made of American wood; that Fedallah will precede his captain in death; and finally, that only hemp can kill Ahab. Ahab interprets these words to mean that he will not die at sea, where there are no hearses and no hangings.

As the *Pequod* approaches the equator, Ahab scolds his quadrant for telling him only where he is and not where he will be. He dashes it to the deck, leaving no way to fix the location. That evening, a typhoon hits the ship. Lightning strikes the mast, setting the doubloon and Ahab's harpoon aglow. Ahab delivers a speech on the spirit of fire, seeing the lightning as a portent of Moby Dick. Starbuck sees the lightning as a warning, and feels tempted to shoot the sleeping Ahab to end the mad quest. After the storm ends, one of the sailors falls from the ship's masthead and drowns—a grim foreshadowing of what lies ahead.

Ahab's fervent desire to find and destroy Moby Dick continues to intensify, and the mad Pip is now his constant companion. The *Pequod* encounters two more whaling ships, the *Rachel* and the *Delight*, both of which have recently had fatal encounters with the whale. The *Rachel*, commanded by Captain Gardiner from Nantucket, is seeking survivors from one of her whaleboats that had gone after Moby Dick. Among the missing is Gardiner's son. Ahab refuses to join the search.

Twenty-four hours a day, Ahab now stands and walks the deck, while Fedallah shadows him. In the ninth and final gam, the *Pequod* meets the *Delight*, badly damaged and with five of her crew left dead by Moby Dick. Her captain shouts that the harpoon that can kill the white whale has yet to be forged, but Ahab flourishes his special lance and once more orders the ship forward. Ahab shares a moment of contemplation with Starbuck. Ahab speaks about his wife and child, calls himself a fool for spending forty years on whaling, and claims he can see his own child in Starbuck's eye. Starbuck tries to persuade Ahab to return to Nantucket to meet both their families, but Ahab simply crosses the deck and stands near Fedallah.

On the first day of the chase, Ahab smells the whale, climbs the mast, and sights Moby Dick. He claims the doubloon for himself, and lowers his boat, leaving Starbuck on board. The whale breaks Ahab's boat in two, tosses the captain out of it, and scatters the crew. On the second day of the chase, Ahab leaves Starbuck in charge of the *Pequod*. Moby Dick smashes the three boats that seek him and tangles their lines. Ahab is rescued, but his ivory leg and Fedallah are lost. Starbuck begs Ahab to desist, but Ahab vows to slay the white whale, even if he would have to dive through the globe itself to get his revenge.

On the third day of the chase, Ahab sights Moby Dick at noon. Ahab lowers his boat for a final time, leaving Starbuck again on board. Moby Dick breaches and destroys two boats. Fedallah's corpse, still entangled in the fouled lines, is lashed to the whale's back, so Moby Dick turns out to be the hearse Fedallah prophesied.

"Possessed by all the fallen angels," Ahab plants his harpoon in the whale's flank. Moby Dick smites the whaleboat, tossing its men into the sea. Only Ishmael is unable to return to the boat. He is left behind in the sea, and so is the only crewman of the *Pequod* to survive the final encounter. The whale now rams the *Pequod* and sinks it. Ahab then realizes that the destroyed ship is the hearse made of American wood in Fedallah's prophecy.

The whale returns to Ahab, who stabs at him again. As he does so, the line gets tangled, and Ahab bends over to free it. In doing so the line loops around Ahab's neck, and as the stricken whale swims away, the captain is drawn with him out of sight. Queequeg's coffin comes to the surface, the only thing to escape the vortex when the *Pequod* sank. For a day and a night, Ishmael floats on it, until the *Rachel*, still looking for its lost seamen, rescues him.

THE GREAT AMERICAN NOVEL

In his introduction to the 1998 Oxford World's Classic edition of *Moby-Dick*, Tony Tanner suggests that the novel could only have been written in America and only in the mid-nineteenth century. The country then "seemed to stand at a new height, or new edge, of triumphant dominion and expansionary confidence in the western world." Tanner and others point out that, during Melville's life, the United States emerged from a colonial society to a world power with its own significant history and mythology. There were also tremendous advances in technology—the development of the railroad, telegraph, and telephone enabling easier travel and communication. Democracy was on the rise, and the country was ready to produce literary voices of its own. Tanner's salient point is that America in the mid-nineteenth century was an ideal place and time to "generate its own epic and myth—in effect find its own Homer."

As the nineteenth century reached its middle years, the American nation yearned for a national literature commensurate with the burgeoning size of the country itself, a great American novel that might confound British literary hegemony, a native author who might outdo the great Shakespeare himself. Whether the "Master Genius" would be recognized was the moot point of Hawthorne's quizzical parable, *A Select Party*, where a youthful and poorly dressed newcomer with glowing eyes is scornfully ignored by the abstract celebrities. "And who was he? Who, but the Master Genius for whom our country is looking anxiously into the mist of time, as destined to fulfil the great mission of creating an American literature. Hewing it, as it were, out of the unwrought granite of our intellectual quarries. From him, whether molded in the form of an epic poem, or assuming a guise altogether new, as the spirit itself may determine, we are to receive our first great original work, which shall do all that remains to be achieved for our glory among the nations."[2]

Melville read these lines while he was composing his review of the book in which they appeared, Hawthorne's *Mosses from an Old Manse*. More importantly, he was also then composing *Moby-Dick*, the book Melville would dedicate to Hawthorne. Melville's review of Hawthorne echoes Hawthorne's patriotic argument for the second coming of Shakespeare. *Moby-Dick* would diverge from the messianic hopefulness by heavily underlining the Shakespearean madness, the intuitive truth that flashes forth from the mouths of Shakespeare's darkest characters, Hamlet, Timon of Athens, and particularly King Lear.

POINTS TO PONDER IN *MOBY-DICK*

An early proponent of the Melville revival, the British author E. M. Forster remarked in 1927, "*Moby-Dick* is full of meanings," adding that determining its meaning was difficult and inconclusive. *Moby-Dick*, like its author, is usually discussed in books on the American novel, but is that categorization correct? According to Howard Mumford Jones, *Moby-Dick* "is not a novel, it was never intended as a novel, and it should not be read as a novel."[3] In this regard, we recall that Melville once described his book as "a romance of adventure." Keeping in mind Hawthorne's distinction between a novel and a romance, neither adequately defines *Moby-Dick*.

This discernment brings to mind an experience I had several months ago, when I visited a public library in search of several film adaptations of

2. Hawthorne, *Tales and Sketches*, 952.
3. Jones, "Commentary," 566.

novels I was considering for this book. While there, I asked about the film version of *Moby-Dick*. They had a copy of the 1998 version, directed by Franc Roddam and starring Patrick Stewart as Captain Ahab, but it was currently signed out. Wishing to help, the receptionist suggested another version instead, featuring an actual whale hunt. I politely declined, noting that I was not interested in watching *Moby-Dick* as a whaling adventure, but rather for its symbolism.

As we explore *Moby-Dick's* symbolism and central themes, we become aware that, unlike with writing novels, Melville was not faithful to Hawthorne's description of the novel as a literary work aimed at a "minute fidelity . . . to the probable course of man's experience." For how likely is it for one to sleep with a tattooed cannibal, or to have on a ship three harpooners named Queequeg, Tashtego, and Daggoo, or a stowaway Parsee named Fedallah with a phantom boat crew, a mad sea captain, and a first mate who meditates in Shakespearean blank verse? For this reason, when asked to write an introduction to *Moby-Dick*, Joseph Conrad, who knew a great deal about sailing vessels, refused, because there was very little actual realism in these three volumes. If the term "novel" is not adequate for *Moby-Dick*, the term "romance" seems equally inadequate. What has all of the information Melville attaches to *Moby-Dick* about ectology, or about capturing and butchering whales, or about gams between whaling vessels, have to do with the spirit of "romance"?

To Henry A. Murray in 1929, *Moby-Dick* was an exploration of the unconscious. To R. P. Blackmeer in 1938, it was a "profound and obsessive image of life." To Charles H. Foster in 1961, it seemed to be an antislavery allegory. To Alan Heimert in 1963, it was a piece of American political symbolism. To Howard Mumford Jones in 1976, it was a journey book—not simply about adventure, but in the category of books such as the *Odyssey*, *Gulliver's Travels*, Dante's *Divine Comedy*, and Darwin's *Voyage of the Beagle*.

It is true that Melville once referred to *Moby-Dick* as a "romance of adventure," but "romance," as we have seen, has a special meaning. Furthermore, Melville seems also to have been haunted by the fear of being classed as a mere novelist. In a striking passage, he noted that the secret motto of his book is "*Ego non baptize te in nomine patris, sed in nomine diaboli*," a black mass parody of part of the Christian rite of baptism.[4] Melville had

---

4. This passage, meaning "I do not baptize you in the name of the father, but in the name of the devil," appears at the end of chapter 113 of *Moby-Dick* ("The Forge"), in reference to Ahab's consecration of the weapon he creates to spear the white whale, a weapon baptized in the blood of the three dark-complexioned harpooners.

earlier written to Hawthorne, speaking of his book as having been broiled in hellfire. Melville had just read Hawthorne's *The Unpardonable Sin* (that is, the story of Ethan Brand), and he was not above pulling Hawthorne's leg a bit by his contrast between the Christian assumptions behind the unpardonable sin and the diabolic quality of Captain Ahab.

Accepting Jones's categorization of *Moby-Dick* as a journey book, I would add that Melville's book is not so much a physical adventure as a spiritual one, not so much a journey of the body as a journey of the psyche—of the human soul. In 1999, Melville biographer Laurie Robertson-Lorant identified epistemology as the book's theme, contrasting Ishmael and Ahab's attitudes toward life, viewing Ishmael's open-minded and meditative stance as antithetical to Ahab's monomaniacal adherence to dogmatic rigidity.[5]

According to Nathalia Wright, Melville's characters are all preoccupied with an intense, eternal quest for "the absolute amidst its relative manifestations," a search central to Melville's work: "All Melville's plots describe this pursuit, and all his themes represent the delicate and shifting relationship between its truth and its illusion."[6] As Ishmael tries, in the opening pages of *Moby-Dick*, to offer a simple collection of literary excerpts mentioning whales, he discovers that, throughout history, the whale has taken on an incredible multiplicity of meanings. Over the course of the novel, he makes use of nearly every human discipline in his attempts to understand the essential nature of the whale. Each of these systems of knowledge, however, including art, taxonomy, and phrenology, fails to give an adequate account. The multiplicity of approaches that Ishmael takes, coupled with his compulsive need to assert his authority as a narrator and his frequent references to the limits of human observation (humans cannot see the depths of the ocean, for example), suggest that human knowledge is always limited and insufficient. When it comes to Moby Dick himself, this limitation takes on allegorical significance. The ways of Moby Dick, like those of the Christian God, are unknowable to man, and thus trying to interpret them, as Ahab does, is inevitably futile and often fatal.

It is not clear, however, what the moral and metaphysical implications of this quest for the absolute might be, because Melville did not distinguish between these aspects. Throughout his life, Melville struggled with and gave shape to the same set of epistemological doubts and metaphysical issues these doubts engendered. An obsession for the limits of knowledge

5. Robertson-Lorant, *Melville*, 279–80.

6. Wright, *Melville's Use of the Bible*, 77.

led Melville to the question of God's existence and nature, the indifference of the universe, and the problem of evil.

Melville's fiction bounces us back and forth between two visions of reality—naturalism and supernaturalism, the known and the unknown—that, though interwoven, are arranged in such a way that from within one of them we simply cannot see the other. For that reason, John Bryant and Haskell Springer, in their analysis of *Moby-Dick*, suggest perception as a central theme, namely, the difficulty of seeing and understanding, which makes deep reality hard to discover and truth hard to pin down. In chapter 36 ("The Quarter-Deck"), Ahab explains that, like all things, the evil whale wears a disguise: "All visible objects . . . are but as pasteboard masks," and Ahab is determined to "strike through the mask! How can the prisoner reach outside except by thrusting through the wall? To me, the white whale is that wall."[7] This theme pervades the novel, perhaps never so emphatically as in chapter 99 ("The Doubloon"), where each crewmember perceives the coin in a way shaped by his own personality.

Melville biographer Andrew Delbanco cites race as an example of this search for truth beneath surface differences, noting that all races are represented among the crew members of the *Pequod*. Although Ishmael initially is afraid of Queequeg as a tattooed cannibal, he soon comes to the conclusion that it is "Better [to] sleep with a sober cannibal than a drunken Christian."[8] While it may be rare for a mid-nineteenth-century American book to feature Black characters in a nonslavery context, slavery is frequently mentioned. The theme of race is primarily carried by Pip, the diminutive Black cabin boy. When we think of race and racism, one aspect Melville had in mind involved the dignity of Native Americans and their mistreatment by white colonizers. He names the whaling vessel the *Pequod*, honoring the Pequod Indian tribe that was massacred in 1637. Ishmael sees her as "a noble craft, but somehow a most melancholy! All noble things are touched with that."[9]

While race is an important topic today, and rightly so, it is a subset of a much larger topic, which concerns humanity as a whole, binding together all who belong to the human race. Melville approaches this deeper issue symbolically, through the spectrum of color, with whiteness and blackness not simply polarities, but somehow together encapsulating reality.

7. Hawthorne, *Moby-Dick*, 164.
8. Hawthorne, *Moby-Dick*, 26.
9. Hawthorne, *Moby-Dick*, 69.

Blackness, understood morally, overshadows *Moby-Dick*. Applying the touchstone of Shakespeare's tragedies to Hawthorne and Melville, the crucial trait that fascinates them is the "power of blackness," a power that derived its force from the Puritan appeal to that Calvinist sense of innate depravity. Though darkness is a virtual obsession with Hawthorne, becoming his trademark after Melville had pointed it out, it is hardly less characteristic of Melville and, as he asserts, of all thoughtful intellects.

The "blackness of darkness" (Jude 1:13 KJV), translated as "deepest darkness" in the NRSV, that intensive phrase that Melville uses twice in *Moby-Dick*, had also been invoked by Edgar Allan Poe in both *The Pit and the Pendulum* and *The Narrative of Arthur Gordon Pym*. This innate darkness is also evident in Hawthorne's *Young Goodman Brown*, particularly in the heartcry of the husband, recognizing his wife as led astray into a witches' Sabbath or black mass, for her name is Faith, and it is faith itself that Hawthorne calls into question. In *The Minister's Black Veil*, the minister speaks on behalf of Hawthorne to declare that behind every individual lie secret sins: "I look around me, and lo! on every visage a Black Veil!"[10] In *The Celestial Railroad*, Hawthorne's parody of Bunyan's *The Pilgrim's Progress*, the narrator comments on the differences between the train ride and typical pilgrimages. The passengers' bags are in a rack, not on their back, and the passengers mock true pilgrims walking along the road, carrying their own bags. However, when the narrator finally reaches the ferry that is to take him to the Celestial City, he finds that the engineer is actually the devil, and the railroad and ferry are not taking him to heaven but toward perdition.

When William Butler Yeats speaks of "the foul rag-and-bone shop of the heart," it is tempting to think of Hawthorne rummaging there; but not only Hawthorne. Herman Melville seems, at first glance, simpler: not so haunted by memories as Hawthorne, not so driven to extremes as Poe. As the youth who went to sea, the man of action relating his adventures, impulsive rather than compulsive, self-taught and extroverted, Melville seems to live up to the pioneering ideals of the American character. However, he was not content to remain merely a reporter. He wanted, as he asserted in a poem, "To wrestle with the angel, Art."

Every person has two saddles, as Melville writes in *Pierre*, one for the land and the other for the sea. *Moby-Dick* oscillates between the sea and the land, the respective extreme of danger and security, the exotic and the

---

10. Hawthorne, *Tales and Sketches*, 384.

familiar. The sea, however, is the place of discovery; "in landlessness alone resides the highest truth, shoreless, indefinite as God" (chapter 23, "The Lee Shore").[11] Moving from the known to the unknown, proceeding as we must from light toward dark, into the untried and unshored, it is noteworthy that Melville's journey starts on Christmas Day. Melville's sea is everywhere and nowhere, and his subject is timeless. He is taking us on a spiritual quest, and the spiritual journey means leaving the homeland behind. The ship is a melting pot, a joint venture. The ship is seasoned and weather-beaten, and its decks are "like the pilgrim-worshipped flagstone in Canterbury Cathedral, where Becket bled" (chapter 16, "The Ship").[12] In short, the Pequod is an appropriate stage for tragedy.

Symbols in literature are usually objects used to represent or suggest important concepts that inform and expand our appreciation of the work. *Moby-Dick* offers some of the most widely known symbols in American literature, its symbols ambiguous in enriching way: Father Mapple's pulpit; Queequeg's coffin; the *Pequod*; the white whale. Its characters are symbolic as well. Like the multivalent doubloon that Ahab offers for the white whale's capture, every character has a different meaning. No two characters are alike, symbolically or spiritually. Ishmael, the young teacher yearning for adventure, is not only Melville in his definitive role; he is also the spiritual seeker. In the Bible, Ishmael was a child born to Hagar, a mistress whom Abraham impregnated because he feared that Sarah was too old to conceive. When Isaac, the "promised" child finally arrived, Ishmael and Hagar were driven into the wilderness. Ishmael both was and was not a "child of Abraham": he occupied an anomalous position on the boundary line separating God's chosen people from the rest of humanity, thereby undoing the religious claim making that boundary absolute.

In the haunting opening sentence of *Moby-Dick*, "Call me Ishmael," Melville identifies Ishmael as an outcast seafaring "Everyman." The opening invites readers to think not what the name means but rather who Ishmael is, for the "I" in this book is not an identifiable individual. Ishmael is a larger than life representation of the individual self questing for defining insight. Melville establishes his intention early on by observing that the sea and meditation "are wedded for ever."[13] The events in which Ishmael participates amount to a series of tests that define his angle of vision and

11. Melville, *Moby-Dick*, 105.

12. Melville, *Moby-Dick*, 69.

13. Melville, *Moby-Dick*, 4.

morally justify his survival. The *Pequod*'s sole survivor, having been reborn from the watery vortex by clinging to Queequeg's coffin, Ishmael lives to tell the tale of Ahab's search for the white whale. The sole survivor, he is also the true Christian disciple, tied by a genuine bond of fraternity to a pagan "other," who in turn bequeaths him the means of survival.

Although heavy with references to the Bible and Christianity, Melville's *Moby-Dick* does not favor one race or espouse one religion, instead suggesting that goodness can be found in people of all races and creeds. Religious tolerance is a notable part of life on board the ship, with so-called heathens and Christians working side by side. The *Pequod*'s crew, a heterogeneous group of individuals whose united efforts are harnessed toward an overriding goal, is a microcosm of the social order. The chief mate is Starbuck, a Nantucket Quaker with a realist mentality whose harpooner is Queequeg; second mate is Stubb, from Cape Cod, happy-go-lucky and cheerful, whose harpooner is Tashtego, a proud, pure-blooded Indian from Gay Head; and the third mate is Flask, also from Martha's Vineyard, short and stout, whose harpooner is Daggoo, a tall African residing in Nantucket.

Despite their general inability to think for themselves, Melville gives the harpooners noble attributes: Queequeg represents essential human nature as one of nature's nobles; Daggoo, a huge black, embodies physical strength; Tashtego, the Indian, primitive spirituality; and Ahab's personal harpooner, Fedallah (his name suggests faithfulness to Allah), the essential mystery of the primitive. With his white hair wrapped in a turban like Muhammad's, Fedallah is Ahab's religious counselor. The richness and suggestiveness of Melville's details even in representing minor characters such as these serve to magnify the tragedy as a comprehensive portrait of the human condition.

While there are many notable characters in the story, the drama pivots around Ishmael and Ahab. Both, can be argued, are universal aspects of the human character: both are "Everyman." As Ahab's character unfolds, it undergoes subtle changes that mark stages in withdrawal, disorientation to reality, and ultimate delusion. The name, like Ishmael, is both biblical and archetypal. The warning of doom at the outset by a ragged stranger named Elijah identifies him with the Old Testament prophet who denounced the abominations of Ahab, king of Israel, who defied God by worshipping idols and taking the law into his own hands. Ahab, at once "ungodly" and "godlike" in his lawless defiance, is prefigured by Prometheus and Lucifer.

The dissociation in Ahab's temperament is physically represented by his loss of a leg from an earlier encounter with Moby Dick, and a lightning-caused scar running down his body. Despite his wounds scars, it is not his body but his nature that is scarred.[14] Ahab's spiritual schism is further reflected in the view of nature he sets forth on deck as he announces his intention to pursue the white whale. All visible objects, he declares, are but masks for a malevolent evil in the world. In speaking of the evil he perceives behind the perceived benign surface of experience, the irony is that he misses the evil within himself. He would strike through the mask with his harpoon to reach what is the "inscrutable malice" behind it. This is what he hates, he tells the astonished Starbuck, whose prudence prevents him from effectively responding. In the chapter "Moby Dick" (chapter 41), Ahab becomes a tragic hero of epic stature, as the image of the whale swims in his imagination as "the monomaniac incarnation of all those malicious agencies which some deep men feel eating in them, till they are left living on with half a heart and half a lung."[15] At this stage, with his thought so polarized, Ahab is enslaved by hatred that consumes him internally like a fire burning inside a lightning-struck tree. Ironically, the angler become the fish, the hunter the prey. With this insight, Melville prepares us for the final encounter between Ahab as the white whale and the whale as Ahab.

As blackness overshadows the tale, so too does whiteness. At the center of *Moby-Dick*'s concern, and organizing its fictional presentation, is the conflict between blackness and whiteness, two attitudes toward and two visions of the nature of the world. This is the opposition Ishmael formulates most clearly in "The Whiteness of the Whale," Melville's essay on whiteness (chapter 42). Whiteness is the symbol of innocence, virginity, love, happiness, and the throne of God. But whiteness is also associated with death, fear, the albatross, phantom animals, ghosts, snow-capped mountains, breakers in a storm, and other destructive items. These paradoxes are capped by a rhapsodic passage on whiteness as the enigma of the universe itself: "whiteness is not so much a color as the visible absence of color, and at the same time the concrete of all colors; all the other earthly hues . . . are but subtle deceits," so that a "palsied universe" becomes a leper, and atheists, like willful Lapland travelers failing to wear glasses, are blinded by a universal

14. As a wounded leader, physically and spiritually, Captain Ahab reminds us of the Fisher King, the wounded king of the Grail Castle. As long as the King is wounded, his kingdom remains in desolation. As a land mirrors the condition of its ruler, so a ship mirrors the condition of its captain.

15. Melville, *Moby-Dick*, 183.

shroud. "And all of these things the Albino whale [is] the symbol."[16] Whiteness is colorless, yet an all-color; its qualities thereby cancel out, leaving the blankness of nothing, which inspires our dread. We might also note that, however implicitly affirmative Ishmael's answers might be, his words putting forth these negations are questions, not answers. Questions create a waiting, an emptiness, a void to be filled by the future. Ishmael will not supply answers because the heart of his emotion-conveyed insights is absence, not presence.

In *Moby-Dick*, whiteness becomes a unifying force, suggesting the omnipresence of the White Whale, though the whale appears to Ahab and his crew only in the book's final three chapters. Until then, it exists as images in the minds of characters, not only aboard the *Pequod*, but also on the whalers she meets. One after another, in responding to Ahab's probing questions about the whale, the sailors of all levels of humanity indicate their limited angles of vision toward nature.

To some, the White Whale is a myth; to others, he is immortal. Since he is an irreducible symbol, an archetype of archetypes, there is no cogency in the varying labels with which his interpreters have attempted to tag him. But what is the White Whale to Ahab? Ishmael grants that Ahab views the whale as an embodiment of evil, though Ishmael himself is not so sure. He often sees both sides of a question, never more so than in "The Whiteness of the Whale," where he tells us that Moby Dick's whiteness might represent good or evil, glory or damnation, all colors or the "visible absence of color."

For Ahab's interpretation, it is helpful to consider his comments in the pivotal chapter 36. There, the captain says he sees Moby Dick as a "mask," behind which lies a great power whose dominance Ahab refuses to accept. Ahab sees that inscrutable power as evil. Some scholars argue that it is not the whale, or the force behind the whale, that is evil; the evil is in Ahab. Others see the captain as simply insane. Ahab is obsessed as he rants about attacking the force behind the façade of Moby Dick. He wants to kill the whale in order to reach that force. Ahab seems to want to be a god. As great and charismatic a man as he can be in his finest moments, the captain is destructively egocentric and mad for power. To Ahab, the White Whale represents that power that limits and controls man. Ahab sees it as evil incarnate; but perhaps it is simply the inscrutable and unconquerable power of Nature, embodied in a smart fish!

16. Melville, *Moby-Dick*, 195–96.

That the biggest fish should end by getting away is the conventional conclusion to an angler's yarn. That this particular monster of the deep should confound his pursuers, with a flip of his ship-sinking tail, is foreordained by the very conditions of the three-day chase. When the voice speaks out of the whirlwind to Job, saying, "Can you draw out Leviathan with a fishhook? . . . Can you . . . pierce its jaw with a hook?" (Job 41:1–2), the whale—which Puritans identified with the devil—is the final instance of divine inscrutability. If *Moby-Dick* holds any answer to the enigmas that perplex humankind, he disappears into the depths without disclosing it.

Chapter 11

Fyodor Dostoyevsky's
Notes from Underground

WHENEVER THE TOPIC OF SPIRITUALITY (or religion) and modern literature arises, one of the first authors that comes to mind—perhaps the first—is the great Russian novelist Fyodor Dostoyevsky (1821–1881). Unquestionably, the novel that best exhibits the connection between his literary artistry and his spiritual impulse is *The Brothers Karamazov*. We have it on Dostoyevsky's own testimony that he wished this, his last novel, to serve as a vehicle for the vindication of Christian Orthodox faith. That book, however, does not serve as our focus here. Rather, our thoughts turn to an earlier work, to his novella *Notes from Underground*.

In life and in death, Dostoyevsky was a brooding religious thinker, neither theologian nor philosopher, yet somehow both. He came from a pious Russian family, and knew the gospels from earliest childhood. As a child, he would be called upon to recite prayers in the presence of guests. His brother Andrei recalled that the family unfailingly attended Mass every Sunday and on saints' days, with vespers the previous night, in the church attached to the Moscow hospital where his father worked as a doctor. His parents were not conventional congregants, but deeply religious. In his *Diary of a Writer* (the series of journalistic essays in which, in the last decade of his life, he bares his soul), Dostoyevsky describes how before he learned to read, his imagination was fired by events from the lives of Christian saints, modeling asceticism, compassion, suffering, humility, and self-sacrifice, based on the example of Christ. Dostoyevsky's mother taught him to read from a religious primer. Intended to be learned by heart, it contained many of the Bible stories that later played a key role in Dostoyevsky's novels. It was also in childhood that he learned to associate the Russian people with deep spirituality.

From 1838 to 1843, Dostoyevsky studied at the Military Engineering Academy in St. Petersburg, where he was known for spending his free time reading. An officer at the academy noted that Dostoyevsky was very religious and faithfully observed all the obligations of the Orthodox Church. After lectures on religion, he would stay behind and engage in long conversations with his professor. His version of Christianity, free from dogmatic content but focused on applying Christian love socially, earned him the respect of his fellow students. Enlisting in the army, he resigned in 1844 for the precarious life of a professional writer.

For a while, Dostoyevsky wavered in both his religious views and his religious observance, finding himself caught between two irresistible imperatives: his commitment to Orthodoxy and the example of Christ, and his rage at the oppression of the lower social classes. His radical political views led to his arrest in 1849. Arrested for belonging to a literary group that discussed and promoted banned books critical of tsarist Russia, he was sentenced to death, but the sentence was commuted at the last moment. He spent four years in a Siberian prison camp, during which time he, like his fellow convicts, was given a copy of the New Testament, the only book they were allowed in prison.

His imprisonment was followed by four additional years of compulsory military service in exile. His outlook on life, and with it his spirituality, underwent lasting change as a result of his suffering and exile. During this time his faith in Christ was revived, and, like the Russian people, actually sustained and strengthened through long periods of suffering. On his release in 1854, he wrote a now-famous and much quoted letter to Natalia Fonvizina, from whose hand he had received his copy of the New Testament: "I have heard from many sources that you are very religious ... [and] it is because of what I experienced and felt myself, that I tell you that there are moments when one thirsts for faith like 'parched grass,' and finds it, for the very reason that truth shines more clearly in affliction." Then he concludes, "Even if someone were to prove to me that the truth lay outside Christ, I should prefer to remain with Christ than with the truth."[1]

1. Cited in Leatherbarrow, *Cambridge Companion to Dostoevskii*, 155–56.

In the following years, Dostoyevsky worked as a journalist, publishing and editing several magazines. He began to travel around western Europe, intrigued by progressive European ideas. In spite of the occasional moments of tranquility and his ecstatic commitment to Christ, the picture we have of Dostoyevsky as he returned to Russia at the close of the 1850s is that of a troubled, questing spirit, open to intense momentary mystical experiences, who became progressively convinced of the spiritual treasures in the soul of ordinary Russian people and of the damage done to the Russian spirit by Westernization.

At this time he developed a gambling addiction, which led to financial hardship, but eventually he achieved fame, becoming one of the most widely read and highly regarded Russian authors. His most acclaimed novels include *Crime and Punishment* (1866), *The Idiot* (1869), *Demons* (1872), and *The Brothers Karamazov* (1880), in addition to a body of work consisting of twelve novels, four novellas, sixteen short stories, and other works. Many literary critics rate him as one of the greatest novelist in world literature, and some of his works are considered highly influential masterpieces. His 1864 novella *Notes from Underground* is considered to be one of the first works of existentialist literature.

In his later years, while accepting the need to take the best of Western civilization, he called for a return to Russian values. Europe, he believed, had long ago sold its soul to the principle of abstract rationalism, legalism, and individualism, which the Catholic Church had inherited from Rome and passed on to Protestantism and then to socialism, which inevitably became atheistic. Russian Orthodoxy, on the other hand, with its ideals of universality and reconciliation, and its abilities to unite diverse peoples in a grand synthesis, had preserved its sense of organic community in its conception of "*sobernost*" (spiritual oneness). There is no doubt that the development of a coherent worldview along these lines helped to stabilize Dostoyevsky's intellectual and emotional life and to restore his respectability in Russian high society. In later years, he gained not only the admiration of Russia's political and religious leadership, but also of the general populace. His funeral in 1881, conducted at Alexander Nevsky Monastery in St. Petersburg, was attended by over thirty thousand people.

Despite his fame, it must be noted that many non-Russian admirers of Dostoyevsky have not found his Slavophile ideas persuasive. In the first place, there is a strident, nationalistic tone to these ideas. Furthermore, this ideology casts little light on what is original and insightful in Dostoyevsky's major fiction, having little in common with those qualities that establish him as a world-ranking author. Actually, not a single character in Dostoyevsky's great novels—and that includes the narrators—subscribes to his personal philosophy as a whole. In fact, it is not the ideology of the later Dostoyevsky but the struggles of the earlier Dostoyevsky that give us the most valuable clues to the reading of his novels. And this should not surprise us, for as Dostoyevsky regularly reminds us, it is not the destination but the journey that matters.

What one observes in Dostoyevsky's novels and particularly in the hero of *Notes from Underground* (the Underground Man, as he is known, is both narrator and protagonist in this novella), is a reflection on the process of discovery—or rediscovery—of the Christian tradition, in the face of its opponents. It is a process of rethinking Christianity in dialogue, a process that reached no final conclusion in his novels, whatever may have been the case with his own spiritual pilgrimage. Writing *Notes from Underground* in 1864, on the occasion of the death of his first wife, Dostoyevsky reflects in his notebooks for that year that to love another person as oneself according to Christ's commandment is impossible, due to resistance by one's ego. That, however, is not the end of the matter, for Dostoyevsky affirms that Christ alone was able to do this, and he is the perpetual ideal toward which we must strive, for Christ represents the ultimate development of the human personality. Noting that annihilating the ego is not possible for humans in this life, Dostoyevsky made this argument the cornerstone of his belief in immortality. Therefore, on earth the individual is in development, transitional and unfinished. When Dostoyevsky says that affliction (which includes spiritual despair) prompts faith, that becomes the key to understanding his fiction. It is as if his major works revolve around some contemporary challenge to Christianity, some expression of unbelief, to which Dostoyevsky expects his readers to work out the appropriate Christian response. This is certainly true of *Notes from Underground*.

NOTES FROM UNDERGROUND: PLOT AND RESPONSE

Notes from Underground is about a man who is disenchanted with society, and seeks to explain his alienation through a series of journal notes and fragments from his daily life. The isolated, bitter individual, whom critics call the Underground Man, is a retired civil servant living in St. Petersburg, and his "notes" consist of a confused and often contradictory set of memoirs describing his alienation from modern society. The story is divided into two sections.

The first part, entitled "Underground," is set in the 1860s, when the Underground Man is forty years old. This part of the story is told in monologue form, with ideological allusions and complex rants challenging the political climate of the period, including nihilism, rational egoism, utilitarianism, and particularly the utopian idealism displayed in Russian philosopher Nikolay Chernyshevsky's popular novel, *What is to Be Done?* This section introduces the protagonist, explaining his theories about his antagonistic position toward society. The second part, entitled "Apropos of the Wet Snow," describes specific events in the Underground Man's life in the 1840s, when he was twenty-four years old. In a sense, this section serves as a practical illustration of the more abstract ideas the Underground Man sets forth in the first section.

The narrator introduces himself as a man who lives "underground." He refers to himself as a spiteful person because every act is dictated by his spitefulness. Then he suddenly admits that he cannot truly be spiteful, because he finds it is impossible to be anything at all: he can't be spiteful or heroic; he can only be nothing. This is because he is a man of acute consciousness, and such a person is automatically rendered inactive because he considers too many consequences of an act before he performs it, and therefore never gets around to doing anything. In contrast, a person who is not very intelligent can constantly perform all sorts of actions because he never bothers to consider the consequences.

The first words we hear from the Underground Man tell us that he is "a sick man . . . a wicked man . . . an unattractive man," whose self-loathing and spite have crippled and corrupted him. Being a highly intelligent and well-read man, he believes that his knowledge of modern society accounts for his misery. While he appreciates the Romantic idea of "the beautiful and lofty," he is aware of its absurdity in the context of his narrow, mundane existence. Disillusioned with all philosophy, he has reached a point of inactivity and ennui.

It is easy for other people to classify themselves, but the Underground Man knows that no simple classification can define the essence of one's existence. Therefore, he can only conclude that he is nothing. Yet in society, the scientists and the materialists are trying to define exactly what a person is in order to create a society that will function for people's best advantage. The Underground Man has great contempt for nineteenth-century utilitarianism, a school of thought that appears to him as deterministic, attempting to use mathematical formulas and logical proofs to align human desires with social progress. The Underground Man objects to this utilitarian trend, maintaining that no one can actually know what a person's best interest is. Such a society would have to be formulated on the theory that humans are rational beings who always act for their best advantage. However, history proves that humans seldom act this way.

The Underground Man then points out that some people love things that are not to their best advantage. Many people, for example, need to suffer and are ennobled by suffering; yet, the scientist and the rationalist want to remove suffering from their utopian society, thereby removing something that humans need. What the Underground Man wants is not scientific certainty but the freedom to choose his own way of life. Simply put, the rule that two plus two equals four angers him because he wants the freedom to say two plus two equals five. However, nature's "stone wall" stands before him, thwarting his free will.

The Underground Man concludes that for the person of conscious intelligence, the best thing to do is to do nothing. His justification for writing these *Notes from Underground* is that every person has some memory they wish to purge from their being, and the Underground Man is going to tell his most oppressing memory. The second part of the novella consists of three segments that describe such specific events. This section describes interactions between the Underground Man and various people who inhabit his world: soldiers, former schoolmates, and prostitutes. The Underground Man is so alienated from these people that he is incapable of normal interaction with them. He treats them with a mixture of disgust and fear that results in his own remorse and self-loathing. He lives an isolated and gloomy existence with no friends or contacts other than his colleagues at work. To escape the boredom of this life, he turns to a life of imagination. There he can create scenes in which he has been insulted and also create ways of revenging himself. These events, however, never take place, for he is unable to fulfill his conceptions.

The first segment of the second part of the novella describes the Underground Man's obsession with an officer who once insulted him in a pub. This officer frequently passes him on the street, seemingly without noticing him. He sees the officer on the street and thinks of ways to take revenge, eventually borrowing money to buy an expensive overcoat and bumping into the officer to assert his equality. To the Underground Man's surprise, the officer ignores him.

In the second segment, the Underground Man follows some school acquaintances who are planning a party for Zverkov, one of their number, who is being transferred out of the city. He decides to meet them for dinner at the appointed hour, but they fail to tell him that the time has been changed to six instead of five, so he arrives early. He gets into an argument with them, alternately insulting them and craving their attention and friendship. Later that evening, the others go without him to a secret brothel, and in his rage, he follows them there. He arrives at the brothel to confront Zverkov, but he and the others have already retired with prostitutes to other rooms. At that point he encounters an attractive young prostitute named Liza.

The third segment begins with Liza and the Underground Man lying silently in the dark together. The Underground Man confronts Liza with an image of her future, delivering impassioned words about the terrible fate that awaits her if she continues to sell her body. Liza believes she can survive and rise up through the ranks of her brothel as a means of achieving her dreams of functioning successfully in society. However, as the Underground Man points out in his rant, such dreams are based on the utopian trust of the societal systems in place as well as of humanity's ability to avoid corruption and irrationality in the process. He ends by giving her his address and leaves.

Back in his apartment, he is overcome by the fear of Liza coming to his dilapidated apartment after appearing such a "hero" to her, and in the middle of an argument with his servant, she arrives. He then curses her and takes back everything he had said to her at the brothel, telling her he had actually been mocking her. Near the end of his rage, he wells up in tears after admitting that he had only sought to control and humiliate her. He starts criticizing himself, admitting that he was in fact horrified by his own poverty and embarrassed by his situation. Liza realizes how pitiful he is and embraces him. The Underground Man cries out "They—they won't let me—I—can't be good!"

Despite his confession, he contrives to demean her, and, before she leaves, he stuffs a five ruble note into her hand, which she throws onto the table (it is implied that the Underground Man engaged in sexual activity with Liza and that the note is compensation for her). Hurt and confused, she goes out to the street. He tries to catch her as she goes out but cannot find her and never hears from her again. Dismayed, the Underground Man decides to end his notes. In a footnote at the end of the novel, Dostoevsky reveals that the Underground Man is unable to make even the simple decision to stop writing, as Dostoevsky states that the notes continue beyond the point at which he has chosen to cut them off.

POINTS TO PONDER IN *NOTES FROM UNDERGROUND*

Several years ago, a group of students joined Dr. John Mark Scott, popular Professor of Russian Studies, at the Union Grill, a popular hangout a block from the Washington & Jefferson College campus in downtown Washington, Pennsylvania. Dr. Scott often met informally with students at designated local spots for conversation and lively banter, and that afternoon's gathering was typical. Hearing the name Dostoyevsky, a brash sophomore joined the group and informed those gathered that he fully understood Dostoyevsky's literary work, at which point Dr. Scott invited the student to visit him in his office, noting, "I did my doctoral dissertation on Mr. Dostoyevsky, and I'm not sure I understand him at all!"

Thinking of what Dr. Scott might have said to the impetuous sophomore, I recall my first encounter with Dostoyevsky's novels when, as a college sophomore enrolled in a course in psychology, I was required to read Dostoyevsky's psychological thriller, *Crime and Punishment*. Distressed and intrigued by the novel's exploration of the deteriorating mental stability of Raskolnikov, the impoverished former student who murdered an old pawnbroker, I engaged in long conversations with my psychology professor about Dostoyevsky's intentions, particularly as they related to the issue of religion and truth.

Dr. Scott's point about the inscrutability of Dostoyevsky's works is particularly relevant regarding *Notes from Underground*, for this novella can be understood politically, morally, psychologically, philosophically, and spiritually. Furthermore, in each of these categories, scholarly interpretations are legion. The book's nameless hero is a profoundly alienated individual, in whose brooding self-analysis there is a search for the true and the good in a world of relative values and few absolutes. Moreover, the novel introduces themes—moral, religious, political, and social—that dominate Dostoyevsky's later works. Aside from its own compelling qualities, *Notes from Underground* offers readers an ideal introduction to the creative imagination, profundity, and uncanny psychological insights of one of the most influential novelists of the nineteenth century. While all of Dostoyevsky's novels are challenging to read, *Notes from Underground* is perhaps Dostoyevsky's most difficult work, in part because Dostoyevsky included diverse ideas succinctly, expressing them with great intensity but without elaboration. In recounting the condition of his Underground Man, whose remarkable intellect is thwarted by a rebellious and fugitive will, Dostoyevsky created a literary protagonist whose illogical caprice and defiant suffering anticipate tendencies of modern thinkers such as Nietzsche, Freud, and Sartre.

In the 1860s, Russia was beginning to absorb the ideas and culture of Western Europe at an accelerated pace, nurturing an unstable local climate. Russia experienced growth in revolutionary activity accompanying a general restructuring of tsardom where liberal reforms, enacted by an unwieldy autocracy, only induced greater social and political tension. Many of Russia's intellectuals were engaged in debate with both Westernizers and Slavophiles over whether to import Western reforms or promote pan-Slavic traditions. Although Tsar Alexander emancipated the serfs in 1861, Russia was still a post-medieval, traditional peasant society.

When *Notes from Underground* was written, there was an intellectual ferment regarding religious philosophy and utopian ideals. Dostoyevsky's work challenged the implications of the ideological drive toward a utopian society. Utopianism largely pertains to a society's collective dream, but what troubles the Underground Man is this very idea of collectivism. The point the Underground Man makes is that individuals will ultimately rebel against a collectively imposed idea of paradise; utopian ideals will always fail because of the underlying irrationality of human beings.

In the early 1860s, Russian philosopher Nikolay Chernyshevsky's *What is to Be Done?* was widely discussed and debated. Written in response to Ivan Turgenev's *Fathers and Sons* (1862), Chernyshevsky's chief character, Vera Pavlovna, escapes the control of her family and an arranged marriage to seek economic independence. The novel advocates the creation of small socialist cooperatives based on the Russian peasant commune, but one oriented toward industrial production. The book became an ideal of the early socialist underground in Russia. Despite his minor role, Rakhmetov, one of the characters in the novel, became an emblem of the philosophical materialism and nobility of the Russian laboring masses. Chernyshevsky promoted the idea that the intellectual's duty was to educate and lead the masses in Russia along a path of socialism that bypassed capitalism.

In *Notes from Underground*, Dostoyevsky reacted against the utopian and utilitarian politics of Chernyshevsky's novel, but he did so novelistically, for Dostoyevsky's artistry operates novelistically far better than systematically. Dostoyevsky reacted angrily against the fact that Chernyshevsky's characters fulfilled the needs of egalitarianism but had no psychological or inner motivation for doing so. To counter Chernyshevsky's heroes, Dostoyevsky invented an anti-hero, an unnamed person so insignificant that he tends to be ignored, and so insecure about existing at all that he regularly and offensively demands attention. The Underground Man challenges Chernyshevsky's doctrine in many ways, particularly his writing a novel made up of exemplary characters and commendable actions but lacking an interior life.

In practice, Dostoyevsky's Underground Man does nothing exemplary. Rather, he theorizes about determinism and disagrees with its implication that human actions are entirely behavioristic and external in origin, reacting to stimuli like "piano keys," that is, as predictably as logarithms. As is evident, the Underground Man often acts contrary to his external interests, at times ignoring them altogether.

Like *Crime and Punishment*, Dostoyevsky's *Notes from Underground* is profoundly psychological. In Dostoyevsky's time, the boundary between psychology and philosophy was still indistinct, and the study of the psyche merged inseparably with that of religion, politics, and the scientific study of the natural world. As a person of his time, Dostoyevsky was familiar with the classic Greek theory of the four humors or body fluids—blood, black bile, phlegm, and yellow bile—their diversity within individuals was believed to determine their temperament. If the fluids were balanced, the individual was said to possess a balanced personality, but if one element dominated the rest, this resulted in four less-balanced personality types, called Sanguine, Melancholic, Phlegmatic, and Choleric.

In the fourth century BCE, Plato had written in *The Republic* of four kinds of character that clearly corresponded with these four temperaments. Plato was more interested in the individual's contribution to society than in underlying temperament, so he named the Sanguine temperament the Artisan, endowed with artistic sense (driven by imagery and likely drawn to the arts, crafts, and creativity in general) and playing an aesthetic role in society. He named the Melancholic temperament the Guardian, endowed with common sense (driven by honor, duty, and trust in others and drawn to traditional leadership roles) and playing a caretaking role in society. He named the Phlegmatic temperament the Rationalist, endowed with reasoning ability (driven by cold and calm reason and likely drawn to logical, mathematical fields) and playing the role of logical investigator in society. And he named the Choleric temperament the Idealist, endowed with intuitive sensibility (driven by intuition and insight and likely drawn to activities involving ethics, relationships, and establishing harmony) and playing a moral role in society. A generation after Plato, Aristotle defined character in terms of happiness and not, as his mentor Plato had done, in terms of virtue. Aristotle identified four sources of happiness: sensual pleasure, acquiring assets, logical investigation, and moral virtue.

This background on temperament was known by Dostoyevsky, and may help explain why, when he refers to the Underground Man's liver as diseased at the start of *Notes from Underground*, it is a way of saying that he is psychologically unstable. In the 1850s and 1860s, around the time Dostoyevsky wrote his psychological novels, humorism began to fall out of favor, due to the advent of germ theory, which showed that many diseases previously thought to be humoral were caused by pathogens.

Dostoyevsky was also acquainted with Plato's theory of the tripartite soul, with reason, passion, and appetite competing for control. However, like most of his contemporaries, Dostoyevsky drew his psychological understanding from two great traditions, both ancient yet influenced by competing nineteenth-century schools of thought: the tradition of the neurologists and that of the alienists. Philosophically, the neurologists were materialists; they reduced perception and consciousness to activity of the nerves and senses, setting the stage for positivists and behaviorists such as Ivan Pavlov (1849–1936).

Philosophically, Dostoyevsky rejected this neurological psychology, along with the varieties of nihilism, rationalism, positivism, scientism, atheism, socialism, internationalism, and feminism that contemporary materialists favored. He felt closer to the work of the practical healers of psychic ailments, then called alienists, a tradition having both religious and secular roots. In the eighteenth century, the idea of "animal magnetism" had been popularized by Friedrich Anton Mesmer (1733–1815), who claimed to use techniques for controlling bodily fluids, a process similar to what makes magnets work. He held séances where he hypnotized people and sometimes produced certifiable cures. Hypnotists of that time explored dreams, hallucinations, memories, and aberrant actions, using the concept of the unconscious to explain diseases and strange behavior, a process still used today by hypnotists, psychotherapists, psychic healers, and spiritual healers.

Alienism and the sensationalist techniques practiced by alienists had a profound influence on Romantic writers such as E. T. A. Hoffman, Alexandre Dumas, Charles Dickens, Nathaniel Hawthorne, Edgar Allan Poe, and the English Gothic novelists, all of whom used the hypnotic tradition to shape their plots, their imagery, and the relationships among their characters. We see this blurring of the line between fantasy and reality in Dostoyevsky, some of whose characters lose contact with reality. While there is nothing new in Dostoyevsky's use of the novel to explore unusual states of mind, he made it a major instrument for investigating one of the key elements of psychology, which Poe called the perverse and Dostoyevsky called the paradoxical. In this regard, Dostoyevsky is often associated with modern existentialist writers such as Sartre and Camus, for like them, his fiction involves gloom, paradox, suffering, violence, self-will, self-pity, hysteria, and other exaggerated and sometimes pathological emotions. As noted above, these topics also became the stock in trade for most popular authors of the nineteenth century, including the Gothic and sensationalist novelists of that period. In Dostoyevsky's case, however, victims turn into victors. (If classic tragedy is about the weakness of the strong, Dostoyevsky's novels are about the power of the weak.)

This insight was not original with Dostoyevsky. Jesus, for example, and his follower Paul of Tarsus, often spoke about strength in weakness, and Dostoyevsky was deeply Christian. Dostoyevsky's contribution to psychology and spirituality lies not in the originality of his discoveries, but rather in the way he made the psychological novel an instrument for exploring the relation between characters' ideas and their drives and personalities. And because his novelistic, religious, social, and psychological imperatives each reinforced the others, he could control the elements of his fiction to achieve the integrity of impact that made his vision of humanity particularly contagious.

Although religious motifs are difficult to find in *Notes from Underground*, religion is central in the Underground Man's obsession with philosophical questions. Like the Underground Man, Dostoyevsky's characters grapple mightily with ultimate questions, functioning as surrogate for their author and his philosophical opponents. Dostoyevsky's audience, prompted by the richly nuanced expression of his spiritual and philosophical interests in *Notes from Underground*, *The Brothers Karamazov*, and other novels, have long accepted him not only as a consummate artist, but also as a great visionary. To Nikolai Berdyaev, the great Russian existentialist, Dostoyevsky was "one of Russia's greatest metaphysicians."

As is well known, Dostoyevsky was both a philosopher and a philosopher's problem, for his principal characters do not necessarily represent Dostoyevsky's point of view. Furthermore, they often disagree radically with one another on fundamental questions. While his characters employ different points of view, this does not mean Dostoyevsky was uncertain or conflicted. He depicted such tension in his fiction for dramatic purposes. He was, as Victor Terras pointed out, an excellent "devil's advocate."[2] Dostoyevsky laid out contradictory views so fairly and forcefully that there is a temptation to think he wanted to believe all of them. He did so, not only artistically, but also for spiritual reasons—to make his readers think. To existentialists, Dostoyevsky resembles Søren Kierkegaard, the Danish philosopher, for on the subject of faith versus reason, Dostoyevsky is much like Kierkegaard, siding with faith and pushing the opposition between the two to the point of paradox.

It is obvious from Dostoyevsky's writings that he did not consider himself a rationalist, a designation he typically reserved for his philosophical antagonists, the Russian representatives of Western European Enlightenment thinking. There is something higher, he noted, than the conclusions of reason. He believed that some fundamental religious issues could not fully be apprehended by reason and hence could only be resolved with certainty by faith. Yet Dostoyevsky was not an "irrationalist," as commonly claimed. For him, reason is simply not final or infallible. Something more is required. Hence, his devotion to Christian faith.

Unlike most Christians, Dostoyevsky was not interested in systematic theology; indeed, he was not much interested philosophically in debating or even in comprehending God. His philosophy, however, does have a singular focus: it is decidedly anthropocentric. In other words, his worldview was not prompted by abstract cosmological or epistemological consensus, but rather by an obsession with humanity. More precisely, he wished to understand the condition of being human, or, as he put it in a notebook, to find the "man in man," that is, the essence of humanity.

At an early age, Dostoyevsky viewed humanity as a mystery to be solved. Over the years, his writings suggest that he grew increasingly confident that he had solved the puzzle of humanity, at least to the extent that

2. Terras, *Reading Dostoevsky*, 6.

anyone in the world could solve it. We see this realization incipiently in *Notes from Underground* and more fully in *The Brothers Karamazov*, his last novel. In *Notes from Underground*, Dostoyevsky originally included a passage in chapter 10 of part 1 that spoke of the need for faith and Christ, but censors deleted it. Aesthetically and rhetorically, it was best to leave the content of Dostoyevsky's ideal in his hero's existentialist malaise. For had the Underground Man realized that he needed faith in Christ, he would have ceased to be "underground."

As scholars indicate, Dostoyevsky conceived the Underground Man as a "satirical parody," one who exemplifies the dire consequences of taking to the limit the radically deterministic and materialistic ideas of the 1860s, but without having anything to replace or transcend them. He is also a cautionary figure of universal significance who, despite his cynical wit, suffers from genuine existential dilemmas, a person of intense feelings who protests against being regarded as an object, against being reified in the name of science. Dostoyevsky's depiction of an acutely self-conscious person registering his awareness of the far-reaching implications of science and technology on his thoughts and feelings is what makes this work seem so astonishingly modern, and so relevant to present dilemmas.

In this respect, I recall how in the 1950s and 1960s, amidst cultural upheaval and moral confusion, the American theologian Francis Schaeffer relocated to Switzerland to establish his L'Abri Center, a place of refuge and retreat where a generation of young, liberally educated Christians could go to debate and ponder the future of Christianity and theism. In the United States, R. C. Sproul took a similar approach at his Ligonier Center.

Schaeffer, a theological conservative, took an intellectual approach to his faith, asking his protégés to rethink medieval theology, choosing Augustine over Pelagius, Aquinas, and eventual Liberal theologians. In Pelagius, he found too much humanism and not enough grace, and in Aquinas, too much rationality and not enough evangelical faith. As it turned out, Schaeffer's apologetic was simply an intellectualized variant of fundamentalist evangelism, but he cautioned his audience not to get to the answer—trust in Jesus' saving work—too quickly. Christian evangelism, he argued, was adequate for the apologetic task, but it should devote its focus on the problem—sin and reliance on reason—and only then, to speak of the answer—salvation grounded in grace alone. For that reason, Schaeffer encouraged his students to immerse themselves in modern culture and thought, not in order to accept its methodology and values, but in order to understand its weakness and ultimate bankruptcy. The answer, he assumed, would be evident to anyone willing to explore the problem—the failure of human autonomy to satisfy the longings of the human soul. While Schaeffer would have faulted much in Dostoyevsky's Christianity, as we learn in *Notes from the Underground*, both he and Dostoyevsky provide an apologetic to Christianity by focusing on the questions. The answers, both agreed, would be evident to those willing to explore the problem.

While *Notes from Underground* leaves the answers to the Underground Man's problems unspoken, the book poses the question, "What happens to modern intellectuals who lose their sense of the holy and become wholly committed to fashionable secular ideas?" The Underground Man is Dostoyevsky's answer. In creating a weird, irrational, convoluted character, Dostoyevsky uses a negative route to counter strong modern challenges to religion such as rationalism, deterministic physics, historical optimism, utilitarian ethics, nihilistic amoralism, and the inadequacy of human language to convey ultimate truth. He does so in this novel by displaying the dreadful consequences for the individual and for society of such ideas taken to their logical conclusion, and by hinting that there is a better way. He accomplished his intention by creating an unattractive anti-hero—the antithesis of a spiritual person—who lives in the underworld, viewing life "through a crack under the floor."

In later novels, we come closer to Dostoyevsky's "answer." In *The Idiot*, he produces a Christlike figure in Prince Myshkin, who displays all the qualities emphasized in the Beatitudes of the Sermon on the Mount. At first sight, *The Idiot* seems an exception to the rule that Dostoyevsky's novels focus on the "mutinous crew" rather than on the captain of faith. The mutinous crew eventually does come forth as the novel progresses, at the expense of Myshkin's saintliness. Nevertheless, Dostoyevsky succeeds in holding up to the other characters an image of the best in themselves and a hint of a supernatural realm beyond the natural world.

The Devils, Dostoyevsky's next major novel, contains many religious motifs, some notable dialogues on religious topics, hallucinations of the devil, and a holy fool. There is, however, little doubt that the mutinous crew is in command here as well, and it is therefore not surprising that many of Dostoyevsky's religious motifs are apocalyptic. In *The Brothers Karamazov*, much is made of the Grand Inquisitor, set in the time of the Spanish Inquisition. Into this scene steps the figure of Christ who, having performed a number of acts that echo the gospel narrative, finds himself in the Inquisitor's cell, where the latter proceeds to justify his procedure at great length. The Church, offering mystery, miracle, and authority, has replaced Christ, the Inquisitor declares. Christ has no right to come back and interfere. In Dostoyevsky's account, Christ makes no answer, but kisses the aged Inquisitor and is allowed to leave. In his segment on the Grand Inquisitor, Dostoyevsky includes powerful and irrefutable arguments against the Christian faith: the first, that a God who permits severe human suffering is unworthy of worship; the second, that Christ fundamentally overestimated the spiritual resources of the human race and the ability of human beings to act as morally free agents. Dostoyevsky was aware of the strength of these arguments, but as he relates later on, the source of the Christian life is not the atheist's abstract love for humanity, but rather the active love that comes to believers from beyond the natural world. For Dostoyevsky, if humans view the world with agape love, they will come to love all things, and in so doing, comprehend the divine mystery more every day.

Such a view corresponds with the apophatic strain in Orthodox theology, according to which the essence of God is unknowable, but that a sense of the presence of God is attained through tranquility and inner silence, for which all mental images are obstacles. Such an approach certainly harmonizes with Dostoyevsky's view that human language is incompetent to express the deepest truths. As noted earlier, Dostoyevsky always insisted that the important thing was not the achievement of the goal but rather the process of striving to reach it. And this may well be the treasure of Dostoyevsky's legacy. What we cannot doubt, in reading Dostoyevsky, is that we are in the presence of a genius wrestling with the problems of rethinking Christianity in the modern age.

CHAPTER 12

D. H. Lawrence's *The Rainbow*

DAVID HERBERT LAWRENCE (1885–1930) was a gifted writer, but more than his story-telling ability, he had a great deal to say. Admired as an author, he had a philosophic mind, using fiction as his medium. He had much to say, not only literarily and philosophically, but also spiritually. Many of his major novels, particularly *Sons and Lovers*, *The Rainbow*, and *Women in Love*, do not end well, so if you like happy endings, his novels are probably not for you. However, if you like to keep thinking about topics and characters long after you have finished a novel, Lawrence's writings might well belong high on your list of required reading.

If asked about Lawrence's writings, most people base his reputation on *Lady Chatterley's Lover*. The story of Lady Chatterley and her gamekeeper broke new ground in describing sexual relationships in explicit yet literary language. Because of its controversial nature, the novel was first published privately in 1928 in Italy and in 1929 in France. Although pirated copies of the novel were made, a censored and abridged edition was published in Britain and in the United States in 1932, two years after Lawrence's death. When a complete and unexpurgated edition was published in Britain in 1960, its publication led to a court case, where it became a test case of the 1959 Obscene Publication Act, which made it possible for publishers to escape conviction if they could show that a work displayed literary merit.

One of the objections to *Lady Chatterley's Lover* was its frequent use of four-letter words, such descriptions of sex viewed to be lewd and vulgar. Lawrence hoped to challenge the British taboos around sex, enabling both male and female characters to think fully and honestly about sex. His earlier novel, *The Rainbow*, had been briefly banned due to the frank and relatively straightforward manner in which he wrote about sexual attraction, in particular due to the mention of same-sex attraction between Ursula and a female teacher, resistance he also encountered in describing the attraction between two principal male characters in *Women in Love*.

The British obscenity trial in 1960 of *Lady Chatterley's Lover* resulted in a verdict of "not guilty." This verdict, issued by twelve jurors—three women and nine men—resulted in a far greater degree of freedom for publishing explicit material, not only in Britain but also across the English speaking world. In the United States, the ban on *Lady Chatterley's Lover*, along with Henry Miller's *Tropic of Cancer* and John Cleland's *Fanny Hill*, was overturned in court in 1959, establishing the standard of "redeeming social or literary value" as a defense against obscenity charges.

Speaking against the accusation of pornography in his work, Lawrence denied the charge, arguing that in writing about Eros, he was going beyond superficial eroticism to the "Eros of the sacred mysteries." And if the latter, he writes in his foreword to *Women in Love*, "why not respect, even venerate? Let us hesitate no longer to announce that the sensual passions and mysteries are equally sacred with the spiritual mysteries and passions. . . . Lewdness is hateful because it impairs our integrity and our proud being. We are now in a period of crisis. Every man [Lawrence's usage is clearly generic, that is, inclusive] who is acutely alive is acutely wrestling with his own soul. The people that can bring forth the new passion, the new idea, this people will endure. Those others, that fix themselves in the old idea, will perish with the new life strangled unborn within them."[1] In 1916, after publishing *The Rainbow*, Lawrence wrote to his confidante Lady Morrell, "At present my real world is the world of my inner soul, which reflects on the novel I write."

How should one "read" Lawrence? His views on sexuality seem contradictory and hard to process. In speaking about sex, is he referring to heterosexual relationships—such as between males and females, husbands and wives—about homosexual and lesbian relationships, or about human relationships in general, including between friends, and children and parents? Furthermore, does he have in mind primarily individual wholeness and integrity, or modern civilization and social regeneration? As one writer wisely noted, it is possible to trace certain of the major developments in

1. Lawrence, *Women in Love*, vii.

culture over the last century on the basis of how people have read Lawrence or what they have chosen to take from his works.[2]

Major creative writers are rare, and Lawrence was unique in this regard. While the artistry in his short stories and tales is compelling, his novels, unfortunately, have been misread and miscomprehended by many readers since their publication, largely looking for features that earned him notoriety. Overall, Lawrence must be read as an astute observer of human nature, for in his writings he explores issues such as sexuality, emotional health, vitality, spontaneity, and instinct. However, he was principally a social critic, his collected works representing an extended reflection upon the dehumanizing effects of modernity and industrialization. Considered neurotic and perverted by "proper folk," he was likely more maligned than any artist of his time was. Those who knew him best considered him a genius, with an idealist bent.

The American author Henry Miller, in preparation for his study, *The World of Lawrence*, found in him three superb qualities: vision, courage, and integrity. Lawrence's opinions earned him many enemies and led to official persecution, censorship, and misrepresentation of his creative work, much of it written during a voluntary exile he called his "savage pilgrimage." At the time of his death, his public reputation was that of a pornographer who had wasted his considerable talent. Many literary critics disagreed. The British author E. M. Forster, in an obituary notice, challenged this widely held view, describing Lawrence as "the greatest imaginative novelist of our generation."

Many of his novels are autobiographical in nature, using material from his own or his friends' lives and experience to develop his plots and characters. For example, in 1910, during the writing of his novel, *The White Peacock*, Lawrence's mother died of cancer. The young man was devastated, and his close relationship with his mother became the basis for his novel *Sons and Lovers*, a work that draws upon much of Lawrence's provincial upbringing. Essentially concerned with the emotional battle for Lawrence's love between his mother and "Miriam" (in reality Jessie Chambers, with whom Lawrence had a brief intimate relationship), the book's publication and the portrayal of Chambers in the novel ended their friendship. After the book's publication, they never spoke again.

In 1912, Lawrence met Frieda Weekley, with whom he shared the rest of his life. Six years his senior, she was married to Ernest Weekley,

2. Trilling, "Moments of Modern Culture," 1.

Lawrence's modern language college professor. She and Lawrence eloped and left England for Frieda's parents' home in Germany, where he was briefly arrested and accused of being a British spy. From Germany, the couple walked across the Alps to Italy, where Lawrence completed various works, including the final version of *Sons and Lovers*, published in 1913, several travel books, and a series of love poems titled *Look! We Have Come Through* (1917). While in Italy, Lawrence wrote a draft of what would later be two of his best-known novels, *The Rainbow* and *Women in Love*, in which unconventional female characters take center stage. Both novels explore grand themes and ideas that challenged conventional thought on the arts, politics, economics, gender, sexuality, friendship, and marriage.

Eventually, Frieda obtained her divorce from Ernest Weekley. Lawrence and Frieda returned to Britain shortly before the outbreak of World War I and were legally married in 1914. Frieda's German parentage and Lawrence's open contempt for militarism caused them to be viewed with suspicion, which may have contributed to *The Rainbow* being suppressed and investigated for its alleged obscenity in 1915. Later, the couple were accused of spying and signaling to German submarines off the coast of Cornwall, where they lived briefly. In late 1917, after constant harassment by the civil and military authorities, Lawrence was forced to leave Cornwall. Earlier, his fragile health greatly affected his wellbeing, and during this period, he barely survived a severe attack of influenza.

After the wartime years, Lawrence began his time of voluntary exile from his native country. He left Britain and returned only twice for brief visits, spending the remainder of his life traveling with Frieda, a pilgrimage that took him to Australia, Italy, the United States, Mexico, and the South of France. In 1922, the Lawrences left Europe behind, sailing to the United States by way of Ceylon and Australia. In the United States, they settled in Taos, New Mexico, a town where numerous bohemians had settled. Lawrence had often talked of setting up a utopian community, and in New Mexico he and Frieda eventually acquired a 160-acre ranch. They remained there for two years, with extended visits in Mexico. While in the United States, Lawrence published *Studies in Classic American Literature*, a set of critical essays on authors such as Poe, Whitman, and Melville later described by Edmund Wilson as "one of the few first-rate books that have ever been written on the subject." These interpretations were a significant factor in the revival of the reputation of Herman Melville during the early 1920s.

In 1925, Lawrence suffered a near fatal attack of malaria and tuberculosis while on a visit to Mexico. Although he eventually recovered, his condition obliged him to return once again to Europe. He was dangerously ill and poor health limited his ability to travel for the remainder of his life. The Lawrences made their home in a villa in northern Italy, where he wrote various versions of *Lady Chatterley's Lover*, his last major novel, published in 1928, a book that reinforced his notoriety. During his final years he produced several works dealing with religious subjects, such as *The Man Who Died*, an unorthodox reworking of Jesus Christ's resurrection, and his reflection on the biblical book of Revelation, entitled *Apocalypse*. He died in 1930, only forty-five years of age, from complications of tuberculosis.

THE RAINBOW: PLOT AND RESPONSE

The Rainbow tells the story of three generations of the Brangwen family, a dynasty of farmers and artisans who live in provincial England. The book spans a period of roughly sixty-five years from the 1840s to 1905, and shows how the love relationships of the Brangwens change against the backdrop of the increasing industrialization of Britain. The first central character, Tom Brangwen, is a farmer whose experience of the world does not stretch beyond his provincial region, while the last, Ursula, his granddaughter, studies at university and becomes a teacher in the progressively urbanized, capitalist, and industrial world.

Tom is a man of the soil, and he lives alone on his farm with only an elderly woman as company and as housekeeper. Then a Polish widow, Lydia Lensky, becomes housekeeper for the vicar of the local church. She brings her small daughter, Anna, with her. One evening a few months later, Tom finds the courage to present the widow with a bouquet of flowers and to ask her to be his wife. Judged by the standards of the world, their marriage is satisfactory. They have two sons, and Tom is kind to his stepdaughter, Anna. Knowing her, however, is easier for him than knowing Lydia. There are times when one or both feels that their marriage is not what it should be and that they are not fulfilling the obligations imposed upon them by marriage.

Anna is a haughty young girl who spends many hours imagining herself a great lady. In her eighteenth year, Will, a nephew of Tom, comes to work in a factory in the nearby village of Ilkeston. Anna and Will fall in love, with a naïve affection for each other. When they announce to Tom and Lydia that they wish to be married, Tom leases a home for them in the village and gives them a present of twenty-five hundred pounds so they can manage financially, given Will's meager salary. After the wedding, the newly married couple spend two weeks alone in their cottage, ignoring the world and existing only for themselves. Anna is the first to come back to the world of reality. Her decision to give a tea party bewilders and angers her husband, who has not yet realized that they cannot continue to live only for themselves. Shortly after the marriage, Anna becomes pregnant, and the arrival of the child brings to Will the added shock that his wife is more a mother than she is a married lover. Each year, a new baby comes of their marriage.

The oldest is Ursula, who remains her father's favorite. The love that Will wishes to give his wife is given to Ursula, for Anna refuses to be physically intimate with him when she is expecting another child, and she is not happy unless she is pregnant. In the second year of his marriage, Will tries to rebel. He meets a young woman at the theater and flirts with her. After this incident, the intimate life of Will and Anna gains in passion, enough to carry Will through the daytime until the night when he can be passionate with his wife. Gradually, he becomes free in his own mind from Anna's influence.

The last and most extended part of the novel deals with Ursula's struggle to find fulfillment for her passionate spiritual and sensual nature against the confines of the increasingly materialist and conformist society around her. In high school, she excels in her study of Latin, French, and algebra. Before she finishes her studies, her academic interests are divided by her relationship with Anton Skrebensky, the son of a Polish friend of her grandmother and a lieutenant in the British army. During a month's leave, he falls in love with Ursula, who is already in love with him. On his next leave, however, he becomes afraid of her because her love is too possessive.

After finishing high school, Ursula decides to teach school for a time, to become financially independent. Anna and Will deny her decision to leave home. Ursula spends two thankless years teaching at the village elementary school, at which time she is ready to continue her education. One day, Ursula receives a letter from Anton, who writes that he wishes to see her again while on leave. Shortly thereafter, he visits her, during which time their love is rekindled with greater intensity than they had known previously. During the Easter holidays, they go away for a weekend at a hotel, where they pass as husband and wife. Anton increasingly presses for marriage, wanting Ursula to leave England with him when he returns to service in India, but she wants to return to college to earn her degree.

Ursula so neglects her studies during this time that she fails the final examinations for her degree. Anton urges her to marry him immediately. In India, he insists, her degree will mean nothing anyway. One evening, at a house party, they realize that there is something wrong in their relationship and that they lack what it takes for a successful marriage. They leave the party separately. A few weeks later, Anton leaves for India as the husband of his regimental commander's daughter.

Ursula then learns that she is pregnant. Not knowing that Anton is married, she writes to him and promises to be a good wife if he still wishes to marry her. Before his answer comes from India, Ursula contracts pneumonia and loses the child. One day, as she is convalescing, she observes a rainbow in the sky, seeing in it a promise of better times ahead.

POINTS TO PONDER IN *THE RAINBOW*

Whatever his faults, Lawrence was a creative thinker, famously lamenting the moment when, in his view, philosophy and fiction became distinct and separate modes of knowledge. They used to be one, he notes in an essay on "The Future of the Novel," in the days of myth, but then they parted, like a nagging married couple, at which time the novel became sentimental and philosophy abstract.

As Lawrence makes clear in his literary essays, it is essential for novelists to write metaphorically, and for readers to think metaphorically when reading his novels. Lawrence's profoundly metaphorical style is how he challenges the rationalistic and dehumanizing influences of modern culture. An artist, Lawrence replaces the logical with the poetic. In writing *Lady Chatterley's Lover*, for example, he did not wish Lady Chatterley's affair with her gamekeeper to be read as an essay in pleasure, but rather as an escape from her crippled and impotent husband, who represents the dehumanizing effects of modern technology and civilization. As Lawrence intended, the book must be read as the negation of society that produces a Clifford Chatterley, not of Clifford Chatterley himself. In his novels, sexual freedom represents a return to a more primitive consciousness; not a wish for the annihilation of society, but for Lawrence's vision of social regeneration.

In 1913, Lawrence wrote to Edward Garnett, his publishing contact and valued friend, that the problem of the day was the establishment of a new relation between men and women, and it is primarily these relationships of women and men—with all their tensions and conflicts—that Lawrence presents so powerfully in *The Rainbow*. On one occasion Lawrence was asked about his religion, and he replied, "My religion is equality," meaning egalitarianism between male and female. The novel, then, presents an account of this journey toward a "new world," an "unknown land" of equality. Lawrence's conception of women in history makes *The Rainbow* a great feminist novel, as he knew—Lawrence clearly saw it as a contribution to the women's movement. In this novel, Lawrence makes women the thinking and aspiring part of his humanity, life's true visionaries. In *The Rainbow*, the account of the three generations of Brangwens reaches a structural climax with Ursula, the thinking and feeling woman, the heroine of the family narrative. Yet even in his expansionary vision, Lawrence remains a man of his class and age, denigrating lesbianism even while describing Ursula's brief attachment to Winifred Inger, her teacher.

In this novel, Ursula's vision stands for Lawrence's. Ursula sees herself as a naked kernel striving for new roots, "to create a new knowledge of Eternity in the flux of Time."[3] It is she who becomes the traveler; a version of both Homer's Odysseus and Bunyan's pilgrim, Christian, Ursula becomes a type of Lawrence's search for psychic wholeness. Into the character of Ursula went the frustrations, jealousy, desire, and joy of his own love-life, especially his struggles to "come through" with Frieda.[4] Able to reimagine himself as a woman, Lawrence insists on the need to grasp the presence of otherness. This imaginative ability on Lawrence's past makes *The Rainbow* unique. In a sense, *Women in Love*, its sequel, is artistically anti-climactic, for in it women lapse back into a conventional social construction, men reassuming the lead.

In *The Rainbow*, Ursula is given a glimpse of the Rainbow at the end of the book, but the bulk of the narrative describes the Flood, the deluge that precedes its appearance. Whatever else Ursula's experiences mean to her, they reveal to her that beneath her outward, conscious, social self she has another true and real self. Lawrence's main intent, then, lay not in ego-determined personalities, or in their fixed, socially determined relations, but in the living, changing relationships of essential human beings below the level of their fully conscious selves. The central argument of the novel is

3. Lawrence, *Rainbow*, 457.

4. Like Ursula, Lawrence endures relational failures and his own frightening destructiveness, and yet survives.

not about male or female sexuality, for, as we see in Ursula, sexual experience alone is not redemptive. The literary critic A. L. Clements convincingly argued that the quest for the self is the central and unifying theme of *The Rainbow*. However, he underestimated the importance of human relationships in the novel, and mistakenly set up the quest for selfhood against the subject of relationships. The two themes are closely related and interdependent.

In particular, Lawrence is concerned with the nature of relationships within industrialized, modern society. Though often classed as a realist, Lawrence used his characters to give form to his personal philosophy. His depiction of sexuality, though seen as shocking when his work was first published, has its roots in a highly personal way of thinking and being. He describes his way of thinking in "The Crown," an essay written in 1915, soon after the completion of *The Rainbow*. In that essay, he speaks of two infinities upon which human life is based: the darkness (the Beginning or the infinity of the past, that is, the Pagan infinity), and the light (the End or the infinity of the future, that is, the Christian infinity). Individuals must know both eternities in order to achieve consummate being. In Lawrence's view, a person's fulfillment is dual: in flesh and in spirit, in darkness and in light. As he writes in "The Crown," "There are two eternities fighting the fight of Creation, the light projecting itself into the darkness, the darkness enveloping herself within the embrace of light. And then there is the consummation of each in the other . . . : our bodies cast up like foam of two meeting waves, but foam which is absolute, complete, beyond the limitation of either infinity, consummate over both eternities."[5]

In Lawrence's essay, a lion and a unicorn are fighting beneath a Crown. They are not fighting for the Crown, but beneath it. The lion is "the king of the beasts"; the unicorn is "the defender of virgins." The two are opposites, and, for Lawrence, a perennial pacifist, it is the fight of opposites that is holy, not the fight of like entities, such as between nations, which is evil.[6] In the fight, it is the conflict that is holy, not winning or losing. The consummation comes from perfect relatedness. To this, a person may win. However, those who triumph, perish. When the opposition is complete on either side, then there is perfection. If the lion or the unicorn wins, and the other loses, then the Crown pressing on the winner would kill it. If the two remain friends and refuse to fight, then the Crown will fall upon both and

5. Lawrence, "Crown," 12.
6. Lawrence, "Crown," 18.

kill them. The Crown is not the prize; rather, it is "the *raison d'être* of both. It is the absolute within the fight."[7] It is wrong to make the lion lie down with the lamb. In Lawrence's estimation, eliminating the conflict between eternal opposites is the supreme sin, the "unpardonable blasphemy."

In speaking of the foam of two meeting waves, Lawrence calls it "the iris between the two floods." In Greek mythology, Iris was the goddess of the rainbow, a goddess of sea and sky. In "The Crown," Lawrence describes the rainbow as the song midway between heaven and earth, as the Holy Ghost between the two opposite Infinities, the Absolute Timelessness made visible between the two Eternities—past and future, Beginning and Ending. As we know, the rainbow is represented on earth by the iris flower, known in Christianity as "the Virgin's flower" and in French as the *fleur-de-lis*, a symbol often placed on political and family coats of arms.

For Lawrence, human beings are timeless and absolute. He likens human life to a flower that comes into blossom and passes away. However, like the perennial iris, death is only temporary, not final, for resurrection is in the human's spiritual DNA. Lawrence views human nature, both physical and spiritual, as a conjunction of darkness and light, a unity of opposites. In the beginning, light touched darkness and darkness touched light, and life began. Light enfolds darkness, and darkness receives and interpenetrates the light. In drawing near, "they are more finely combined, till they burst into the crisis of oneness, the blossom, the utter being, the transcendent and timeless flame of the iris."[8] For the male, the female is the doorway to the Creator's power. Individually, they are "the relative parts dominated by the strange compulsion of the absolute." United with the female in intimacy, the male opens his eyes and knowns "the goal, the end, the light which stands over the end of the journey, the everlasting day, the oneness of the spirit."[9] Nevertheless, as Lawrence wrote later in *Women in Love*, the goal of earthly love is "mutual unison in separateness," not union in surrender.[10] Perhaps it is this anomaly that leads to Lawrence's utterly unorthodox view that a man's love ideally is fulfilled not in an exclusive relationship with a woman but through two kinds of love, spiritual wholeness achieved through commitment to another male and female equally and simultaneously. Speaking through Birkin, a male protagonist in *Women in Love*, Lawrence tells his

7. Lawrence, "Crown," 17.
8. Lawrence, "Crown," 22.
9. Lawrence, "Crown," 26.
10. Lawrence, *Women in Love*, 257.

friend Gerald. "A permanent relation between a man and a woman isn't the last word. . . . I believe in the *additional* perfect relationship between man and man—additional to marriage."[11]

The human source is in the two eternities, and between them is the rainbow—the iris of being. For Lawrence, the process of individuation is essential to the quest for wholeness. In his view, the soul does not come into being at birth, but rather in the midst of life, "just as the phoenix in her maturity becomes immortal in flame. This is not her perishing: it is her becoming absolute: a blossom of fire. If she did not pass into flames, *she* would never really exist. It is by her translation into fire that she is the phoenix. Otherwise she were only a bird, a transitory cohesion in the flux."[12]

While most people have never read or even heard of "The Crown," this essay may well represent the core of Lawrence's thinking. Written while he was still a young man, it contains the whole of his philosophy and vision of life. All the themes he elaborated in his novels, all the symbols he employed, appear here in seed form. The antagonism between the lion and the unicorn, for example, symbolizes his own struggle, first to be, and then to know himself.

Lawrence believed his intrinsic sexual nature was dual and not wholly male, and that his male and female elements were in conflict, not in balance. This perception gave him great insight into the female, a considerable advantage to a creative writer. However, it also caused him to see sexual relationships in terms of struggle rather than harmony, and led to a fear of merging rather than a confidence in union. In this regard, Lawrence's novels frequently describe mutually destructive conflicts between men and women, as well as an alternative search for satisfying relationships between men. Ultimately, for Lawrence, women are from Venus and men are from Mars, forever uniting yet forever opposite. Lawrence's conflicting attitudes about the possibility of male love are expressed throughout his works, but in all cases, they are modeled on the biblical friendship of David and Jonathan and not on the Greek ideal of male love.

Despite describing homosexual scenes in his novels, whether Lawrence ever had homosexual relations is unclear. However, given his enduring and robust relationship with Frieda, it is likely that he was primarily

---

11. Lawrence, *Women in Love*, 345; see also Lawrence's conclusion, when Ursula tells Birkin, "You can't have two kinds of love," and Birkin responds, "I don't believe that." *Women in Love*, 473.

12. Lawrence, "Crown," 38.

"bi-curious," intrigued by love in all its manifestations. Lawrence recognized consciously that he was born a divided self—not yet fully human, somehow spiritually incomplete. He had within himself a strong element of femininity, identified by some as a homosexual tendency, an element he did not fully comprehend. As we know from the Swiss psychiatrist Carl Jung (1875–1961) on the *anima* (the female aspect of a male's nature), Lawrence's creative genius was the result of his unrecognized sexuality. Had he been fully aware, he would have recognized the bisexual character of his makeup. This he refused to do. However, it was this conflict, like all the other conflicts in his nature, which nourished his remarkable creativity.

In order to attain "wholeness of being," a person must find fulfillment in two directions, represented in fictional terms in the first few pages of *The Rainbow* by "the teeming life of creation" on the Marsh Farm in which the men are immersed and "the activity of man in the world at large" to which the women on the Farm aspire. In a way, the development of the entire novel is suggested in its very first paragraph, which deals with the life of the Brangwens on the Marsh farm: whenever one of the Brangwen men working in the fields lifts his head from his work, he sees on a hill two miles away the church tower at Ilkeston. It is this "something unknown," as yet above and beyond the Brangwens, which must be added to their life for it to be complete. The women on the farm already yearn for this "finer, more vivid circle of life"—if not for themselves, then for their children. The horizontal of the land and the vertical of the church tower must be brought together in the complete arch of the rainbow. Both men and women, in their own way, seek to achieve a higher form of being. In *The Rainbow*, this conflict between the individual's human and divine self comes to a resolution. The very title is significant of the human necessity to bridge the two extremes of each person's duality. The mystic unity that Ursula catches, which enables her to visualize the two halves of herself, becomes Lawrence's basic criterion for all human dichotomies. Henceforth, all of Lawrence's characters are constructed from the standpoint of possession or non-possession of this essential unity.

This insistence on wholeness is essential to Lawrence's presentation of relationships. The main threat to marriage and love affairs is the growth of industrialization. The colliery, the machinery, the soulless work, the houses of the brick city, all are elements that destroy human wholeness. Ursula's rainbow is her hope for the New Human, particularly the New Woman, a daring metaphor joining earth and sky. Ursula has become the new Noah, the mediator of a new covenant, the promise of a new beginning. The novel's last sentence completes the pattern of the interrelated imagery of rainbow and arch: "She saw in the rainbow the earth's new architecture." The rainbow transforms the architectural arch into an image of openness, like the novel's structure, "fitting to the over-arching heaven."

As novelist, Lawrence utilized a double method, that of the realistic social narrative and what T. S. Eliot called the mythological pattern. As medium for his artistry, Lawrence articulated a new kind of language—lyricized prose fiction—poetry joining prose to recognize two dimension of existence. As intended, Lawrence's reader too must oscillate between ordinary events and moments of vision. To accomplish this union between opposites, Lawrence used sexual acts, desires, and relationships symbolically. The old conventional distaste for Lawrence and for *The Rainbow* as perverse, orgiastic, or beastly, is grossly misplaced. Lawrence held sex sacred, like nature, and like intuition, impulse, and the unconscious, which we should trust. The view of sex as a mere physical act, disconnected from emotional intimacy, comes far short of what Lawrence considered the ideal. For Lawrence, sexuality as an end in itself, like religiosity disconnected from life, is symptomatic of modern, increasingly mechanized and industrialized society. Lawrence's characters work hard at their sexuality in order to escape, or try to escape, institutional falsification and distortion. They do so by trying to create their own narratives, both realistic and poetic. Even their failures are honorable. Lawrence understood, profoundly, that it is always failure that shows the way forward.

In composing novels, Lawrence wished to go beyond where anyone had ever gone in a novel. In addition to what an ordinary novel might do—tell a grand story—Lawrence desired (at least from *The Rainbow* onward) to seek to go beyond human feelings and sentimentality to the spiritual realm of life. His interest was not in emotions or personal feelings and attachments, but in the larger, unknown forces of life, forces coming into us unseen and driving us—even destroying us, he wrote in a letter—"if we do not submit to be swept away." For Lawrence, behind all living characters stands a felt but unnamed and unknown God-flame, and if novelists make their characters "too personal, too human," the flame dies out and what we are left with is something common, lifeless, and trite.

In the period of *The Rainbow* and *Women in Love* (during which time he also wrote "The Crown"), Lawrence comes increasingly to speak of the role of the Holy Ghost in his mission to save the world. In his view, the savior type is a religious male with an unusual portion of femininity in his character, which comes to represent his spiritual nature. For this reason, Lawrence's artistic goal is to recreate his personality. His language increasingly becomes one of "identification with the universe," first in the effort at unity, and then in the effort to arrive at absolutism, that is, to become one with God.

In Lawrence's evolution, we see the trend toward fulfillment through sex, which proves a failure; then, through friendship, also a failure; and finally, through mysticism. The mystic is the opposite of the scientist, for whereas the scientist wishes to confront and explain reality, the mystic wishes to preserve mystery and obscurity. The mystic, or in the case of Lawrence, the artistic genius, is not one who adapts to reality but rather one who adapts reality to him/herself.

Instead of avoiding the religious issue of meaning, Lawrence accepted it unqualified. He sought to reestablish the sacred character of life, to re-enthrone God, to make God the only issue. He rejected the psychologists' explanations because they nullified the God-element in life. For Lawrence, humanity's sole problem is God, not society, not solidarity, not anything else. The next era, he believed, would be the era of the Holy Ghost—not of the Father, the Son, or of the third member of the Christian Trinity, but that unknown area of the self of which the gods as well as humans are born. Union with this cosmic spirituality, he believed, would result in the restoration of human divinity, which requires a new birth, a new flowering of the human iris.

Repeatedly, Lawrence came face to face with the mysterious dimension of life, experiencing the union and dissolution of the mystic who momentarily becomes one with the universe. He tried to give his readers what he had experienced, which is impossible, since each person must experience it uniquely and alone. As Lawrence demonstrated, victory and defeat are identical, simultaneous, and inseparable. For the artist, victory and defeat are immaterial—the important thing is the struggle. Either way, God is essential, for when human beings eliminate God, either by denying God's existence or through mystical union with God, there is no longer any struggle. And without struggle, the basis of existence is removed.

Frail physically and unstable temperamentally, Lawrence can easily be reduced to a Chaplinesque role. Rather, we should see him as a modern Don Quixote, tilting against the windmills of technological reductionism and social conformity. When we consider not only the quantity of his work but its quality, when we consider the age in which he wrote, so hostile to artistic genius, Lawrence burned so vividly and intensely that, just as the phoenix in its maturity, he became immortal in flame.

CHAPTER 13

Hermann Hesse's *Demian*

THE FIRST HALF OF THE TWENTIETH CENTURY witnessed lasting individual and social trauma, experiencing vast social, political, and psychological change precipitated by pandemics, two world wars, and a global Depression. As a way to chronicle the transition to a new and better world, novelists increasingly resorted to the psychological novel, a work of fiction in which the thoughts, feelings, and motivations of the characters were of equal or greater interest than the external action of the narrative. In psychological novels, the emotional reaction and internal states of the characters are interrelated.

This emphasis on the inner life of characters was not new in the twentieth century, but the psychological novel only reached its full potential in that era. Emphasis on the inner life went back to Augustine's *Confessions* and had been illustrated in dramatic form in William Shakespeare's *Hamlet* and in English novels such as Samuel Richardson's *Pamela* (1740), which is told from the heroine's point of view, and Lawrence Sterne's introspective first-person narrative *Tristram Shandy* (1759–1767).

While the development of the psychological novel coincided with the growth of psychology and the psychoanalytic discoveries of Sigmund Freud (1856–1939), it was not necessarily a result of expansion in this field. The penetrating insight into psychological complexities and unconscious motivations characteristic of the works of the Russian novelists Fyodor Dostoyevsky (1821–1881) and Leo Tolstoy (1828–1910), the detailed recording of external events inspiring an individual consciousness in the novels of the

American writer Henry James (1843–1916), the associative memories of French novelist Marcel Proust (1871–1922), the stream-of-consciousness technique of James Joyce (1882–1941) and William Faulkner (1897–1962), and the continuous flow of experience used by Virginia Woolf (1882–1941) was each arrived at independently.

In the psychological novel, plot is subordinate to a protagonist's inner journey or subjective experience. Events may not be presented in chronological order but rather as they occur in a character's thoughts, memories, fantasies, reveries, contemplations, and dreams. For instance, the action of Joyce's *Ulysses* takes place in Dublin in a twenty-four-hour period, but the events of the day trigger associations that take the reader back and forth through the characters' past and present lives. In the complex work of Franz Kafka (1883–1924), the subjective world is externalized, and events that appear to be happening in reality are governed by the subjective logic of dreams.

As many writers we have examined, Herman Hesse (1877–1962) used the novel as a creative way to expand his ideas of the self, utilizing an approach Princeton professor Ralph Freedman calls the "lyrical novel." In this stepchild of the psychological novel, writers recreate a novel's world as a metaphoric vision of mental and spiritual phenomena. But why choose this genre? Why not turn to poetry? By accepting qualities of the novel, such as using narrative to describe human experience in the external world but then focusing on the conditions of knowledge and awareness, doesn't the lyrical novel function as antinovel? The decision to use novelistic form, of course, is to the reader's benefit, for prose attracts more readers than poetry. Furthermore, lyrical novelists are not disinterested in the questions of human conduct in the world; they simply choose to view this activity in a different light.

While spiritual and intellectual quests generally take place in concrete settings, lyrical novelists often prefer to filter these quests through inner monologue or stream-of-consciousness techniques, as in Joyce's *Ulysses* (1922), Woolf's *To the Lighthouse* (1927), or Dostoyevsky's *Crime and Punishment* (1866). As in Melville's *Moby Dick* and Conrad's *Heart of Darkness*, the format of adventure can be used lyrically, psychologically, morally, or politically, although the most influential forms utilized by lyrical novelists are the picaresque, the episodic romance, and the allegorical quest. In German literature, the episodic narrative is typical and widespread. As we find in Hermann Hesse's work, protagonists serving as the writer's mask wander through worlds of spiritual encounter. While some modern authors rely deeply on inner monologue and stream-of-consciousness, others are more narrowly lyrical, such as Hesse, who prefers romantic allegory.

With the success of *Demian* (1919), Hermann Hesse became his era's spokesperson of German youth, such as Thomas Mann had been for the immediately preceding generation. In that novel, Hesse used romanticism as a tool for analyzing the self and the meaning of personal identity, exploring them in contemporary terms. To understand *Demian*, we must first become acquainted with central aspects of Hesse's life, for the novel is autobiographical.

Hesse was born in a small village in southern Germany, on the edge of the Black Forest. A poet and painter as well as a novelist, Hesse is best known as the author of *Demian*, *Siddhartha* (1922), *Steppenwolf* (1927), *Narcissus and Goldmund* (1930), and *The Glass Bead Game* (1943). In 1946, the Nobel Prize in Literature honored his body of work. Hesse grew up in a Pietist Lutheran household, within a religious sect that insulated members into small, deeply thoughtful groups. His maternal grandparents served as missionaries in India, where Hesse's mother was born. His grandfather, a linguist, acquired a large library of books about Eastern thought and became a master of Indian languages. Hesse's father, after briefly working as a missionary in India, returned to Germany to work in a religious publishing house.

As a child, Hesse was subjected to many religious influences, both to the narrow views of Protestantism and to the wider scope of Eastern religions and philosophies. Both views were formative of his later thought; his interest in Buddhism led eventually to the publication of his influential *Siddhartha*, a masterpiece that deals with the self-discovery of an Indian named Siddhartha during the time of the Buddha. Hesse's home was frequently the scene of visitations from foreigners, ranging from Buddhists to Americans. At his disposal was his grandfather's rich library. Hesse later stated that all of his writing was spiritual autobiography, religious not in an orthodox sense but in a larger, universal way.

From childhood, Hesse was headstrong and hard for his family to handle. It was determined early that he would study theology, but though he showed remarkable intellectual promise, young Hesse disliked school, especially the stifling rigidity of the German educational system of his time. Showing signs of serious depression, he turned to music, painting, and poetry, and by the age of thirteen, he decided he was going to be a poet. Rebellious at school and conflicted with his parents at home, he attempted suicide and was briefly institutionalized. In 1893, upon completing his schooling, he befriended older companions and took up drinking and smoking.

After various apprenticeships, he began working in a bookshop in Tübingen, where he began reading widely, including the works of Friedrich Nietzsche (1844–1900), and that philosopher's idea of dual impulses of passion and order in humans became influential in many of his novels. Nietzsche's questioning of the "herd instinct" and "mass morality" also guided Hesse's ideas in his novel *Demian*. In 1900, Hesse was exempted from compulsory military service due to eye problems that, along with nerve disorders and persistent headaches, affected him his entire life.

In 1902, his mother died after a prolonged illness, and Hesse could not bring himself to attend her funeral. After writing several minor works, he achieved literary success in 1904 with the publication of *Peter Camenzind*; from then on, Hesse knew he could make a living as a writer. This novel became popular throughout Germany, and was praised by Sigmund Freud as one of his favorite reading. Financially independent, Hesse secretly married Maria Bernoulli and they began a family, eventually having three sons. In 1914, Hesse became associated with pacifist writers and even wrote essays against growing nationalism in Germany. For the first time, he found himself in the middle of serious political conflict, attacked by the German press, the recipient of hate mail, and distanced from old friends.

A turning point in Hesse's life occurred in 1916, when his father's death, coupled with the illness of his son Martin and his wife's schizophrenia, led him to receive psychotherapy treatments in a Swiss sanatorium. From 1916 to 1917, he underwent more than seventy sessions with J. B. Lang, a disciple of the famous psychiatrist Carl Jung, eventually coming to know Jung personally. The result was beneficial for Hesse, leading him to new creative heights. The works following this period, particularly *Demian*—written during a three-week period in 1917—cannot be fully understood without recognizing the Jungian influence. After 1919, we cannot appreciate Hesse without a knowledge of such terms as "unconscious," *anima*, and "archetype." By the time Hesse returned to private life, his marriage had failed. After his wife's severe episode of psychosis, their home was divided and their children were accommodated in boarding houses or by relatives. In 1922, his novel *Siddhartha* was published, and the following year he divorced his wife and adopted Swiss citizenship.

In 1924 Hesse married the Swiss writer Lisa Wenger, but that marriage failed as well. The years 1924–1927 saw the publication of various autobiographical works, including *Steppenwolf*, and in 1930 Hesse married Ninon Dolbin, forming a solid relationship that endured until his death in 1962. During World War II, Hesse again became the subject of German ostracism because of his anti-nationalist views. In the late 1930s, German journals stopped publishing his works, which the Nazis eventually banned altogether. However, after receiving the Nobel Prize in 1946, his writings again became popular in Germany. Hesse's works had long enjoyed popularity outside of Germany, especially in southern Europe and Latin America. However, he remained virtually unknown in the United States until the 1960s, when he became a cult hero, particularly within the youth culture, which identified with his alienated protagonists. His works became bestsellers, and *Steppenwolf* became a virtual Bible for the 1960s counter-culture. *Siddhartha* and *Demian*, particularly, were added to the curricula of many progressive high schools and colleges. By the early 1970s, Hesse became the most widely read and translated European author of the twentieth century.

DEMIAN: PLOT AND RESPONSE

Demian, a coming-of-age *Bildungsroman*, presents the reflections of an older man on his childhood and upbringing. In this book, Emil Sinclair recounts the various episodes of his childhood that led to a profound change in his self-understanding and worldview. Emil was raised in Germany in a traditional home at the turn of the twentieth century. His family is rather wealthy and they have a reputation as a godly family. As a boy, Sinclair views the world within the walls of his home as representing all that is good, pure, innocent, and godly. However, starting at a young age, he feels a constant inner conflict between this world, which he refers to as the "world of light," and the outside world or "forbidden realm," which represents sin, loneliness, deceit, and insecurity. Although his mother, father, and two sisters remain within the "world of light," Sinclair constantly feels drawn to the outside realm and is in this way somewhat estranged from his family and their sphere of security. He ends up vacillating between both and not belonging to either.

Sinclair's struggle between those two worlds manifests itself when he is about ten years old. While playing one day with some fellow schoolmates, an older boy, Franz Kromer, joins them. In an effort to impress the older boy and his schoolmates, Sinclair makes up a story in which he and another unnamed accomplice stole a bag of apples from a fellow neighbor. Although the story is untrue, Kromer threatens Sinclair with exposure if Sinclair does not pay him off. Unable to pay the full amount, Sinclair is forced to become Kromer's slave, ultimately sending Sinclair into depression and paranoia. Sinclair feels trapped by Kromer, forced to live within the "forbidden realm" by lying and stealing for Kromer, which in turn exiles him from the "world of light." This experience is traumatic for Sinclair and he is haunted by nightmares, is unable to eat, and becomes sullen and withdrawn. His personality alters as he tries to cope with the bondage of his slavery to this troublemaking kid, but he sees no escape and reluctantly succumbs to what he believes to be his fate.

The arrival of a new kid in town, Max Demian, is noticed by everyone due to the strange aura that surrounds him and his recently widowed mother. From the start, Sinclair feels a type of fascination for Demian, a confusing feeling filled with animosity and love. "He was in every respect different from all the others, was entirely himself, with a personality all his own, which made him noticeable even though he did his best not to be noticed; his manner and bearing was that of a prince disguised among farm boys, taking great pains to appear one of them."[1] The first encounter between Sinclair and Demian occurs one day after school as the two boys are walking home. Sinclair had learned the biblical story of Cain and Abel from the book of Genesis that day in class. Demian starts a conversation about the story and challenges Sinclair to look at the account from a different perspective. Demian proposes that Cain carried a mark of distinction because he was feared by others due to his strength, and that Abel had been killed simply because he was the weaker of the two. Sinclair is impressed and at the same time overwhelmed by this radical perspective, which challenges the traditions and teachings with which he had been raised. He therefore denounces the idea as absurd, thereby protecting himself and all he knows to be true.

At a later date, Sinclair once again comes in contact with Demian. It is in the town square after Sinclair had a troublesome meeting with Kromer, who still plagues his life. Through mere observation, Demian assesses the situation between Kromer and Sinclair, and Demian confronts Sinclair about his fear of Kromer. Angered by Demian's accurate insight, Sinclair

---

1. Hesse, *Demian*, 27.

brushes Demian off out of fear and frustration, but within the next couple of days Sinclair is freed from his bondage to Kromer when Demian intervenes without Sinclair's knowledge, causing Kromer to leave Sinclair alone for good. Sinclair feels an immense sense of gratitude and indebtedness toward Demian, but due to fear and immaturity, he is unable to express this to Demian. Instead, Sinclair confesses everything to his parents and regresses into a childlike state within the "world of light." This provides momentary comfort and security, but due to the severity of the experience and consequent loss of innocence, Sinclair realizes that he can never really be a model child, dwelling exclusively in the "world of light."

After a number of years of only peripheral contact, Sinclair and Demian are reunited in a religious Confirmation class. Though they do not spend much time together at first, their relationship is rekindled after the teacher discusses Cain and Abel in class one day. Demian switches his seat to be next to Sinclair and they spend much time discussing the human will and exploring Demian's uncanny ability to affect how other people act. During this time, Sinclair's religious faith begins to wane. Demian presents him with the idea that worshipping the God of the Bible is not sufficient. The God of the Bible represents all that is sanctified and good in the world. Nevertheless, Demian insists, one ought to worship the entire world—the evil as well as the good. Sinclair is elated that Demian has touched on these thoughts—that the world is divided in two realms, light and darkness, good and bad.

Sinclair enters boarding school, confused and unsure of what he thinks and believes. One day he is approached by an older boy, Alfons Beck, who invites him to a bar. They go off together, drink wine, and chat. This marks the beginning of a rebellious streak and a new group of friends for young Sinclair. He often goes out late into the night, drinking and carousing. However, he refrains from one of the activities popular among his friends: he refuses to go with them when they visit women, for Sinclair has a yearning for love, not sex. One day, Sinclair sees a girl at the park who is, for him, the paradigm of beauty. She has some male features, but is surrounded by an alluring air. Though he never speaks to her, he names her Beatrice, and she becomes an ideal for whom he acts. Immediately he reforms his behavior and ceases his activities with his friends. He begins to take up painting and paints a picture of this girl. Days later he realizes that the picture is also a picture of Demian.

In class one day, Sinclair finds a note that speaks about breaking free; it also mentions a god named Abraxas. Sinclair is certain that the note is from Demian. Only partly paying attention to the day's lecture, Sinclair perks up when he hears his teacher mention Abraxas. The teacher says that Abraxas is an ancient God who contains both divine and satanic elements.[2]

Strolling through town one day, Sinclair hears organ music emanating from a small, locked church. He is moved by the music and sits outside to listen for a while. He does this many times and eventually decides to trail the organist as he leaves after playing. Sinclair follows him to a bar and sits beside him. They begin to chat and Sinclair mentions Abraxas. At once, the organist, Pistorius, takes a great interest in Sinclair. This is the start of an intense relationship between the two men. Pistorius becomes a mentor to Sinclair, helping him to learn further things about himself and teaching him about Abraxas.

Eventually, Sinclair comes to see that Pistorius has limitations. He tells him that he is too "antiquarian." He brings Pistorius to recognize that he can only teach Sinclair about old gods and ideas of the past—he is not creative enough to invent new ones. Their relationship ends as Sinclair concludes his time at preparatory school. Before entering university, Sinclair visits Demian's old house. There, the new owner shows him a picture of Demian's mother. Sinclair realizes that she looks exactly like the portraits he has been drawing, and he unsuccessfully searches for her.

Upon entering the university, he is disappointed by his philosophy courses, which offer him no new knowledge or enlightenment. Then one night, as he strolls through town, which is filled with the sounds of drunken fraternities in the bars and taverns, he comes upon two men having a conversation about the absurdity of the fraternities, since they only lead to conformity. Sinclair is overjoyed to realize that the voice he is listening to is that of his beloved old friend Demian. Demian is not surprised to find Sinclair, knowing that he would eventually come because he had wanted him there. Sinclair is even more overwhelmed to learn that not only Demian but Demian's mother also awaited his arrival. Demian tells him to visit their house whenever he is ready to see her.

2. Abraxas, depicted as a bird breaking out of the world as if it were a gigantic egg, may be viewed as a bird, a lyrical equivalent of the enlightened self. This Gnostic deity, used symbolically throughout the text, idealizes the interdependence of all that is good and evil in the world. Demian argues that Jehovah, the Jewish God, is only one face of God. Jehovah rules over all that is wholesome, but there is another half of the world, and an infinite God must encompass both sides of the world.

Demain's monologue at this point becomes a turning point in the novel as well as in Sinclair's fate as Sinclair realizes that his destiny is tied to all those around him. Demian condemns the society of Europe as being lost and afraid, and he predicts the coming of a catastrophic event that will change the world. "He spoke about the spirit of Europe and the signs of the times. Everywhere, he said, we could observe the reign of the herd instinct, nowhere freedom and love. All this false communion—from the fraternities to the choral societies and the nations themselves—was an inevitable development, was a community born of fear and dread, out of embarrassment, but inwardly rotten, outworn, close to collapsing."[3]

The next day, an excited Sinclair goes to the Demian household, where he and Demian's mother Frau Eva bond at once. Sinclair soon becomes a regular in the Demian household. He is immensely happy to be spending his time with Demian, Demian's mother, and others of their type who pass through. Sinclair becomes a part of the family and joins in at all the meetings that take place in the house, the gatherings of those with the mark of Cain. Those in the circle believe in every sort of religion and God, and Sinclair learns about many ways to explain God through these fellow seekers. Sinclair spends that summer with the Demian family, further strengthening his bond with Demian and Frau Eva. One day, Sinclair summons his mental energy to call Frau Eva telepathically. She hears his call and sends Demian to him. Sinclair is ecstatic that mental telepathy works.

Sinclair falls deeper in love with Frau Eva. She understands everything about him. She is able to make sense of his dreams; at times, she even remembers them better than he himself does. Sinclair is in constant conflict with himself over his love for her. She encourages him in his desire, telling him not to be afraid. However, she also tells him that her love must be won, and for her to be attracted to his love he must be confident and unafraid. His love probably would have attracted her, had it not been for the events that came about in the summer of 1914.

Shortly before the war begins, Demian realizes what is to come, the tragic event that would change European society forever. It meant the death of the old world, an end to conformity and the coming of a new age. Demian and Sinclair will be a part of this new world; they will be leaders because they accept fate.

War begins, and Demian, now a lieutenant, is called to serve. Before Sinclair too goes off to war, Eva tells him that he now knows how to call her

3. Hesse, *Demian*, 139–40.

and whenever he needs to, he can do so and she will send somebody like her to his side. Wounded in battle, Sinclair is stunned to find Demian by his side in the infirmary. Demian tells Sinclair that if he ever feels like he needs help, he no longer needs to call Demian. He simply needs to look inside himself and he will see that Demian is within him. With that, Demian gives him a light kiss on the lips—a kiss that he says is from Frau Eva—and vanishes into the night of Sinclair's death.

POINTS TO PONDER IN *DEMIAN*

What a wonderful book this is to read and to end our study—a book at once frustrating and confusing, but even more so intriguing, compelling, and exhilarating. I write this chapter in October: fall is here, the leaves are falling, and frost will soon be on the ground. However, after reading *Demian*, I now see spring in the fall, newness in death, beginnings in endings. In introducing Abraxas, Hesse is suggesting a new way to think, see, and believe: a nondualist, integrative, hopeful way to live.

For those of us who now see ourselves in Cain, his mark subtle beneath our foreheads, we realize, as D. H. Lawrence did, that humans, like God, are neither good nor evil; we only are. And, like John Milton states in *Paradise Lost*, "The mind is its own place, and in itself can make a Heaven of Hell and a Hell of Heaven" (Book 1). The nature of our lives is decided by our outlook and attitudes. Though the world is the same for all of us, our individual mentality changes perception and with it, reality. If we believe in ourselves and have a positive attitude toward life, we can be happy and satisfied. On the other hand, if we are unsure of our abilities, or are excessively controlling, we may never be satisfied in life. Thus, it is our attitude that decides our happiness and satisfaction in life, our salvation or condemnation, and the concepts of heaven and hell in our minds.

Published in 1919, *Demian* is crucial to understanding Hermann Hesse. The title, which came to Hesse in a dream, is a direct outgrowth of Hesse's psychoanalysis of 1916–1917. It marks a new direction in both the tone and message of his works. If, as Timothy Leary declared, Hesse may be seen as "the poet of the interior journey," *Demian* is the beginning of Hesse's introspection and of his turning to the "inward way." It is also the start of the enduring influence of Carl Jung on Hesse's thinking. *Demian* is replete with Jungian archetypes, elements of the collective unconscious, and with Jungian symbolism such as the *anima* and the shadow self.

Dreams, of course, are an important part of the development of one's personality—a process Jung called individuation. Jung saw dreams as the psyche's attempt to communicate important things to the individual, and he valued them highly, primarily as spontaneous products of the unconscious psyche, outside the control of the human will.

In my earlier book, *Dark Splendor*, I spoke of a form of dream interpretation developed by Gestalt therapists, which views every aspect of a dream, including every character and situation, to be an aspect of the dreamer's self. Since dreams are not controlled by the will, they don't have to be reasonable. Dreams are free from authoritative strictures and authorities, be they societal, moral, parental, or religious. Dreams are free to take us to interior places we can't imagine, and to challenge the way we run our lives, or the way life runs us. They can be daring, zany, playful, or simply frightening. They speak truth as they point to our particular needs to growth. They highlight the changes we are able to make, but also parts of us that we have denied.

According to Gestalt pastoral therapist Tilda Norberg, whatever we disown in ourselves shows up in our dreams. Fritz Perls used the term "polarities" to speak of the parts that function as opposites of how we think of ourselves; Jung called this disowned material "the shadow." Keep in mind that our shadow includes "good" qualities as well as "bad" or "shameful" qualities that we deny. As we make room for our polarities, we become healthier and more open to transforming grace.

If dreams express a person's natural spirituality, they also provide a venue in which God's presence may be discerned. For this reason alone, reading Hesse's *Demian* is invaluable, for the entire book has a Jungian, dream-like quality. Near the end of the book, Demian tells Sinclair about his dream of climbing up a ladder placed against a tree trunk or tower.

"When I reached the top I saw the whole landscape ablaze—a vast plain with innumerable towns and villages. I can't tell you the whole dream yet, everything is still somewhat confused."

"Do you feel that the dream concerns you personally?" Sinclair asks.

"Of course," Demian replies. "No one dreams anything that doesn't concern him personally."[4]

When Hesse first published *Demian*, he did so pseudonymously, using the pen name Emil Sinclair. He did so on account of his anti-nationalist views, to avoid the disfavor with which he was held by the German public.

---

4. Hesse, *Demian*, 159–60.

Had he published the novel under his real name, it would have been ignored. Under this guise, however, it was not only a success, but Sinclair was also awarded the Fontane Prize for new authors. When the truth became known, Hesse could not accept the prize, for he was already an established author. Even his friend, the renowned Thomas Mann, could not believe that this was the work of Hermann Hesse, so radical was the departure from his earlier work.

Structurally, the book falls loosely into three stages of Sinclair's growth from childhood to maturity. The first is Emil's sudden awareness of anxiety and guilt at the threshold of puberty, as he realizes that the universe is divided into the respectable world of "light," inhabited by his parents and sisters, and the sinister, yet always subconsciously attractive world of "dark," which looms at the fringes of his middle-class existence. This loss of his innocence can be paralleled with the biblical fall from grace. At this critical juncture Max Demian, his boyhood friend and lifetime guide, emerges to teach him the need to realize himself at all cost and to transcend the conventional dichotomies of good and evil.

The second, intermediate stage, which is the longest, concerns itself with the period of anguish and despair that follows the fall. Sinclair's recognition of pure love at this stage of sexual awakening comes to him through a vision of feminine beauty—a girl whom he identifies with a picture and then seeks to paint, that is, to recreate as an internal image. Abruptly, this experience leads him to sever his connections with the world of "dark" and to turn toward guides and teachers who might show him the way to higher stages of self-realization. This phase is also marked by his important relationship with Pistorius, who, knowing "Abraxas," shows Sinclair the importance of the inner vision and of the efficacy of the human will in transcending the external world.

In the third phase, the protagonist experiences some degree of enlightenment. When Sinclair meets Demian again as a young adult, this reunion with his friend becomes equivalent to the union of the self with its ideal image, now broadened to include not only Demian but also the figure of the universal Mother, significantly named Frau Eva. However, his love for Frau Eva is not consummated until, wounded, he receives from Demian her saving kiss. At this point Sinclair realizes that all the figures and visions that had appeared to him on the road to salvation had really been images within his own soul.

Within the allegorical structure, the stages of the hero's progress are marked by three characters, both guides and also pictures of his own changing condition. An ultimate unity, this triad of figures embodies Hesse's thesis of the "manifold within unity." Demian is the most inclusive figure, supplemented by Pistorius and Frau Eva. Although on the surface Demian is described realistically, supernatural traits are not far beneath the surface. Passages showing him as a person of insight and character are soon matched by accounts of his truly supernatural wisdom. Possessed of supernatural intuitions, only he can recognize the Sign of Cain on Sinclair, discover the emblem of the sparrow-hawk (a symbolic figure of opposing worlds), or communicate with the hero in occultic ways. As a figure both timeless and acting in time, Demian's function is also internal. He appears and disappears, but even in his physical absences, he is a symbol in Sinclair's mind, ready to be called upon whenever he is needed. His final reappearance coincides with Sinclair's deepest understanding, and he is eventually joined with him at death. An inner voice, Demian is a controlling conscience, Sinclair's *daemon* directing him from awakening to maturity and liberating him from himself at crucial junctures. His presence and absence mark stages in a process of deepening awareness. Like the ideal of much romantic thought, the transcendent self can only be joined with the natural self after death.

If Demian is a pervasive symbol in the protagonist's consciousness, Pistorius is a temporal, visionary symbol leading to transcendence of the social abyss between good and evil. Pistorius makes mistakes, and the inevitable break occurs after Sinclair has reached an advanced point of self-recognition, at which occasion Sinclair indulges in discursive lectures about antiquarian religions. The final image of salvation, Frau Eva, is also the most shadowy figure of the triad. A symbol for the union of opposites, she includes the male and the female, light and dark. On a primary level, she is an allegorical figure representing the eternally feminine, origin of all life. On another level, she is also the juxtaposition of sensual and spiritual love. In the end, Sinclair's salvation takes place in notably un-Christian terms, for salvation coincides with self-awareness. As Demian, and temporarily Pistorius, taught Sinclair "to live out completely what seeks to break out of me," so Frau Eva taught final self-discovery within the mirror of oneself. Together, these three major figures portray through their contrived actions the conflicts and images within Sinclair himself. The allegory is shaped by the idea, which they express, that the self must render itself completely, reconciling the oppositions that divide inner and outer nature.

Of the many symbols used in the novel, one of the most fascinating is that of the painting Sinclair makes. Beginning with reproductions of Beatrice, Sinclair finds that each successive painting of her face resembles more and more an image of his dreams. With each fresh start, the painting comes to mirror more closely a unity of his inner and outer visions. The "picture" moves progressively outward from Beatrice to Demian, and eventually to Frau Eva. Moreover, as his self-recognition deepens, he realizes that he has drawn not only Beatrice or Demian or Frau Eva but also himself: "Not that the picture resembled me . . . but it was what determined my life, it was my inner self, my fate or my *daemon*."[5] Once the painting of Beatrice is joined with the Abraxas motif, new attitudes emerge: the enlarged picture is now also a challenge to its creator. "I often saw the beloved apparition of my dream with a clarity greater than life, more distinct than my own hand, spoke with it, wept before it, cursed it. I called it mother and knelt down in front of it in tears . . . I called it devil and whore, vampire and murderer. . . . All pointed toward Abraxas. But none of these dreams, none of these thoughts obeyed me . . . . I was . . . their vessel."[6]

Such a conversion of a picture of one person's creation into an icon, finally into an antagonist, illustrates Hesse's technique. After intense inner concentration, Sinclair's painting becomes a higher vision of the self. In the final phase, the painting or picture, which dominates the novel's center, is displaced by the inner vision. Frau Eva teaches Sinclair the value of dreams; this enables him to achieve more successfully a concentrated vision of himself. In the end, Sinclair's longing for Eva is so concentrated, that "for a few moments I felt something contract within me, something bright and cool which felt like a crystal in my heart"—and then he recognized Eva as his own self.[7]

At the point of death, at which all significant images unite, Sinclair witnesses a constellation of pictures that become the ultimate self-portrait, the inner landscape of the self. Under the veneer of a novel of development, the reader has followed the transformation of a hero into a symbolic hero. Progressing from childhood to maturity, Sinclair regularly redraws his own

5. Hesse, *Demian*, 86.

6. Hesse, *Demian*, 99–100.

7. Hesse, *Demian*, 164.

image, ascending from his awareness of a perceived object to its image in his mind and finally to its symbol with which he wholly identifies.

In *Demian*, Hesse succeeds in drawing a spiritual self-portrait leading the reader through successive stages to the attainment of a symbolic vision of a "new world," born of catastrophe. Using portraiture as a lyrical form, Sinclair becomes a symbolic representative of Hesse and his world on the "road to salvation."

Appendix

Miguel de Unamuno's
San Manuel Bueno, Martyr

While our study ends appropriately with Hermann Hesse's *Demian*, bookended with James Joyce's coming-of-age *A Portrait of the Artist as a Young Man*, I wish to conclude with one of my favorite short stories, *San Manuel Bueno, Martyr*, written by the distinguished Spanish thinker Miguel de Unamuno (1864–1936). I first encountered Unamuno's writings as a young college student majoring in Modern Foreign Languages, and the study of Spanish culture and literature has been a lifelong passion of mine.

Spanish essayist, novelist, and philosopher, Unamuno worked in all major genres, and as a Modernist, contributed greatly to dissolving the boundaries between genres. In addition to his writing, Unamuno played an important role in the intellectual life of Spain. He served as rector of Spain's prestigious University of Salamanca from 1900 to 1924 and again from 1930 to 1936, at a time of great social and political upheaval. During the 1910s and 1920s, Unamuno became a passionate advocate of Spanish social liberalism. He was removed from his post by the dictator General Miguel Primo de Rivera in 1924, at which time he was exiled in the Canary Islands, later living in southern France. He returned to Spain in 1930, after the fall of Primo de Rivera's dictatorship, to resume his rectorship, only again to come into conflict with government officials, including longtime Spanish dictator Generalissimo Franco, who placed Unamuno under house arrest until Unamuno's death.

Unamuno's *nivola*, as he called it, was written in 1930, just after the fall of military dictator Primo de Rivera. It tells the story of a Catholic priest (Don Manuel) in Spain through the eyes of Angela, one of the townspeople in the fictional Valverde de Lucerna. Throughout the course of the story, Manuel is adored by the people of the town. He constantly serves the townspeople, refraining from condemning anyone, and regularly going out of his way to help people marginalized by society. Instead of refusing to allow the holy burial of someone who committed suicide, he explains that he is sure that in the last moment, the person would have repented for his or her sin. In addition, instead of excommunicating a woman who had an illegitimate child, as the Catholic Church would have done, Don Manuel arranges a marriage between the woman and her ex-boyfriend, so that order will return to the town and the child will have a father figure. The people of the town consider him their "saint" because of all of the good deeds he does.

What makes Don Manuel unusual is that he may well be the only priest in the world who doesn't believe in God. He agrees with the statement that religion is the opium of the people, and he feels burdened with his responsibility of being the one who administers this opium. Most of the story is told from the perspective of Angela Carballino, a woman around fifty years old who records the memories of her early years. In her confessional memoir, she reveals that Don Manuel, the great man who had loved helping other people, had lived a life full of spiritual turmoil himself.

As a child, Angela was raised by a deeply religious woman, and she was taught to be obedient and to love God. When Angela meets Don Manuel, she realizes immediately that the man is not like other people—he holds a special, important role as the spiritual anchor for the villagers, a role that he successfully fulfills. Don Manuel is beloved by everyone in the village, as he works hard to mend broken families, heal the sick, and clothe the poor. Angela soon develops a close bond with Don Manuel, coming frequently to confessionals and talking to him about her worries and doubts.

Angela also has a brother, Lazaro, who spends many years living in the New World. When Lazaro comes home, he is dismayed by what he sees as his family's backward and rural lifestyle, and tries to convince his mother to move the family to a big city. However, their mother refuses to leave; she is attached to her village, and to Don Manuel.

In addition to not believing in God, Don Manuel also believes religious officials to be corrupt and wicked. However, even Lazaro cannot help but admire Don Manuel's kind spirit upon meeting him. The turning point for Lazaro comes when his mother becomes deathly ill. On his mother's deathbed, Lazaro is moved by Don Manuel to promise that he will pray for her. This experience brings Lazaro and Don Manuel close together, and soon Lazaro joins the parish under Don Manuel.

As Lazaro becomes closer to Don Manuel, the priest tells him his deepest secret: he also doesn't believe in God. Furthermore, he believes that religion is a lie meant to disguise a terrible truth: humans are born for no other reason than to die. Finding common ground in this belief, the two men grow even closer. Angela is horrified when she discovers this shared belief. However, through conversations with Don Manuel and Lazaro, she grows to accept that it is necessary that the villagers of Valverde de Lucerna never discover this truth about Don Manuel.

The epilogue reveals that this memoir is being read to us not by Angela herself, but by a separate narrator. This narrator, who could be Miguel de Unamuno or someone else, believes Angela Carballino's account to be true, and that even if nothing is resolved through this memoir, hopes that the story will persist and endure throughout the world and "in the divine novel of our existence."

In his *nivola*, Unamuno explores the idea of truth, primarily religious or metaphorical truth, published at a time of economic downturn and political instability, when anti-clericalism was rapidly gaining support in Spain. Unamuno utilized both form and content to portray the elusive nature of truth and the importance of perception and belief when dealing with the question of truth. Don Manuel commits himself to a life of intentional falsehood because he believes some truths are too awful to be told. He believes that life can be lived either in ignorance of humanity's mortal, temporal nature through belief in God and an afterlife, or in knowledge of the fact we are ultimately doomed to die. This, in turn, raises the question of the value of religion and blind faith in the modern world.

In this respect, *San Manuel Bueno, Martyr* stands against the progressive cause. Lazaro's spiritual death is associated with his exposure to progressivism in America. There is a line in the story when Manuel echoes Karl Marx: "Opium . . . opium, yes! Let's give them opium, and let them sleep and dream," and it appears that Unamuno is endorsing happiness based on blind faith and tradition, simply as a way for common people to live their live in contentment and without fear. However, as Unamuno noted in 1897, "My religion is to seek for truth in life and for life in truth, even knowing that I shall not find them while I live." For Unamuno, that search required a Christian context. It is clear in this story that Manuel is a representation of Jesus Christ himself, and Lazaro's conversion a representation of the story of Christ and Lazarus in John 11:1–45.

However, in his short story, Unamuno paints a new picture of saint-hood, a new understanding of what it means to be christlike. In Manuel, we see a thoroughly spiritual individual whose compassion, social vision, and spiritual sensibility are enhanced—not diminished—by doubt. In the end, readers are left pondering the nature of truth, acknowledging that they cannot reach a core of certainty, for truth is frustratingly out of reach. As an intellectual, Unamuno spent much of his life facing the tragic nature of the human condition while also shaking people out of their complacency, forcing them to question the fictional truth that he was laying before them.

San Manuel Bueno, Martyr, like many of the works we have studied, explores truth in many of its different facets. Unamuno focuses on the elu-sive nature of truth in literature because anything that is written or spoken is always a matter of perception. Hence, the reader can never reach a point of certainty. At a time of political turmoil in Spain, Unamuno's novel was particularly relevant because it questioned people's accessibility to the truth behind public discourse, while also raising questions about the benefits and problems with organized religion and its use and abuse by politicians and pundits.

Unamuno also reminded his readers that compassion is more impor-tant than belief, that doubt can function as a portal to a more mature and fruitful kind of faith, and lastly, that truth is stranger than fiction.

Bibliography

Abanes, Richard. *Harry Potter and the Bible*. Camp Hill, PA: Horizon, 2001.

Bergonzi, Bernard. *T. S. Eliot*: New York: Macmillan, 1972.

Birzer, Bradley J. *J. R. R. Tolkien's Sanctifying Myth: Understanding Middle-earth*. Wilmington, DE: Intercollegiate Studies Institute, 2003.

Bradley, Marion Zimmer. *The Mists of Avalon*. New York: Knopf, 1982.

Brodhead, Richard H. *Hawthorne, Melville, and the Novel*. Chicago: The University of Chicago Press, 1976.

Carpenter, Humphrey. *The Letters of J. R. R. Tolkien*. Boston: Houghton Mifflin, 1981.

Chesterton, G. K. *The Everlasting Man*. Garden City, NY: Image, 1955.

Conrad, Joseph. *Heart of Darkness*. Edited by Robert Kimbrough. 3rd ed. New York: Norton, 1988.

Cornils, Ingo. *A Companion to the Works of Hermann Hesse*. Rochester, NY: Camden House, 2009.

Davis, Merrell R., and William H. Gilman. *The Letters of Herman Melville*. New Haven, CT: Yale University Press, 1960.

Delbanco, Andrew. *Melville: His World and Work*. New York, Knopf, 2005.

Dostoyevsky, Fyodor. *Notes from the Underground*. New York: Dover, 1992.

Eliot, T. S. "A Commentary," *The Criterion* 13 (April 1934), 451–54.

———. *On Poetry and Poets*. New York: Noonday-Farrar, Straus, & Giroux, 1961.

———. *Selected Essays: New Edition*. New York: Harcourt, Brace, 1950.

Eliot, Valerie. *The Waste Land: A Facsimile and Transcript of the Original Draft*. New York: Harcourt Brace Jovanovich, 1971.

Freeman, Ralph. *Studies in Hermann Hesse, André Gide, and Virginia Woolf*. Princeton, NJ: Princeton University Press, 1963.

Granger, John. *The Deathly Hallows Lectures: The Hogwarts's Professor Explains the Final Harry Potter Adventure*. 2nd ed. Wayne, PA: Zossima, 2008.

———. *Looking for God in Harry Potter*. 2nd ed. Carol Stream, IL: Tyndale House, 2016.

———. *Understanding Harry Potter: Five Keys for the Serious Reader*. Wayne, PA: Zossima, 2007.

Harkness, Marguerite. *A Portrait of the Artist as a Young Man: Voices of the Text*. Boston: Twayne, 1990.

Hart, Dabney Adams. *Through the Open Door: A New Look at C. S. Lewis*. University, AL: The University of Alabama Press, 1984.

Hawthorne, Nathaniel. *The House of the Seven Gables*. Edited by Robert S. Levine. New York: W. W. Norton, 2006.

————. *The Scarlet Letter*. New York: Norton, 1962.

————. *Tales and Sketches*. New York: Library of America, 1982.

Hesse, Hermann. *Demian: The Story of Emil Sinclair's Youth*. Translated by Michael Roloff and Michael Lebeck. New York: Harper & Row, 1965.

————. *Narcissus and Goldmund*. Translated by Ursule Molinaro. New York: Farrar, Straus and Giroux, 1968.

Jones, Howard Mumford. "A Commentary." In *Moby-Dick; or, the Whale*, text and notes prepared by Harrison Hayford and Hershel Parker, 565–575. New York: Norton, 1976.

Joyce, James. *A Portrait of the Artist as a Young Man*. Edited by Hans Walter Gabler. New York: Garland, 1993.

Killinger, John. *God, the Devil, and Harry Potter*. New York: St. Martin's, 2002.

Lawrence, D. H. "The Crown." In *Reflections on the Death of a Porcupine*, 1–100. Bloomington, IN: Indiana University Press, 1963.

————. *The Rainbow*. New York: Knopf, 1995.

————. *Women in Love*. New York: Viking, 1960.

Leatherbarrow, W. J. *The Cambridge Companion to Dostoevskii*. Cambridge: Cambridge University Press, 2002.

Levin, Harry. *The Power of Blackness: Hawthorne, Poe, Melville*. New York: Knopf, 1967.

Lewis, C. S. *The Discarded Image*. Cambridge: Cambridge University Press, 1964.

————. *An Experiment in Criticism*. Cambridge: Cambridge University Press, 1961.

————. *The Great Divorce*. New York: Macmillan, 1946.

————. *The Screwtape Letters & Screwtape Proposes a Toast*. New York: Macmillan, 1962.

Mabinogion, The. Translated by Gwyn Jones and Thomas Jones. Amsterdam: Dragon's Dream, 1982.

Martin, Jay. *A Collection of Critical Essays on "The Waste Land."* Englewood Cliffs, NJ: Prentice-Hall, 1968.

McLaren, Brian. *Faith After Doubt*. New York: St. Martin's, 2021.

————. *A New Kind of Christian: A Tale of Two Friends on a Spiritual Journey*. San Francisco: Jossey–Bass, 2001.

Melville, Herman. *Moby-Dick; or, the Whale*. New York: Norton, 1976.

Miller, Henry. *The World of Lawrence*. Santa Barbara, CA: Capra, 1980.

Miller, Jr., James E. *T. S. Eliot's Personal Waste Land: Exorcism of the Demons*. University Park, PA: The Pennsylvania State University Press, 1977.

Newell, John Philip. *Listening for the Heartbeat of God: A Celtic Spirituality*. Mahway, NJ: Paulist, 1997.

Otto, Rudolph. *The Idea of the Holy*. Translated by John Harvey. Oxford: Oxford University Press, 1923.

Plimpton, George. *Writers at Work: The Paris Review Interviews (Second Series)*. New York: Viking, 1963.

Rainey, Lawrence. *The Annotated Waste Land with Eliot's Contemporary Prose*. New Haven, CT: Yale University Press, 2005.

Robertson-Lorant, Laurie. *Melville: A Biography*. New York: Clarkson Potters, 1996.

Rowling, J. K. *Harry Potter* Series. 7 vols. New York: Scholastic, 1997–2007.

Scanlan, James P. *Dostoevsky the Thinker*. Ithaca, NY: Cornell University Press, 2002.

Schwarz, Robert L. *Broken Images: A Study of The Waste Land*. Lewisburg, PA: Bucknell University Press, 1988.

Terras, Victor. *Reading Dostoevsky*. Madison, WI: University of Wisconsin Press, 1998.

Tobias, Ariana. "Ending Dualism at Hogwarts." No pages. Online: http://eportfolios. macaulay. cuny.edu/hpapocalypse/thesis/.

Tolkien, J. R. R. *The Hobbit, or There and Back Again*. Rev. ed. New York: Ballantine, 1966.

————. *The Lord of the Rings*. 3 vols. New York: Houghton Mifflin, 1994.

Trilling, Diana. "Lawrence and the Moments of Modern Culture." In *D. H. Lawrence: Novelist, Poet, Prophet*, edited by Stephen Spender, 1–7. New York; Viking, 1973.

Unamuno, Miguel de. "Saint Manuel Bueno, Martyr." No pages. Online: www. armandbaker. com>unamuno>san_manuel_bueno_martir.

Van de Weyer, Robert. *The Letters of Pelagius: Celtic Soul Friend*. New York: Arthur James, 1997.

Vande Kappelle, Robert P. *Dark Splendor: Spiritual Fitness for the Second Half of Life*. Eugene, OR: Resource, 2015.

————. *Wading in Water: Spirituality and the Arts*. Eugene, OR: Wipf & Stock, 2021.

————. *Walking on Water: Living into a New Way of Thinking*. Eugene, OR: Wipf & Stock, 2020.

Walker, Franklin, *Heart of Darkness and The Secret Sharer*. New York: Bantam, 1981.

Walton, Evangeline. *The Mabinogion Tetralogy*. New York: Overlook Duckworth, 2004.

Wikipedia. "Harry Potter." No pages. Online:http://en.wikipedia.org/wiki/Harry_Potter.

Wright, Nathalia. *Melville's Use of the Bible*. Durham, NC: Duke University Press, 1949.

Yeats, William Butler. *Essays and Introductions*. New York: Macmillan, 1959.

Index